"Powerful.... Makes a persuasive case for inclusion, compassion, and welcoming of those seeking a meaningful Jewish life."
   —Dr. Ron Wolfson, Fingerhut Professor of Education, American Jewish University; author, *Relational Judaism*

"Optimistic ... visionary ... prescient ... belongs in the hands of our leadership, especially the American rabbinate and rabbinic students."
   —Rabbi Jerome K. Davidson, rabbi emeritus, Temple Beth-El of Great Neck

"Shares the stor[ies] of ... so many ... who have felt unwanted or unappreciated by the Jewish community because of intermarriage. Forces readers to consider whether existing approaches designed to protect the tradition actually do more to threaten its future. For leaders of the Jewish community, this book provides food for thought as your organization considers how to create a home that feels right for everyone."
   —Winnie Sandler Grinspoon, president, Harold Grinspoon Foundation

"The Jewish community faces a stark choice: build walls or build bridges. In relation to intermarriage, the former posture is doomed to failure. The latter can create a community that is enriched by an influx of partners from different faith traditions who see the beauty of Jewish life and creating a Jewish home. Ed Case has made this case to the Jewish community for more than twenty years. Now we have his playbook on how to do it with sensitivity and intelligence."
   —Rabbi Sid Schwarz, senior fellow, Hazon; author, *Jewish Megatrends: Charting the Course of the American Jewish Future*

"A seriously well-documented analysis of the most pressing issue facing the North American Jewish community.... [P]lac[es] this important issue into a context where community leaders and family members can more fully understand how Judaism addresses modernity."
   —Rabbi Charles Simon, former executive director, Federation of Jewish Men's Clubs

"Taking a hard look at what's lacking in efforts to engage interfaith families now, Ed Case advocates forcefully on behalf of an expanded vision of inclusion and ... takes on the full array of thorny issues to lay out a path to carry that vision into the world. Read it; then let's do it together!"
>—Dru Greenwood, former director, Department of Outreach, Union for Reform Judaism; founding director, SYNERGY: UJA-Federation of New York and Synagogues Together

"The recommendations clearly outlined in this must-read book are solutions we can act on immediately. Young Jews, both children of interfaith families and those married to or dating someone from another background, want to feel embraced by the Jewish community and want to be given the opportunity to make a significant contribution to Jewish life."
>—Becky Voorwinde, executive director, Bronfman Fellowship

"Ed Case's work helped change the way interfaith families are viewed and outreach become normative in many parts of the Jewish community.... I don't agree with some of his conclusions, but he raises important issues with passion and clarity."
>—Barry Shrage, former president and CEO, Combined Jewish Philanthropies of Boston; Professor of the Practice, Brandeis University, Hornstein Jewish Professional Leadership Program; and faculty, Cohen Center for Modern Jewish Studies

"Must reading for rabbis, cantors, lay leaders, anyone contemplating intermarriage, those who choose Judaism, and born Jews who want a richer understanding of the history and issues surrounding intermarriage.... Makes a powerful case."
>—Rabbi Stephen S. Pearce, senior rabbi emeritus, Congregation Emanu-El, San Francisco

"A book that every rabbi, every Jewish educator, every executive director of every Jewish institution should read and embrace."
>—Rabbi Steven Carr Reuben, rabbi emeritus, Kehillat Israel Reconstructionist Congregation

"Creating road maps to help create lives of meaning and a strengthened community, Ed Case outlines a better future. This book needs to be widely read."

—**Jeffrey R. Solomon**, president, Andrea and Charles Bronfman Philanthropies

"Provide[s] thoughtful, nuanced, yet realistic approaches to practical and philosophical challenges and opportunities that face those of us who work with all Jewish families."

—**Alicia Schuyler Oberman**, executive director, Jack Miller Family Foundation, Jack and Goldie Wolfe Miller Fund

"Brings together years of experience, significant data, and clear thinking to provide an understanding of the challenges as well as specific methods to strengthen Jewish life. Anyone interested in building a more vibrant community should read this book."

—**Gil Preus**, CEO, Jewish Federation of Greater Washington

"Remarkably clear and concise … an important chronicle of Jewish inter-marriage and outreach in America…. This positive vision for the future of engagement should be required reading for … all Jewish communal professionals."

—**Paul Golin**, executive director, Society for Humanistic Judaism

"Important, timely, thought-provoking—and deeply helpful."

—**Nigel S. Savage**, president and CEO, Hazon

"With wisdom and sensitivity … provides a road map and support for every couple taking the journey. It should be in every clergyperson's and communal worker's library."

—**Rabbi Peter Rubinstein**, director of Jewish community and Bronfman Center for Jewish Life, 92nd Street Y

"A clarion call for making our synagogues and families truly inclusive, inspiring, and engaging. Highly recommended."
—Rabbi Evan Moffic, Makom Solel Lakeside Congregation, Highland Park, Illinois; author, *The Happiness Prayer: Ancient Jewish Wisdom for the Best Way to Live Today*

"Masterful ... wise advice for couples who unite Jewish and often Christian partners.... Will enrich their marriages and help them raise their children with a deeper and more meaningful understanding of their backgrounds and faiths."
—Newton N. Minow, senior counsel, Sidley Austin LLP

"For anyone who is committed to the future of Jewish life and understands what it means to live in the twenty-first century with the reality of interfaith marriage, this book is filled with insights and practical wisdom."
—Rabbi Alvin Sugarman, rabbi emeritus, The Temple, Atlanta, Georgia

"Ed Case is a prophet and a change agent."
—Rabbi Rim Meirowitz, rabbi emeritus, Temple Shir Tikvah, Winchester, Massachusetts

"If you want to understand interfaith families, and the issues they face in engaging in Jewish life, look no further. Essential reading."
—Jodi Bromberg, CEO, InterfaithFamily

RADICAL INCLUSION

ENGAGING INTERFAITH FAMILIES FOR A THRIVING JEWISH FUTURE

EDMUND CASE

CENTER FOR
RADICALLY INCLUSIVE JUDAISM

Radical Inclusion
Engaging Interfaith Families for a Thriving Jewish Future

2019 Quality Paperback Edition, First Printing
© 2019 by Center for Radically Inclusive Judaism, Inc.

Cartoon by Harry Bliss in chapter 2 is used with permission of Pippin Properties, Inc.

Translations from the Torah, unless otherwise noted, are taken from W. Gunther Plaut, ed., *The Torah: A Modern Commentary*, rev. ed. (New York: URJ Press, 2005).

Translation from Pirkei Avot in chapter 6 taken from https://www.myjewishlearning.com/article/pirkei-avot-ethics-of-our-fathers.

Translation from Isaiah 58:6–7 in chapter 6 taken from Edwin C. Goldberg et al., eds., *Mishkan Hanefesh: Machzor for the Days of Awe, Rosh Hashanah* (New York: CCAR Press, 2015), 277.

Book cover design by Tim Holtz. Center for Radically Inclusive Judaism logo by blazar design studio.

Center for Radically Inclusive Judaism
321 Walnut Street, #443
Newtonville, MA 02460
www.CFRIJ.com
Contact the Center at info@CFRIJ.com

ISBN: 978-1-7329388-0-9 Paperback

Library of Congress Control Number: 2018913336

For Wendy, for making everything in my life possible

And for Emily and Adam, Brett and Alicia,
Jonah, Elsa, Ori, and Ben,
for giving me the opportunity to "teach these
words diligently to your children"

CONTENTS

Prologue   1

PART ONE
The Intermarriage Landscape   7

  1 Choosing Love—the Rise of Intermarriage in America   9
  2 Choosing Tradition—the Jewish Community's Response   13
  3 How Many Jews Will There Be?   21
  4 What Will Jewish Life Look Like?   27
  5 Choosing Love *and* Tradition—Couple and Family Dynamics   37

PART TWO
Three Invitations to Extend to Interfaith Families   45

Invitation One
Find Meaning and Spiritual Connection in Jewish Life   47

  6 Jewish Traditions for a Life of Meaning   49
  7 What about Christmas?   57
  8 Expressing Spirituality in Jewish Settings   65

Invitation Two
Find Belonging in Jewish Community   73

  9 *Being* Jewish—Conversion   75
 10 *Doing* Jewish—Radical Inclusion   83

Invitation Three
Raise Children with Judaism   95

 11 Welcoming a Baby   97
 12 Raising Children—Jewish or *Both*?   101

PART THREE
Three Road Maps for Engaging Interfaith Families   111

Road Map One
Attitudes   113

 13 The Discouraging Attitudes That Need to Change   115
 14 Radically Inclusive Attitudes   125

Road Map Two
Policies   137

    15 Radical Inclusion Starts at the Wedding   139

    16 Status—Recognition and Ritual Participation   155

    17 Intermarried Rabbis   167

    18 Working with Families *Doing Both*   173

Road Map Three
A Serious Campaign to Engage Interfaith Families   179

    19 Building a Future of Programmatic Efforts   181

    20 Model Pathways to Engagement   189

    21 The Positive Impacts that Can Be Achieved   199

    Conclusion   Everything Follows from Attitudes   205

    Epilogue   211

      Acknowledgments   215
      Notes   219

PROLOGUE

"If you marry Ed, you'll be stabbing his father in the back with a knife."

That's what the rabbi, whom I had revered growing up, said to Wendy, my Episcopalian fiancée, in January 1974.

I had told my parents that we wanted to marry. My father first said, "I won't go to a wedding in a church," followed by "I won't go to a wedding on a Saturday" (when Jews traditionally did not have weddings), followed by "I suppose I should say congratulations." He then urged me to "go see the rabbi."

The rabbi's statement reduced Wendy to tears. I'm still amazed that she didn't say, "Forget about this Jewish stuff, I want no part of it." Instead, we married, and she honored that Judaism had a powerful claim on me. When our children got to school age, we joined a local Reform synagogue. I got involved in the Reform movement's outreach efforts to welcome interfaith families, and then in similar efforts in the Boston Jewish community. When I found my work as a business litigation lawyer to be lacking in social value, I realized that the cause I cared about most was engaging interfaith families in Jewish life. So I embarked on a new career that led to founding InterfaithFamily, now the only national Jewish nonprofit dedicated to both supporting interfaith families as they explore Jewish life and encouraging Jewish communities to welcome them.

The Jewish concept of *bashert* (intended one) suggests there is one perfect match in the world for every person. Some would say that the *bashert* of a Jew can only be another Jew. But I'm sure Wendy is mine. Each of our children found their *bashert* too; they married the most wonderful spouses who are not Jewish and are now raising our four grandchildren with Judaism.

I wrote this book because after living an interfaith family life personally and working with interfaith families professionally, I have abiding faith in two realities: (1) engaging in liberal Jewish life can be a source of deep value and meaning not only for Jews but also equally for their partners from other faiths and most importantly for their children; and (2) Judaism is a tradition that helps people live better lives and make the world a better place and should be perpetuated.

But while most Jews are choosing love with partners who are not Jewish—almost three-quarters of non-Orthodox Jews are marrying someone from a different faith background—many are not choosing to engage with Jewish tradition. At a time when the liberal Jewish community is swimming in an ocean of interfaith marriage, instead of maximizing efforts to encourage interfaith families to engage, many Jews and Jewish leaders and institutions still question whether Jews can choose *both* to love someone from a different faith background *and* to engage with Jewish tradition.

I say, yes, they can. Moreover, if liberal Judaism is to be vibrant and thrive into the future, yes, they must, in increasing numbers.

While primarily directed toward Jewish lay and professional leaders, this book is for everyone interested in seeing more interfaith families becoming more engaged in Jewish life and community. It describes three invitations that can be extended to interfaith couples to experience and embrace the value and meaning that Jewish life can offer them, and three high-level road maps for what Jews, Jewish leaders, and Jewish organizations can do to facilitate the Jewish engagement of interfaith families.

My central proposition is that the liberal Jewish world needs to adopt radically inclusive attitudes toward interfaith marriage and partners from different faith traditions, and radically inclusive policies that embrace interfaith families.

Judaism is a distinctive tradition, one of many in a multicultural world. We can effectively invite interfaith families to engage in Jewish traditions by promoting how they can help people have lives of meaning, raise grounded children, and fulfill their needs for spiritual expression and community.

Instead of viewing interfaith marriage as a threat to the distinctiveness of Jewish identity and Jewish traditions that will lead to fewer Jews and less Judaism, we can engage interfaith families in Jewish life and community. But that requires changing the Jewish narrative about intermarriage from the fundamentally negative to the confidently positive, and eliminating the borders and boundaries that frown on or exclude partners from different faith backgrounds.

I am inspired by two statements in the Torah. "You shall love [the stranger] as yourself" (Leviticus 19:34) is the ultimate expression of radically inclusive attitudes. "You and the stranger shall be alike before the Eternal; the same ritual and the same rule shall apply to you and to the stranger who resides among you" (Numbers 15:15–16) is the ultimate expression of radically inclusive policies.

Instead of focusing on who is a Jew and who isn't—thereby including those who are and excluding those who aren't—we need to let everyone who wants to, *do* Jewish. Instead of focusing on identifying as a member of the Jewish people—distinguishing and even demeaning others—we need a broad, inclusive concept of a Jewish community made up of Jews and their partners who together are engaging in Jewish traditions.

Paradoxically, to maintain distinctive Jewish traditions, we need to be radically inclusive of partners from different faiths and the children of interfaith families. I hope this book will lead to an opening of hearts and minds for Jews, Jewish leaders, and Jewish organizations, toward embracing a radically inclusive approach—and to a Judaism revitalized by the engagement of interfaith families embracing a beautiful tradition.

A NOTE ON TERMINOLOGY

If you are reading this book, you are probably already aware of the many differences of opinion around the subject of Judaism and interfaith families. Those differences even extend to the meaning of the term *interfaith*. As I use the term, an interfaith relationship is one between a person with a Jewish background and a person with a background from another or no religious tradition. The couple can be married—intermarried or in an interfaith marriage—or not. An interfaith family includes one or more Jews and one or more people from different faith traditions. Interfaith does not connote anything about religious practice. It doesn't necessarily mean a couple that is practicing two faiths or trying to join two faiths together, or a couple where one partner is practicing one faith and the other is practicing no faith, or a couple that is raising children in two faiths (what is referred to as "raising children both").

Some couples don't feel the term describes their relationship well—some are even offended by it—because one is practicing a religion and one isn't, or because they are both practicing the same religion, or for other reasons. I hope that people interested in the issue will come to understand the term as I do: interfaith has become what in the legal field would be called a "term of art," meaning a word that has an acquired meaning that may not be clear from the word itself.

Over the years I've heard many suggestions for different terminology. *Intermarried* isn't a better term because not everyone is married, although the term is used often, particularly in demographic studies. *Mixed*, as in *mixed-married* or *mixed-faith* (*inter-mixed* is a newer variant), is old-fashioned, is negative in tone, and is not more clear or precise than *interfaith*. *Intercultural*, *inter-group*, or *inter-heritaged* (if that's even a term) don't work because Judaism is more than a culture, group, or heritage. No term is perfect; no term is better able to describe couples and families that include people from more than one religious background than *interfaith*.

As used in this book, *interfaith family* is meant to be very inclusive, of both immediate and extended families: couples that include converts to Judaism who still have relatives who are not Jewish, people with one Jewish parent, parents of intermarried children, grandparents of children being raised by intermarried parents, and so forth. An interfaith family may include those who identify their family as Jewish or as more than one religion, as well as those who are unsure of how they identify. I use the terms *intermarried*, *intermarriage*, and *interfaith marriage* interchangeably.

4

Finally, one term you won't see in this book, unless I'm quoting some-one else, is *non-Jew*. I prefer to say "partner from a different faith" tradi-tion or background, with thanks to Rabbi Mayer Selekman, a pioneer in efforts to welcome interfaith families, who promoted use of that term. It is a bit ungainly, and it certainly would be easier and shorter to just say "non-Jew," but as Paula Brody and Kathy Bloomfield, wise Jewish professionals, taught me and many others, people don't identify as "nons." Jews wouldn't want to be identified as non-Christians, non-Muslims, or "non" anything else, so why should people from different faith traditions be defined as non-Jews?

One last definition: *liberal Judaism*, as I use the term, means respect-ing halachah (Jewish law) in various ways but not regarding it as obliga-tory, in contrast to *traditional Judaism*, which considers halachah to be binding.

PART ONE

THE INTERMARRIAGE LANDSCAPE

We need to understand the current landscape of intermarriage in America in order to effectively extend invitations to interfaith couples to engage in Jewish life and draw road maps to engage them. An inevitable consequence of living in a modern liberal society, intermarriage has steadily increased to the point that 72 percent of non-Orthodox Jews are now intermarrying. That growth is the subject of chapter 1. The Jewish communal response to intermarriage has been polarized: one camp seeks to prevent or reduce it; the other, to seize the opportunity it presents. Chapter 2 describes that response, intertwined with my own story of interfaith marriage and my participation at InterfaithFamily in the intermarriage debate that has played out since the 1990s. Many national and local Jewish community demographic surveys shed light on the impact of intermarriage, both on the number of Jews (the subject of chapter 3) and on Jewish attitudes and behaviors (chapter 4). Finally, interfaith couples come to the table with a wide variety of family influences and interpersonal relationship issues. Chapter 5 outlines what we can learn about engaging them from a couple and family dynamics perspective.

1

CHOOSING LOVE—THE RISE OF
INTERMARRIAGE IN AMERICA

By the time of my bar mitzvah in 1963, I had internalized the Jewish community's message that interfaith marriage was wrong. I wrote a letter to my future self, predicting that I would be happily married to a Jewish woman. I remember telling my father, when he picked me up at a bar mitzvah party, that I was going to marry Judy, a girl I knew from Hebrew school.

So how did I come to intermarry in the first place?

To my grandparents, who were part of the large wave of Jews immigrating from Eastern Europe to America around 1900, interfaith marriage would have been inconceivable. My father's mother, Minnie Milkowitz, never learned to read or write English, only Yiddish. My mother's father, Harry Sobol (shortened from Sobolevsky), whom I called Zaide (Yiddish for "grandfather"), would disappear from the table at family gatherings; I would find him davening (reciting Hebrew prayers) in the corner of a room.

Jews have been in America since colonial times, but for a very long time interfaith marriage was rare. Only 2 percent of Jews who married before 1925 intermarried.[1] Inmarriage was the normative behavior of Jews in my grandparents' era—Jews married Jews. With ethnic groups segregated and discriminated against, there weren't many people of other faiths looking for or even open to considering Jews as marriage partners in those days.

When my parents got married in 1942, interfaith marriage was still extremely rare. They had attended different high schools in Hartford but were in the same circle of friends. They started dating when he attended veterinary college in Canada. Although there were many Italians, Irish, Poles, and others in my parents' high schools, all of their friends were Jews. Only 6 percent of Jews who married between 1940 and 1960 intermarried.[2]

When my father returned from service in Asia during World War II, he started his veterinary practice in Wethersfield, a nearby suburb, where very few Jews lived (there were five Jews in my high school class of 350). My parents frequently hosted parties at our house, but their friends were Jews who had moved to another suburb, West Hartford. At the party we held at our house following my bar mitzvah, the only person who wasn't Jewish was our Italian next-door neighbor.

Growing up Jewish in Wethersfield made me feel different from my classmates. In third grade I was asked to talk to a sixth-grade class about Passover; I was too intimidated to agree. In seventh grade my mother wouldn't let me try out for the basketball team because I would miss Hebrew school at the Conservative synagogue in West Hartford, where she schlepped me and my older brother dutifully, twenty-five minutes each way, on Tuesdays, Thursdays, and Sundays. In gym one day, when I missed a volleyball shot that lost a game for my team, a longtime childhood friend called me a "dirty Jew." In the locker room afterward, I pushed him into a bank of lockers, which almost tipped over.

But I loved being a Jew. I was one of the apparently rare kids who liked Hebrew school. I still remember the model Eastern European wooden synagogue I built out of popsicle sticks. I won the sixth-grade essay contest by explaining why Yom Kippur was my favorite Jewish holiday—it really was, but I also thought I was likely to win by saying so. I learned to chant Torah from Pincus Bernikier, a Holocaust survivor; after my bar mitzvah, the temple office would ask me to chant Torah on holidays. After a week at Camp Ramah, a Conservative Jewish summer camp, I came home and began putting on tefillin (leather straps used by traditionally observant Jews during certain prayers) each morning. I told my father he shouldn't have office hours on Saturdays. When I was fourteen, an older cousin took me to see a documentary about the Holocaust; I've never forgotten the images I saw that day. My favorite books were *Mila 18*, about the uprising in the Warsaw Ghetto, and *Exodus*, about the founding of Israel, both by Leon Uris.

While I was growing up, the rate of intermarriage was increasing, from 12 percent of those who married between 1960 and 1964 to over 25 percent of those who married between 1965 and 1970.[3] When I was fifteen, my brother started going out with a Protestant girl. My parents were vehemently upset. Traditional Jews sat *shiva*, a mourning ritual, when someone intermarried; I was told that Zaide sat *shiva* for an older first cousin who had intermarried around the same time.

When I got my driver's license, I started dating girls from West Hartford, the same Judy I had a crush on at thirteen, and others. But in March 1968 my brother was home from college and came to the National Honor Society Assembly, where I gave a speech. Afterward, he said, "You should go out with that Wendy Bosworth [who also gave a speech], she's cute." So I did, and it was love on first date. When I got home, my parents were still up. My asking if it would be okay if I continued to see Wendy elicited an extremely negative reaction. Their disapproval had a powerful impact on me. Despite my feelings for Wendy, at school the following Monday I was cold to her, which she couldn't understand because we'd both had such a good time.

I started going out again with Penny, a Jewish girl from West Hartford. We planned to go to each other's senior prom on consecutive weekends. Following hers, we went to her house, where instead of changing her clothes for the after-party, she went upstairs and fell asleep. While I wasn't that upset, my father and brother were so insulted they insisted I should not go to my senior prom with her. So I broke our date.

In what may be the greatest irony in his life, my father unknowingly reopened the door to my relationship with Wendy. Neither he nor I were thinking about long-range consequences. He wanted to see me go to my prom, and I needed a date. I knew that Wendy didn't have one (we were still friends), so I called her, apologized for the late notice, and asked if she wanted to go with me. She said, "What happened to Penny?" I explained, she accepted, and we had another wonderful time. I was in love again.

That summer I asked my mother why it would be so bad if I kept seeing Wendy. She said, "Well, you might go to college, and you might not meet anyone you like as much. You might keep going out with her, and you might end up getting married." And that is exactly what happened.

During our first two years of college, we dated secretly. Agonized, I sought advice from Seymour Lustman, a wonderful, wise, Jewish psychiatrist who was the head of my residential college. Dr. Lustman told me I needed to do what was right for me, not for my parents.

Our courtship was long (six years) and difficult because of my parents' disapproval of our interfaith relationship. Nevertheless, in 1974 Wendy and I married. By then and throughout the 1970s, the rate of intermarriage was 28 percent—a little more than one in four Jews marrying were intermarrying.[4] Amid all the other drastic changes of the 1960s and 1970s, young adult Jews were increasingly mixing with others, finding people with compatible values in school and at work, losing insecure feelings that the *other* wasn't to be trusted, and encountering less and less prejudice and discrimination, all trends that have accelerated to this day.

While driving to our synagogue in West Hartford, my father would often point to a nearby house and say, "I could have put my veterinary hospital there." If he had, I would have grown up around a lot more Jews and maybe ended up married to one. Critics of interfaith marriage often focus on proximity. They suggest that Jews live in areas highly populated by other Jews to more easily meet and marry. But young adult Jews will come into contact—at universities, in the workplace—with other young adults with similar values and interests but different backgrounds. Outside of self-segregated Orthodox communities, there is no way to prevent this, nor would that be desirable. It has been noted that intermarriage is a sign of the success Jews have had integrating into American society. Most of us wouldn't want to turn back that clock.

Some may say that by marrying Wendy I was rejecting Judaism or perhaps that I was not prioritizing my future family's Jewish involvement. I wasn't particularly focused on my future family's religious life, but I know I was *not* rejecting Judaism. While I wasn't aware of it then, I wanted both love *and* tradition—the love of my life and the beauty and meaning of Jewish traditions to share with her and my future family.

2

Choosing Tradition—The Jewish Community's Response

In 2006 the *Boston Globe* ran the following cartoon:[1]

"Harold, do you hear this? He's marrying a shiksa!"

My parents were unhappy about my marriage, and my rabbi tried to prevent it, in part because of the tribalism so aptly expressed in that cartoon. Because of their upbringing, experiences, and ideologies, they held the deep-seated view that Jews should stick together, be with, and marry other Jews.

My parents and my rabbi, along with other Jews and Jewish leaders like them, were also concerned about the consequences they thought interfaith marriage would have. They wanted there to be Jews and Jewish communities in the world. They wanted Judaism to continue to thrive as an ethnic- and religion-based system. They thought that Jews who intermarried, and more importantly the children of Jews who intermarried, would not identify as Jewish or participate in Jewish religious or communal life. They feared that welcoming interfaith couples would lead to more intermarriage, fewer Jews, and less Judaism in the world.

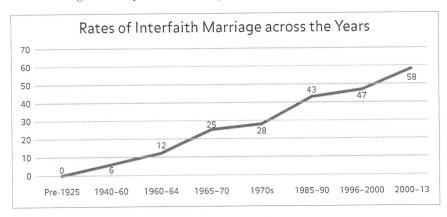

As the rate of interfaith marriage started to increase more rapidly in the 1960s, the main reaction of Jews and Jewish leaders was that this trend would lead to assimilation and the disappearance of Judaism and the Jewish people. The title of a 1964 *Look* magazine article, "The Vanishing American Jew," succinctly summarized their concerns.[2] What Jewish leaders called the first "continuity crisis" started then. During the 1970s, the American Jewish Committee, a leading Jewish policy organization, gathered rabbis for consultations, held a national conference, and sponsored research that resulted in *Intermarriage and the Jewish Future*, a report that took a grim view of the future unless interfaith marriage was curtailed.[3]

At the same time, parts of the Jewish community were responding more proactively. Leading the way, the Reconstructionist movement adopted a 1968 resolution that stated it would consider as Jews the children of a Jewish father and a mother who was not Jewish if the parents "have committed themselves to raise the children as Jews."[4] This was a major change from the "matrilineal descent" of traditional Jewish law, under which only the child of a Jewish mother is a Jew. It served to increase the number of people who would be considered Jewish.

The much larger Reform movement began to follow suit in 1978 when its president, Rabbi Alexander Schindler, announced a movement-wide program of outreach to potential converts, intermarried partners from different faith traditions, and seekers; then in 1983 the Central Conference of American Rabbis, the Reform movement's rabbinic association, adopted what is often called "patrilineal descent," technically that the child of a Jewish mother or father is presumed to be Jewish, with the child's Jewish status to be established through "appropriate and timely formal and public acts of identification."[5] My family was personally impacted by these changes. Our daughter Emily, born in 1978, and our son Adam, born in 1982, were Jewish in the eyes of the Reconstructionist and Reform movements.

The Reform movement created an outreach department, initially led by Lydia Kukoff, which eventually had a national staff and a part-time regional outreach director in each of the movement's then fourteen regions. The idea was to help Reform synagogues be more welcoming to interfaith couples, in hopes that more such couples would join synagogues, raise their children as Jews, and perhaps convert. I got involved in the Reform movement's outreach efforts. Our rabbi asked Wendy and me to help lead an interfaith discussion group that met approximately once every three months for many years and was the source of ongoing friendships. I joined the temple board and chaired a committee that recommended a policy regarding leadership roles for members who were not Jewish, using materials supplied by the Reform outreach department. Wendy and I were panelists at outreach programs at a Reform regional biennial.

In 1985, sociologist Egon Mayer published *Love and Tradition: Marriage Between Jews and Christians*, a groundbreaking book asserting that interfaith marriage did not necessarily mean a rejection of Jewish connections and advocating for the importance of welcoming interfaith families into the Jewish community.[6] In a 1989 interview, Mayer said:

> When Jews spoke of the problem of intermarriage, they would invariably speak in terms of a loss to the Jewish family and the Jewish community. But today, a great many people have come

to acknowledge that it reflects certain positive developments as well. For example, it reflects the great tolerance that America has for religious minorities, it reflects the self-confidence of Jews as individuals and it reflects the unbridled primacy of love in mate selection. In fact, as the rate of intermarriage has grown in the last 20 years, large numbers of the intermarried couples have opted to remain within the Jewish community and to raise their children as Jews.[7]

Then the 1990 National Jewish Population Survey was published and reported that 52 percent of Jews who married between 1985 and 1990 intermarried, launching the second "continuity crisis." Although the percentage was later corrected to 43 percent, the news that apparently more than half of Jews were intermarrying is credited with generating numerous Jewish continuity efforts. The American Jewish Committee developed a 1991 *Statement on Intermarriage* and distributed a 1996 *Statement on the Jewish Future*.[8]

The main concern of the continuity efforts was the children, as sociologist Sidney Goldstein explained in an analysis of the 1990 *National Jewish Population Survey*:

> One of the major concerns about the demographic implications of high rates of mixed marriages is the Jewish identity of the children of such marriages. . . . Of these children, only 25 percent were being raised as Jews at the time of the survey; 45 percent were being raised in another religion; and 30 percent were being raised without any religion. Unless a large majority of the latter opt to be identified as Jews when they reach adulthood, most children of mixed marriages will be lost to Judaism. . . . These potential losses constitute a major challenge to the Jewish community. Seen in the context of the high rate of mixed marriage that has come to characterize the community, the failure to attract more of these children into the Jewish fold could contribute to declines in the number of Jews in the future.[9]

In essays attached to the 1996 *Statement on the Jewish Future*, Jack Wertheimer, then provost of the Jewish Theological Seminary of America, expressed his opposition to interfaith marriage, which has continued to the present:

> The more we try to make intermarried families feel comfortable in Jewish settings, the further we demolish barriers to intermarriage. Why should young people oppose intermarriage if they see interfaith families treated as equals in the synagogue? How can our youth develop a resistance to interdating and intermarriage when the Jewish community is becoming ever more reluctant to stigmatize intermarriage—and on the contrary, is creating a vast population of lobbyists who favor the elimination of barriers to intermarriage because they themselves are intermarried?[10]

In 2001, the American Jewish Committee's Jewish Life Department, directed by Steven Bayme, convened a coalition of twenty-five Jewish leaders determined to "'work together to restore the ideals of inmarriage' and to encourage Jewish leadership to promote it as a norm"; the group, which included Brandeis professor Sylvia Barack Fishman, another prominent critic of intermarriage, adopted the name "Jewish Inmarriage Initiative."[11] Fishman released a study done for the American Jewish Committee, *Jewish and Something Else: A Study of Mixed-Married Families*, with the key finding that interfaith families incorporate "substantial Christian elements" in the home; in the foreword to Fishman's study, Bayme stated that this dynamic was "particularly ominous for Jewish continuity."[12] In 2007, prominent sociologist Steven M. Cohen[13] published *A Tale of Two Jewries: The "Inconvenient Truth" for American Jews*, in which he decried intermarriage as "the greatest single threat to Jewish continuity."[14]

Outside of the Reconstructionist and Reform movements, a handful of communal responses also saw intermarriage as a reality that cannot be prevented and an opportunity to grow and enrich Jewish life and communities. In 1994, a predecessor of the national association of local federations now known as the Jewish Federations of North America issued a task force report that described a process for local federations and their agencies to develop a response to the intermarried.[15] It recognized that interfaith marriage is a fact of life for the American Jewish community, that the number of intermarrieds will increase, and that many participate actively in the Jewish community. It also recognized that whether the intermarried become involved in the community depended in large part on whether the community chose to welcome them. In 1996, Combined Jewish Philanthropies, the Boston federation, commissioned a Task Force on Services to the Intermarried, which resulted in making engaging interfaith families a priority in its 1998 strategic plan.[16]

I became a participant in the debate, as a proponent for greater inclusivity. After leaving my law career, I had earned a master's degree in Jewish communal service from the Hornstein Program at Brandeis University in 1999 with the goal of working in outreach. There were no programs for interfaith families with positions suited to my résumé—I wasn't a rabbi or teacher who could lead classes nor a social worker capable of running a couples group. I was introduced to Yossi Abramowitz, a creative entrepreneur who had started a nonprofit that published numerous Internet magazines. I worked as the publisher of one of them, www.InterfaithFamily.com, for two years. When I found that I wanted to do more work that didn't fit within a publishing model, with Yossi's agreement, I raised funding and purchased the URL and existing content of InterfaithFamily.com.

On New Year's Day 2002, InterfaithFamily began operating as an independent nonprofit with me as president, Ronnie Friedland as half-time editor, and a budget of about $200,000. We expanded organically in response to customer demand, publishing personal narratives of people in interfaith relationships, creating DIY Jewish resources, and producing listings of welcoming Jewish organizations and professionals. Our writers reached a steadily growing number of monthly site visitors who were looking for and finding a positive picture of Jewish engagement. InterfaithFamily.com provided welcoming, nonjudgmental information and resources about Jewish life and the interpersonal dynamics faced by interfaith families. Readers used our discussion boards to reach out to others like them and to seek support for the decisions they were making. They sought information about welcoming rabbis, synagogues, and programs from us and each other.

As I'll describe later, InterfaithFamily expanded beyond the website to offer services and programs for interfaith couples in several cities around the country. From the outset, I wrote and spoke in favor of engaging interfaith families and responded to frequent arguments by critics of intermarriage. Whatever skills I had as a litigator were put to active use. By 2001, Egon Mayer, who had founded the Jewish Outreach Institute (JOI) and been the leader of the pro-outreach approach, shared with me that he had grown tired of fighting with the intermarriage critics. Rabbi Kerry Olitzky and Paul Golin, who became JOI's leaders, remained primary allies in the debate, and the heads of the Reform movement's outreach department, Dru Greenwood and later Kathy Kahn, occasionally joined in.

While the debate went on, the rate of intermarriage continued to increase, from 47 percent of those who married between 1996 and 2000,[17] to 58 percent of those who married between 2000 and 2013.[18] Most important, data from the famous 2013 Pew Research Center report *A Portrait of Jewish Americans* (what I'll refer to as "the Pew report") show an intermarriage rate of 72 percent of non-Orthodox Jews.[19] Looking at all Jews who were married in 2013, not those who got married at any particular time, 44 percent of all Jews who were married in 2013 were intermarried. Data from other countries, including Canada[20] and the United Kingdom[21] confirm that intermarriage among Jews is an inexorable phenomenon in all open, liberal societies.

3

HOW MANY JEWS WILL THERE BE?

Counting the population is a venerable Jewish tradition—Numbers, the fourth book of the Hebrew Bible, begins with the command to "take a census of the whole Israelite community" (Numbers 1:2).[1] Who is counted as "in" and who "out" also has a venerable history—in that first census, it was only males. Jewish communities, both national and local, regularly conduct demographic surveys that measure, among other things, the number of Jews, the extent of interfaith marriage, and whether children are being raised as Jews, as partly Jewish and partly something else, or some other way.[2]

When considering survey research, it is important to remember that advocates of policy can selectively cite social science data. The significance of and conclusions to be drawn from particular data can be quite different, based on what one chooses to focus on or what conclusion one is hoping to find. Critics of interfaith marriage point to the percentage of children not being raised exclusively as Jews to support views that intermarriage should be prevented and that efforts to engage interfaith families are ill-advised. Advocates for inclusion of interfaith families view children being raised both, neither, or undecided as opportunities for potential engagement.[3]

MORE OR FEWER JEWS?

Whether the size of the Jewish population grows or declines depends on how the children of interfaith marriage are raised and identify. In an analysis of the Pew report, sociologist Theodore Sasson wrote that for two decades the general view among social scientists was that intermarriage would drive down the Jewish population because the demographic threshold for breaking even—50 percent of children of intermarriage being raised as Jews—was not being reached.[4]

It's important to understand how that demographic threshold works.

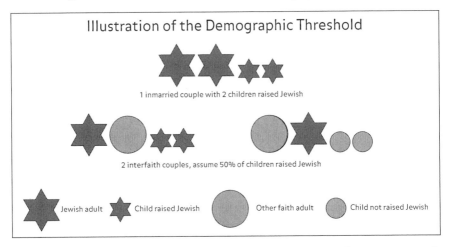

Assume, for purposes of example, in a population of 100 Jews, each marriage produces two children, all children of inmarriage are raised as Jews (as the demographic studies invariably report), and half of the children of intermarriage are raised as Jews:

- If all 100 Jews inmarry, then 50 couples produce 100 children raised as Jews.
- If 50 Jews inmarry, then 25 inmarried couples produce 50 children raised as Jews, and 50 intermarried couples produce 100 children, 50 of whom are raised as Jews, for a total of 100 children raised as Jews.

In other words, so long as 50 percent of the children of intermarriage are raised as Jews, the *same* number of children will be raised as Jews as if all the Jews inmarried.

Now imagine if *more* than 50 percent of the intermarried couples raise their children as Jews: there will be more Jewish children than if all 100 of the Jews had inmarried. Let's say that 60 percent of the intermarried couples raise Jewish children, then 50 children of inmarried couples and 60 children of intermarried couples are raised as Jews, or 110 Jews—that's 10 percent more children raised as Jews.

How Are the Children of Intermarriage Raised?

Before the Pew report, when there weren't enough adult children of intermarriage to survey, data about how the children of intermarriage were raised was provided by their parents. That data from major local and national community studies varies widely:

- The *Jewish Community Study of New York: 2011* (what I'll refer to as "2011 New York study") found that 42 percent of the children in intermarried households were being raised with Judaism: 31 percent being raised Jewish, 11 percent being raised "Jewish and something else"; 13 percent had parents who were undecided, and 46 percent were not being raised Jewish.[5]
- The *2015 Greater Boston Jewish Community Study* (what I'll refer to as "2015 Boston study") found that 69 percent of the children of intermarried couples were being raised with Judaism: 57 percent exclusively Jewish, 12 percent with Judaism and another religion; 21 percent were being raised with no religion and 10 percent in another religion.[6]

The Pew report introduced a wrinkle to this issue by distinguishing between "Jews by religion" and "Jews of no religion." Respondents were asked, "What is your religion?" If they said "Jewish," they were classified as Jews by religion; if they did not, they were asked if they considered themselves Jewish or partly Jewish aside from religion, and if they said yes, they were classified as Jews of no religion. Applying that distinction, the Pew report found that 61 percent of intermarried families were raising their children with some Judaism: 20 percent as Jewish by religion, 16 percent as Jewish but not by religion, and 25 percent as partly Jewish by religion and partly something else (37 percent were not raising their children Jewish at all).[7]

However, the Pew report was the first significant survey to have data showing how the young adult children of intermarriage themselves responded to survey questions about how they identified. Because the data showed that 59 percent of young adult children of intermarriage were identifying as Jews, Sasson concluded that intermarriage has contributed to a Jewish population increase. Moreover, Sasson described a decidedly promising trend toward increased Jewish identification:

> There appears to be a trend of young adults raised in non-Jewish or partly Jewish households opting in [to identifying as Jews]. . . . The propensity of adults with intermarried parents to identify as Jewish [has] steadily increased, from 25 percent in the [Jews who are now] 65-and-older group, to 37 percent in the 50–64 age group, to 39 percent in the 30–49 group, to 59 percent in the 18–29 group.[8]

WHAT ABOUT THE GRANDCHILDREN?

In 2016, Steven M. Cohen wrote in the *Forward* that his analysis of the Pew report data indicated that only 5 percent of children with one Jewish grandparent were raised as Jews by religion.[9] That statement accurately reflects the data, but it does not represent the full picture: another 20 percent of children with one Jewish grandparent were raised as partly Jewish by religion, and another 7 percent as Jewish but not by religion. In all, 32 percent of the grandchildren of intermarriage were, in fact, being raised with Judaism in some way.[10]

Critics of intermarriage also emphasize that the rate of intermarriage is higher among the children of intermarried parents than among the children of inmarried parents. The Pew report, for example, found that while 37 percent of married Jews whose parents were inmarried are intermarried, 83 percent of married Jews whose parents were intermarried are intermarried.[11] This is not surprising. Children of intermarried parents resist ideas that suggest that their parents' kind of relationship is wrong or a problem or to be avoided. An important 2016 study on millennial children of intermarriage reported:

> When asked about future spouses, few [interviewees who were children of intermarriage] seemed to view being Jewish as a critical

characteristic. They see themselves as proof that inmarriage is not a necessary ingredient for having a Jewish home or raising children as Jews. . . . [M]any interviewees expressed their commitment to raising children Jewish—or in some instances, children with exposure to Jewish traditions—regardless of whether they marry someone who is Jewish. As well, interviewees often discussed the importance of giving children multicultural experiences such as they had in their own childhood, and to sharing in cultural/religious traditions [of] their spouse.[12]

It is fruitless to decry the phenomenon of intermarriage. Engagement activists view families with children or grandchildren being raised Jewish not by religion, or partly Jewish, or by undecided parents as susceptible and even predisposed to interventions that might increase their engagement. The same is true of higher rates of intermarriage among the children of intermarriage. That there will be more intermarriage among them only heightens the importance of efforts to engage interfaith families in Jewish life.

4

WHAT WILL JEWISH LIFE LOOK LIKE?

InterfaithFamily's mission was to empower people in interfaith relationships to engage in Jewish life. Jewish leaders would often ask us to define the Jewish life we wanted people to engage in. Should they be religious? Did they need to convert? Must they join a synagogue, of a particular denomination? Keep kosher? What if they were secular? Or just accessed Jewish culture? InterfaithFamily defined Jewish life broadly—no one approach was favored, anything Jewish that people did was good.

We can't understand the impact of interfaith marriage on Jewish life, however, without defining the Jewish life that is being impacted. Yet while volumes have been written expressing various analyses of Judaism as a religion, a civilization, an ethnicity, a culture, there is no consensus on a clear definition of liberal Jewish life. Many Christians would define religious life as having a personal relationship with God. Traditionally observant Jews would say that Jewish life is defined by the obligations of halachah. For liberal Jews, it's more complicated.

It turns out that people who think intermarriage leads to less Jewish behaviors and attitudes have a more traditionally observant, more ethnicity-based definition of Jewish behaviors and attitudes in mind. Those who see intermarriage as an opportunity have a broader conception and more expansive definition that take into account the evolving ways that Jews are expressing Jewishness, including through social justice work, the arts, environmental activities, mindfulness, and more. These different perspectives on what constitutes Jewish life underlie much of the debate about intermarriage and how to respond to it.

DEFINING JEWISH LIFE

In addition to measuring the size of the community and the extent of intermarriage, national and local Jewish community surveys measure

Jewish attitudes and behaviors. All the major surveys since 1990, in varying degree and with varying survey questions, have measured the following categories and corresponding behaviors and attitudes.

Behaviors and Attitudes Measured by Surveys

Category	Behaviors and Attitudes
Religious/Ritual	• Fast on Yom Kippur/attend services on High Holidays • Attend Passover Seder • Light Shabbat and/or Hanukkah candles • Attend synagogue services • Keep kosher
Pride/Salience	• Pride in being Jewish • Importance of being Jewish • Importance of being part of a Jewish community • Sense of belonging to the Jewish people
Social/Organizational	• Belong to a synagogue, JCC, or other Jewish organization • Attend Jewish programs • Donate to Jewish charity and/or federation • Volunteer for Jewish organization/under Jewish auspices • Friends mostly Jewish
Israel	• Emotional attachment to Israel • Follow events in Israel • Visit Israel
Culture/Learning	• Subscribe to Jewish periodical • Read books and/or watch movies with Jewish content • Listen to Jewish music • Use the Internet for Jewish purposes • Participate in adult Jewish education

The 2011 New York study created an index of Jewish engagement based on a selection of these factors.[1]

ETHNICITY

Many of the Jewish attitudes and behaviors measured by the surveys are related to ethnicity, not religion or culture. The pride/salience, social/

organizational, and Israel factors listed in the table above are all part of what Steven M. Cohen has called "Jewish ethnic 'groupiness'"[2] and what a 2016 United Kingdom study called "socially exclusivist."[3] But as Cohen and fellow author Arnold Eisen point out in their important book *The Jew Within: Self, Family and Community in America*, it is well known that ethnic groupiness—whether of Jews or others—wanes in successive generations of immigrants, as societies open and people from different groups are exposed to each other and assimilate in positive ways.[4]

The people who would tend to score high on the Jewish engagement index of these surveys would largely be an *inside* group. Being Jewish and part of the Jewish people and community would be very important to them. They would be synagogue members, support Jewish charities, and attached to and supportive of Israel. Most of their friends would be Jewish. Those attitudes and behaviors were widespread in the 1950s and 1960s and were reinforced to the extent American society was not as open to Jews as it is today and Israel's survival was precarious.

But times have changed. Despite disturbing signs of ongoing anti-Semitism, American society is now completely open to Jews, and Israel's politics are complicated, to say the least. There is also a general trend against joining organizations. Some Orthodox Jews may insulate themselves from exposure to others, but liberal Jews are likely to have many friends who are not Jewish, donate to secular as well as Jewish charities, and volunteer with other-than-Jewish organizations.

While in the past Jews identified as Jews—and Jews only—and stayed that way, the 2011 New York study describes a context of shifting identities. Today identities are fluid, freely chosen, and based on rela-tionships. They are malleable, changing over time. They are hybrid—a confluence of multiple traditions that is the ethos in American society generally.[5] That's not to say that pride in being Jewish, joining Jewish organizations, and giving to Jewish charities are out of date, but looking to the future they will not have as big or exclusive a role in people's lives, nor will they form as much or as exclusive a way for people to express their Jewishness.

RELIGION AND CULTURE

The declines in ethnicity and shifts in identity have been accompanied by changes in religious behavior. To the extent the existing community surveys measure religious factors, they ask about ritual observance and synagogue attendance. The people who would score highest on the survey measures would engage in more frequent and extensive holiday celebrations, keep kosher, and attend religious services—in short, behave more like traditional, religiously observant Jews. But a shift has occurred away from viewing Jewish law as obligatory and adhering to commanded behaviors, toward making personal choices to take on certain obligations.

The Pew report asked if certain qualities were an essential part of what it means to be Jewish:[6]

What Being Jewish Means

Some Essential Parts of What Being Jewish Means	% Saying ___ Is an Essential Part of What Being Jewish Means
Remembering Holocaust	73%
Leading ethical/moral life	69%
Working for justice/equality	56%
Being intellectually curious	49%
Having good sense of humor	42%
Eating traditional Jewish foods	14%

None of these factors have previously been measured by national and local surveys. Respondents who express their Jewishness, and in some cases their spirituality, by remembering the Holocaust, leading an ethical life, working for justice, or the other matters listed—or engaging in environmental activities from a Jewish perspective, another recent development—wouldn't have scored high on Jewish attitudes and behaviors in those surveys.

The authors of the 2015 Boston study referred to "diversity . . . in many types of Jewish identification and means of engagement in Jewish life." They created a typology of five patterns of Jewish engagement— familial, affiliated, cultural, minimally involved, or immersed—based on whether people engaged primarily through family, home-based, ritual, communal, and/or cultural activities. They created the typology because dichotomies such as engaged/not engaged and religious/not religious, and comparisons between denominations "are inadequate descriptors of contemporary Jewish behavior."[7]

In the summer of 2018, a Jewish Telegraphic Agency article about changes in "the field of counting Jews" quoted Lila Corwin Berman, director of Temple University's Feinstein Center for American Jewish History, as saying that the traditional categories "about what makes a good Jewish life . . . have a particular worldview and particular set of values. . . . [Researchers] should ask how Jews experience their own Judaism and go from there." Bethamie Horowitz, codirector of the education and Jewish studies doctoral program at New York University, elaborates that these measures "imply a set of traditional priorities" and agrees that researchers should "ask about how people feel about being Jewish, or how they make meaning about being Jewish . . . letting individuals describe what they experience and what is meaningful to them." Deborah Dash Moore, a professor of American Jewish history at the University of Michigan, says we should "stop assuming that there are gradations of being Jewish that make one better than the other."[8]

In defining Jewish life, existing surveys are not asking all the right questions. Coming from an ethnicity-based, traditionally observant perspective, they measure essentially the ways people have expressed their Jewishness in the past. Given the shifts that increasingly are taking place, we need new measures that reflect the ways that people are currently expressing their Jewishness and how it will be expressed in the future.

THE IMPACT OF INTERMARRIAGE ON JEWISH ATTITUDES AND BEHAVIORS

Despite their shortcomings, what surveys report about the impact of intermarriage on Jewish life has heavily influenced Jewish communal responses to intermarriage. Ever since intermarriage rates started to increase, community surveys have compared the Jewish attitudes and behaviors of intermarrieds to those of inmarrieds and generally shown that all intermarrieds, as an undifferentiated group, demonstrate less of the measured Jewish attitudes and behaviors than inmarrieds.[9] Critics of intermarriage conclude from this data that intermarriage needs to be prevented or reduced and that resources should not be expended to engage interfaith families.

Proponents of engagement say that lumping all intermarrieds together skews the results, because when the attitudes and behaviors of interfaith families who *are* engaged are compared to those of inmarrieds, the gaps are much less significant.[10] Instead of writing off interfaith families, efforts should be made to increase the numbers who engage.

The 2011 New York study generally follows the approach of comparing all intermarried couples and highlighting their relatively low levels of Jewish engagement when compared to inmarried couples. For example, the following chart shows the percentages of inmarried couples and intermarried couples who score low or very low on the study's index of Jewish engagement:[11]

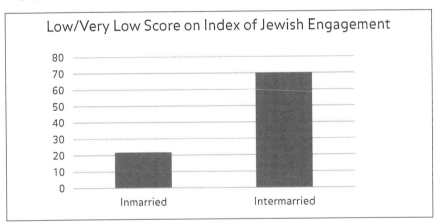

However, when the 2011 New York study compares inmarried couples with intermarried couples who are Jewishly engaged (for example, with the 15 percent of intermarried households that are synagogue members), the results are quite different. The following chart shows the percentages of inmarried and Jewishly engaged intermarried couples who send their children to Jewish supplemental religious schools or day schools:[12]

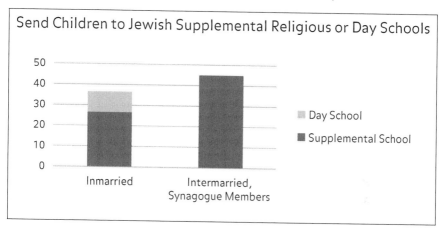

Advocates might use the first chart to support the argument that it is not worth trying to engage interfaith families; the second, to support the argument that increased efforts should be made to attract them.

It is also important to note that to the extent that indices of Jewish engagement overemphasize behaviors that are more formal and collective (e.g., joining and volunteering with a Jewish organization), they understate the Jewish engagement of intermarried families, who tend to be more involved in Jewish behaviors that can be undertaken individually or with friends and family (e.g., cultural activities, and home- and family-based religious/ritual traditions).[13]

Finally, it makes sense that inmarried households would score high on the standard measures of Jewish attitudes and behaviors. Pride in being Jewish, the salience of being Jewish, and a sense of belonging to the Jewish people are factors that can obviously be challenging to interfaith couples, where one partner by definition is not Jewish and, as will be discussed later, Jewish communities have often acted in a way that would tend to make interfaith couples feel excluded. Social/organizational and Israel-related factors can be challenging to interfaith couples for the same reason.

One of the most interesting findings in the Pew report is that 89 percent of intermarried Jews are proud to be Jewish and 67 percent say being Jewish is important to them, yet only 59 percent have a strong sense of belonging to the Jewish people.[14] It is logical that 89 percent are proud but only 59 percent have a sense of belonging, because of the way they either have been treated or perceive they have been treated in the Jewish community. We cannot know how interfaith families would score on these surveys' measures if they had been warmly welcomed starting in the 1990s or earlier. We don't know what the surveys would have shown, for example, if the messages from Jews and Jewish leaders to interfaith couples, and in particular to the partners from different faith backgrounds, had been: "It's wonderful that you are partnering with our child/our relative/a member of our community. We invite you to participate in our traditions. We think Judaism adds a great deal of meaning and value to people's lives, and we hope you'll find that true for yourself."

A VISION OF INTERFAITH FAMILY ENGAGEMENT

It's clear that large numbers of interfaith families are engaging in Jewish life and community. The Pew report data indicates that there were 1.17 million intermarried couples in 2013,[15] and the report says that 14 percent of intermarried Jews were synagogue members,[16] which would mean 163,800 intermarried couples had joined synagogues.[17] Existing survey data provides almost no information about the factors that motivate interfaith families to engage in Jewish life and community. However, the qualitative personal stories of thousands of engaged interfaith families do shed light on that important question.

Because people are interested in and may want to follow what celebrities do, it is significant that well-known children of intermarriage are engaging in Jewish life. David Gregory, the former host of NBC's *Meet the Press* and author of *How's Your Faith*,[18] was "raised Jewish by his Jewish father and non-Jewish mother."[19] His wife, Beth Wilkinson, is not Jewish and decided not to convert but agreed to help educate their children as Jews. She "encouraged Gregory to understand more about Judaism," and her questions prompted David's resolve to find answers through serious Jewish learning:

> If it's Friday night, it's Shabbat with his wife and three young children. . . . Gregory has committed not just to exposing his children to Judaism, but to making it a part of the air they breathe. . . . That includes saying the *Sh'ma Yisrael* prayer with them before bed.[20]

Eric Lesser, another child of intermarriage, while working in the White House,

> looked out over the containers of Thai carryout, the bottles of wine and the Shabbat candles. "Should we do Shalom Aleichem?" he asked, and the whole table began singing a warbled but hearty version of the song that welcomes Shabbat. In Lesser's group house of Obama staff assistants, Friday-night Shabbat dinners have become something of a ritual, a chance to relax and spend a few hours with friends, reflecting on the week. . . . At the end of every Friday dinner, the tradition is that everyone goes around the table and says something from the past week for which they're grateful.[21]

Over the years, InterfaithFamily published hundreds of personal stories of people in interfaith relationships for whom Judaism is a meaningful and visible part of their lives and who demonstrate that by:

- Marking Shabbat with a special dinner; celebrating and understanding the meaning of the holidays; incorporating Jewish traditions in life-cycle celebrations and daily practices.
- Reading Jewish stories and listening to Jewish music with their children; telling their children they are Jewish, in whole or in part; sending their children to Jewish preschool, summer camp, education, or youth groups or programs.
- Engaging in Jewish learning or adult education.
- Feeling connected spiritually to God or something greater than themselves that they think of as part of their or their family's Jewishness.

- Being aware of local Jewish resources and establishing community with other Jewishly engaged people; engaging in social action and social justice activities, the arts, or environmental causes as members of a JCC, synagogue, or other Jewish group.
- Agreeing with each other about their Jewish engagement, and appreciating the similarities and differences in their traditions while maintaining positive relations with both of their families.
- Regarding Jewish traditions as a resource to help them live better lives and motivating them to make the world better.

Some policy makers may not value the personal stories of engaged interfaith families because they're anecdotal rather than data driven. Arnold Eisen, acknowledging that some intermarried couples are living Jewishly and raising children as Jews, once wrote, "[O]ne does not want to base communal policy on what a minority manages to achieve against the odds."[22] However, engaged interfaith families are a substantial minority, and many thousands of their stories amount to a solid basis for a road map of actions that could help to make that minority a majority.

5

CHOOSING LOVE AND TRADITION—
COUPLE AND FAMILY DYNAMICS

My wife, Wendy, converted to Judaism after we had been married for thirty years. Before then, when people asked about her religion, she would say that she lived "Jewishly" but was not Jewish. We celebrated Shabbat and Jewish holidays and were active in our synagogue, and she didn't practice another religion. At the time, we were good friends with another family that we would often see at our synagogue. When you asked the mother what her religion was, she would say her family was Jewish but she was a practicing Catholic—she went to Mass every week.

There is a wide range of ways that the partners in interfaith relationships identify and behave with respect to religious traditions. Reaction and involvement of their parents and extended family are equally wide-ranging. How the partners identify and behave is, of course, determined by many factors, but a key set of influences is how the partners relate to each other and how they interact with their families. Partners come to a relationship with different degrees of connection and attachment to their religious backgrounds, and these connections and attachments can change over time. The parents and relatives likewise have different connections and attachments with their religious backgrounds and involvement with the couple. Efforts to engage interfaith families in Jewish life and community need to be informed by and address all of these interpersonal dynamics.

In an important 1989 presentation on how communication among interfaith couples is influenced by their different ethnic and cultural backgrounds, Esther Perel noted that all couples address issues of identity, commitment, intimacy, and separation from their family of origin.[1] Interfaith couples have the additional challenge of addressing these issues against a backdrop of cultural and religious differences. At times of developmental transition—particularly marriage, birth, and death—people seek the familiarity of their cultural and religious traditions to guide them through change. At those times, interfaith partners come up against different interpretations, symbols, and rituals for managing shared life events and may experience a reawakened cultural identity. To come together as a couple and achieve greater intimacy, the partners need to work out their sense of identity as part of differentiating from their family of origin and draw out and understand the differences between them. This negotiation, which happens periodically at holiday times as well, involves both the content of the tradition and the surrounding emotional and interpersonal dynamics.[2]

Perel found that while interfaith couples generally focus on religious differences, they should not overlook cultural differences with respect to the place of the couple's marriage in the larger family system, the nature of the boundaries around the couple, responses to stress and conflict, patterns of emotional expressiveness and communication, and the meaning of autonomy and dependency. She noted one pattern of "cultural complementarity" around autonomy and togetherness in interfaith marriages: the Jewish partner, coming from a style of family togetherness, is attracted to the style of autonomy and independence of the partner from a different faith tradition, while that partner is attracted to the style of warmth and togetherness of the Jewish partner. Sometimes, a partner is attracted to a trait that the other partner is trying to escape. At other times, what initially attracts may become a source of tension—closeness may come to be felt as intrusion; independence may come to be felt as distance.[3]

Perel writes that for some, intermarriage is an escape from their cultural background, a separation from family, an opportunity to adjust undesired characteristics they attribute to their ethnic background by associating with another group. For others, however,

> paradoxically, [intermarriage] sometimes offers the individual the opportunity to reaffirm his or her ethnic identity and to make creative personal changes. Intermarriage highlights the discontinuity

with one's past and cultural roots. It can disrupt family patterns and connections, yet its very diversity also opens the system to new patterns, connections, and creative changes.[4]

Perel's analysis, which describes couples coming from different cultures and religions, may become less relevant in the future. As more children of intermarriage become the young adult partners in interfaith relationships, differences in exposure to religions and cultures may not be as great. Still, as she says, all couples have issues of identity, commitment, and separation from their families of origin.

Perel says interfaith couples can adopt one of three main strategies:

- Conversion—where one partner adopts the other's religious and cultural background
- Rejection—where the couples seek to abandon their traditions
- Integration—the most common approach, where couples blend the things they find most important from their backgrounds, the observances, rituals, and celebrations that enhance the richness and pleasure of family life

Citing Egon Mayer's *Love and Tradition*, she concludes, "More than a blending, it is a recognition of continuity, where each one grants limited territorial rights for their respective heritages in a jointly shared home."[5]

Twenty-five years after Perel's paper, new qualitative research funded by the One8 Foundation fleshed out the nature of interpersonal dynamics of "interfaith families who have not decided to raise their kids Jewish only, and who operate outside Jewish communities" (called "free roamers" in the study). Those couples prioritized their relationships over religion. As partners they wanted each other to be comfortable, to strengthen their relationships, to make decisions together. They respected their different experiences and points of view and recognized that each parent has a need to leave a legacy and to have equal opportunity to mark their children's identity. The partners showed empathy for each other, including the Jewish partner's concern for the other partner feeling like an outsider, knowing little about Jewish traditions.[6]

The research also provided key insights about the couples' social dynamics. Personal recommendations, especially from others like them, had a strong influence. People preferred to engage Jewishly in small groups close to them and looked to other parents or groups to forge tight relationships that provided emotional connections.[7]

Finally, the research provided key observations about the dynamics of couples' decision making. They needed:

- to know how engaging in Jewish practices could add meaning to their lives
- an explanation of the "why" behind the Jewish traditions in a way that related to their current context and made explicit how the activities related to day-to-day life and what the benefits were on a rational level
- to have Jewish practices made accessible and meaningful to the parent who was not Jewish and address that parent's background
- the "right" Jewish leaders who are warm and supportive[8]

The research stressed the importance of "lasting meaning," which comes from shared emotional feeling between partners and between couples and their close friends, arising from engaging in a Jewish practice at home or in small groups and understanding its meaning and relevance. The research describes a "sparking experience" as a "strong personalized moment that reinforces the relationship and connects to the magic of family and tradition," joins the partners to each other in a Jewish context, and creates a shared vision of the future with both partners. Finally, the research suggests that early decisions about religious traditions are associated with couples being able to "do Jewish and say Jewish"—that is, to say to their children that they are Jewish.[9]

Over the years, what InterfaithFamily heard from interfaith couples was consistent with this theoretical and research-based understanding of couple and family dynamics. One of the main themes was that many Jewish partners express a very strong Jewish identity and commitment to Jewish life, and many partners from different faith traditions are supportive of their families' Jewish involvement. Jewish partners revealed a strong desire to identify as Jews and to perpetuate Jewish life, often arising out of a sense of connection with and obligation to parents, grandparents, and ancestors, and expressing itself within their interfaith relationship. In one moving unpublished essay, an intermarried Jewish man composes a letter to his deceased father, describing how he is raising his five-year-old daughter:

> Dad, you won't believe this, but she speaks Hebrew. She goes to synagogue and observes Shabbat. She almost knows more about our people and our religion than I do, probably because she pays more attention in services than I ever did. She is a Jew, Dad. I want you to know that.

He goes on to say that his wife, Christine, is "very supportive of [their daughter's] Judaism." She sings the *Barechu* "pretty well, too. Oh, and Christine also puts together the synagogue newsletter and is active in our Havurah. Not bad for a Lutheran."[10]

Another important theme was that many partners say that because they are part of an interfaith family, they cannot take their Jewish involvement for granted. They must think about what is important to them, make conscious decisions, and work harder at it. In another unpublished essay, an interdating Jewish woman describes her feelings as she brings her boyfriend to meet her Holocaust-survivor grandparents:

> I desperately wanted my grandparents to know that dating Nathan had not made me any less Jewish and had, in many ways, strengthened my personal commitment to a faith that was easy to take for granted in a Jewish home, a Jewish grade school, and a largely Jewish community.[11]

Today, when everything is a matter of choice and different activities and affiliations compete for people's limited time, many people aren't going to get involved in Jewish life just because they're born Jewish. If we believe that engaging in Jewish life is a great source of meaning, purpose, and fulfillment—and that people who think about and explore Jewish life will agree—then it is a very promising development that people in interfaith families have to make conscious decisions about Jewish life as an option.

In *The Jew Within: Self, Family and Community in America*, authors Steven M. Cohen and Arnold Eisen recognize that interdating and intermarriage often provoke heightened Jewish involvement by the Jewish partner. Thus in every intermarried couple there is potentially a partner who is confident of Jewish identity and susceptible to increased attachment. Cohen and Eisen also write that inmarried couples "often bridged their disparities in Jewish involvement by moving closer to the wishes of the more Jewishly involved spouse"; similarly, in an interfaith marriage, there is the potential for the spouse from a different faith tradition to move closer to the position of a Jewishly involved spouse.[12]

Three key practical lessons for anyone interested in engaging interfaith families Jewishly can be drawn from understanding family and couple dynamics. First, interfaith couples need to negotiate what they will use from their respective religions and cultures at various life-cycle stages and at holiday times. Jewish communities can create space for and help couples to understand their differences and work out what their religious and cultural identity will be. We can provide workshops, discussion groups, and meet-ups—one of the most important kind of programmatic offerings—for this purpose, as discussed in chapter 19.

Second, we need to recognize that interfaith couples regard each other as equal partners in the relationship, respecting each other's views and need to mark their children's identity. This does not mean they won't decide to be Jewishly engaged. It does mean, however, that if they do engage Jewishly, it will be after the views of the partner from a different faith tradition are fully respected. The Jewish traditions interfaith couples engage in will have to be meaningful and relevant to both and accessible to the partner from a different faith tradition. Ideally, their encounters with Jewish traditions will be emotionally fulfilling and experienced with other Jewishly engaged friends.

Finally, we need to recognize that new patterns, connections, and creative changes will continue to arise as interfaith couples choose to integrate their traditions. This does not mean that they won't develop and engage in Jewish attitudes and behaviors, but the attitudes and behaviors they develop and engage in may look different from those of their parents and grandparents. We can choose to view this as discontinuity—a break from the past—or as adaptive continuity, that is, new Jewish attitudes and behaviors that will take us into the future.

PART TWO

THREE INVITATIONS
TO EXTEND TO
INTERFAITH FAMILIES

Today, people identify and engage Jewishly not because they are compelled to or feel obligated to, but because they choose to. That is certainly true of people in interfaith relationships who are engaging Jewishly—both the Jewish partners and the partners from different faith traditions. But *why* do they choose to do so? What do they find meaningful and appealing about Jewish life? How might others who are open to the possibility, or become open to it, be encouraged to make similar decisions? What invitations might we extend to them?

InterfaithFamily was founded on two core beliefs. First, Jewish traditions have a claim on everyone who has Jewish ancestry: whether they have two Jewish parents, or one, or even Jewish grandparents or beyond, they have inherited a set of traditions that can help them live better lives. Second, those traditions can be shared with partners from different faith backgrounds and with children to help them live better lives as well. The goal was to extend a warm invitation to interfaith families to learn about and experience Jewish traditions with hope and confidence that if interfaith families try Judaism, they will like it.

Based on these core beliefs, what follows are three invitations that Jews and Jewish leaders can extend to interfaith families: to find meaning and spiritual connection in Jewish life; to find belonging in Jewish community; and to raise their children with Judaism. In order to effectively lead to Jewish engagement, each of these invitations must be framed with the nature of interfaith relationships and the needs of interfaith families in mind.

Find Meaning and Spiritual Connection in Jewish Life

Engaging in Jewish traditions can help people lead lives of meaning and spiritual connection. Chapter 6 addresses how we can best promote engagement in Jewish traditions, especially holiday celebrations, to interfaith families. Chapter 7 addresses how Jews and Jewish leaders should understand interfaith families celebrating Christmas. Chapter 8 offers steps that Jews and Jewish leaders can take to facilitate interfaith families finding spiritual connection through Jewish practices.

6

Jewish Traditions for a Life of Meaning

Everyone wants to live a life of meaning. Jewish traditions can serve as a framework to help people do just that. They inspire people to seek productive work that helps make the world a better place for themselves and others; to be generous, kind, compassionate, and deeply caring about others; and to learn throughout their lives. They help people raise children to be good and caring, and they teach compelling values. That's what Jewish life has to offer interfaith families and what can be emphasized in order to effectively invite their Jewish engagement. Moreover, Jewish traditions have always adapted to suit contemporary needs and can continue to do so—including the needs of interfaith families.

This approach to finding meaning in life, while not exclusively Jewish, is profoundly Jewish, informed by what the Lippman Kanfer Foundation for Living Torah calls "Jewish sensibilities":

> [They are] lenses that help us make sense of what we are experiencing and guide us in responding emotionally and behaviorally to particular life situations. . . . Jewish sensibilities originate most often in Jewish texts and teachings, in the stories Jews have told from biblical times to the present day, in the experiences that have shaped these narratives, and in the lessons that have been derived about how to live a worthy and fulfilling life. Taken as a set of life approaches, sensibilities offer one way to answer the question: What does it mean to be Jewish?[1]

Irwin Kula, co-president of Clal—the National Jewish Center for Learning and Leadership, writes that religious leaders need to provide wisdom and practice drawn from their tradition that helps people construct lives that are ethical, vital, and loving.[2] Barry Shrage, former president of Combined Jewish Philanthropies, provided one eloquent answer to the wisdom that Jewish traditions offer:

> In a time of rootlessness and alienation our stories are connected to a religious civilization with a 3,500-year-old history and an infinite future and the ultimate responsibility for the betterment of humankind in the name of the God whose story is at the heart of our existence.
>
> In a time of greed and selfishness, our stories are part of an old—a very old—tradition of caring for strangers—love of the poor and oppressed—and responsibility for widows and orphans, the elderly and handicapped.
>
> In a time of forgetfulness, our stories are part of a living chain of learning and literature in the world, inheritors of an ancient and hauntingly beautiful culture.[3]

JEWISH TRADITIONS ARE A SOURCE OF PURPOSE, ETHICS, AND LEARNING

We can invite Jews and their partners from different faith backgrounds to understand and experience distinctive Jewish traditions as helpful ways to fulfill the universal needs that all people have for purpose, ethics, and learning.

The notion that the purpose of life is to make the world better, not to live just for oneself or for rewards in an afterlife, has a distinctive Jewish expression—for example, "You are not obligated to complete the work, but neither are you free to desist from it" (Pirkei Avot 2:21). Over the years, many couples told InterfaithFamily that they found this worldview to be compelling and appealing.

Similarly, interfaith couples often said that Jewish ethical views are a distinctive aspect of Judaism that appeals to them. With the partner from a different faith tradition often viewed as different and *other*, interfaith couples find especially compelling the Torah's emphasis—in a commandment that appears thirty-six times, more than any other—that the stranger shall not be oppressed (Exodus 23:9) or wronged (Leviticus 19:33) but loved as we love ourselves (Leviticus 19:34), all because the Jews were strangers in the land of Egypt. Love the stranger is a key Jewish sensibility.

The relevance to contemporary issues found in Jewish texts is profound; talmudic discussions shed light on civic responsibility, welfare, environmental protection, treatment of immigrants, capital punishment, and many other issues. One indicator of this ever-renewing relevance is the fact that text-based learning is thriving among young adults at Moishe House programs.[4] Another indicator is the revival of Mussar, a Jewish spiritual practice aimed at developing balanced character traits including humility, forgiveness, patience, strength, moderation, equanimity, trust, and gratitude. Opportunities abound to make the extensive storehouse of Jewish wisdom accessible to liberal Jews and their partners from different faith backgrounds.

JEWISH TRADITIONS HELP TO RAISE CARING CHILDREN

Like everyone else, interfaith couples want to raise well-adjusted, grounded children with a strong moral compass—compassionate, caring of others, and eager to learn. Judaism has always placed special emphasis on child-rearing, and engaging in Jewish traditions can be a great way for interfaith couples to raise children with a connection to an ancient and beautiful tradition, a rich system of ethics, and a meaningful structuring of time and the stages of life.[5]

InterfaithFamily developed "Raising a Child with Judaism in Your Interfaith Family," a curriculum organized around eight universal parenting needs and the Jewish practices that address them. For example, parents want their children to be grateful for food and to be aware that others are hungry; the class taught the Jewish practice of saying the blessing over bread, *hamotzi*. In in-house evaluations, parents told InterfaithFamily,

> Usually I find I'm mindlessly eating . . . , to get done, and get on
> with dishes/bath/etc. I love the idea of saying thanks to God first,

and thinking about our connection to the world, about where our meal comes from, before eating. I think this will be a great addition to our nightly meal time—a deep breath so to speak.

We talked about appreciating the food that we have and told the girls that there are people who don't have enough food to eat. This is the first time that we have ever talked about this. A. (age 5) asked, "Can't we share our food with the people who don't have any?" We talked about what a mitzvah it would be to volunteer at a food organization and/or donate from our piggy banks.

Every night at dinner we discuss a mitzvah that we have done during the day.

ADAPTABLE HOLIDAY CELEBRATIONS TEACH COMPELLING VALUES

Rabbi Nicki Greninger explains how Judaism can be a source of meaning and purpose:

> It has a calendar that can give shape and meaning to time, it has rituals that can bring holiness into your life and the world. When you are in crisis or feel like you're free-floating, Judaism can give you roots, a foundation, a structure, texts, stories, prayers, and teachings to give you direction and hope.[6]

The holiday observances of the Jewish calendar provide a prime opportunity to foster interfaith families' Jewish engagement.[7] Jewish holidays can be shared by and become a source of personal meaning for both partners, teaching and reinforcing ethics, good conduct, and positive character traits. As with other Jewish traditions, Jewish holiday celebrations have always adapted to meet contemporary needs and can continue to do so for interfaith families.[8] In one of my favorite InterfaithFamily stories, a woman who grew up in a different faith tradition explained how she used her old Christmas lights to decorate her interfaith family's sukkah.[9]

SHABBAT

Interfaith families have consistently found marking Shabbat to be particularly meaningful. One said:

> When we sit down together, there's a peacefulness that comes over us. Something about it, about the ancient Jewish prayers, about being linked to a worldwide tradition, about sharing it together, all of us, has truly brought the beauty and bond of Judaism into our intermarried home.[10]

Any special effort to mark the time can become a family's Shabbat ritual. One of the participants in a Raising a Child class said:

> We have also started to have "Shabbat dinners." I don't make anything fancy; we just eat what we would normally eat, but we say the prayers over the candles, wine, and bread. When J. is a little older, I would like to introduce the concept of *tzedakah* [righteous behavior, justice] to him and add that to our Shabbat dinners.

THE HIGH HOLIDAYS

When I was twelve I won my synagogue's essay contest by writing that my favorite Jewish holiday was Yom Kippur. Something about self-evaluation, seeking forgiveness, striving to return to right behavior, and taking advantage of a new beginning, the key values behind the holiday, appealed deeply to me. The Torah and haftarah portions read in Reform synagogues on Yom Kippur morning are the most inspiring expressions of Jewish values—from the Torah portion's command to "choose life" (Deuteronomy 30:19) to the haftarah portion's command "to break the bonds of injustice . . . to share your bread with the hungry" (Isaiah 58:6–7). The themes of the liturgy of the day fully apply to both Jews and their partners, making the High Holidays, and Yom Kippur in particular, a great gift that interfaith families can benefit from and fully enjoy.

When our children were young, we modified the traditional practice of *tashlich*, observed by traditional Jews on the afternoon of the first day of Rosh Hashanah by going to a body of moving water and throwing bread or stones into it—a symbolic casting away of sins. At first it wasn't deliberate; looking for something to do on Yom Kippur afternoon with our children, we went to a neighborhood park and threw bread into the Charles River to feed the ducks. As our children got older, however, we started talking with them about the idea of trying to get rid of bad behavior and do better. We ended up clinging to the custom religiously. Every Yom Kippur afternoon, dressed in our finest suits and dresses (which must have looked very curious to the families playing in the park), we cast away our sins, though a lot of the bread was intercepted by hungry ducks before it even hit the water.

PASSOVER

Passover could well be the ultimate holiday expression of a particularly Jewish story and set of customs that are instructive of universal values— teaching children about their tradition, the obligation to care for all and to help liberate all who are oppressed, self-control—which makes the holiday especially appealing to interfaith families. When asked "what are a couple of things you love most about Jewish religion or Jewish culture," former first daughter Chelsea Clinton said she loved how her husband was "so dedicated to ensuring that we start developing our own Seder traditions for Passover . . . so he feels like we ironed out all of the kinks before we are blessed to have children."[11]

When I was a child, my mother's father read the entire Haggadah in Hebrew from beginning to end. At our most recent Seder, there were masks representing each of the ten plagues and items for our grandsons and their young friends to throw (like mini marshmallows representing hail). More seriously, we adopted a new tradition suggested by HIAS (originally the Hebrew Immigration Aid Society). We have a child walk to the door and place a pair of shoes on the doorstep, "to acknowledge that we have stood in the shoes of the refugee . . . [and] that none of us is free until all of us are free and to pledge to stand in support of welcoming those who do not yet have a place to call home."[12]

HANUKKAH

Beyond the fun of lighting candles, playing dreidel games, and exchanging presents, Hanukkah teaches important lessons. In "Why Hanukkah?" Rabbi Steven Carr Reuben explains that "Jewish civilization represents a value system that declares to every single individual human being on earth, that what they say matters, and what they do matters, and who they are matters." The Jews were resisting assimilation into a culture where "the only rule that mattered was that whoever had the most power and carried the biggest club got to make the rules," a culture of bigotry and prejudice based on "might makes right."[13] He concludes:

> Light the lights this year with pride as we continue to stand for the enduring values that celebrate the fundamental spiritual worth of every human spirit. That is why Hanukkah continues to matter.[14]

Many interfaith families find that Jewish traditions provide a wonderful, ever-adapting structure for lives of meaning, purpose, ethics, and values—for the Jewish partner, the partner from a different faith tradition, and for their children. That's one key thing we need to emphasize in extending invitations to interfaith families to engage in Jewish life. There's one more thing those invitations need to accommodate: how interfaith families are celebrating Christmas, the subject of the next chapter.

7

WHAT ABOUT CHRISTMAS?

Christmas has been a flashpoint of contention for as long as I can remember, so much so that the term *December dilemma* regularly appears in the media at this time of year. When I spoke at a synagogue in Santa Barbara in the early 2000s, a woman told me her child was intermarried, belonged to a synagogue, and was raising the children Jewish, but the woman wouldn't go to her child's house at Christmas time because they had a tree. I replied, "Ma'am, I would urge you to look at all that you should be pleased with, and not focus so much on the tree." Another young man, a good friend who was seriously dating a Unitarian woman, said they were deadlocked over their future because he refused to consider ever having a Christmas tree, even though she agreed that their children would be Jewish. I had the same advice for him. Kathy Bloomfield, an outreach professional, once told me that many Jews felt the same way about a Christmas tree as they did about a Nazi swastika. Viewing Christmas and its symbols as an ultimate expression of Christianity, they are reminded of a past when Jews were persecuted, or they resent the near constant exposure to a holiday that they do not consider their own.

Partners from different faith traditions, who grew up with warm family Christmas celebrations, have a difficult time understanding these reactions from Jews.

I grew up feeling very distanced from Christmas. My father gave his kennel man the day off, so I had to clean the kennels at the veterinary hospital on Christmas Day. When I started dating Wendy and was first in the presence of her family's Christmas tree, I remember feeling physically uncomfortable—just like the individuals described above. Nevertheless, we went every year without fail to my in-laws, who, while not particularly religious, had a Christmas tree. We exchanged gifts, and over time I was no longer uncomfortable. Our children, who grew up celebrating Christmas in this way, with many presents, did not experience any religious significance of Christmas. They did not feel it made them any less Jewish. They just felt that it was a nice time to be with their grandparents.

What to do about Christmas is an issue that interfaith couples need to negotiate. In another of my favorite stories, a woman insisted to her Jewish fiancé during their engagement that she would have to have a Christmas tree; he insisted that they would not. Eventually he said, "You know, our relationship is more important than a Christmas tree. If you want to have one, we will have one." Once he indicated that the relationship was more important, which is what they were really negotiating about, she lost interest in having a Christmas tree.[1] This is not an uncommon example.

When my children were preschool age, we had a Norfolk pine all year long as a house plant. At Christmastime we put a few ornaments on it. By the time the children started attending Jewish religious school, Wendy and I were uncomfortable even with that degree of decorating a tree, and we stopped. Our attitudes and practices had evolved. When our children were younger, my wife and I were still negotiating how we would adjust our individual traditions, and that takes time. I think that my agreeing to put some ornaments on the Norfolk pine showed my wife that I respected her tradition, which helped enable us to reach a mutual decision later to celebrate Christmas at her parents' house but not our own.

The key question has always been, what is the meaning of the tree or the Christmas celebration to the participants?[2] I learned from personal experience, InterfaithFamily writers, and ten years of surveys conducted by InterfaithFamily that many intermarried families celebrate Christmas not as a religious holiday but as a family time, like Thanksgiving. They are not affirming any kind of religious doctrine, and their participation does not mean that their children will not be raised with Judaism.

Successfully encouraging interfaith families to engage in Jewish life necessitates that Jews overcome their discomfort with interfaith families celebrating Christmas.

WHAT CHRISTMAS MEANS TO INTERFAITH FAMILIES

Since Sylvia Barack Fishman's 2001 American Jewish Committee study *Jewish and Something Else: A Study of Mixed-Married Families*, critics of intermarriage have argued that interfaith families incorporate substantial Christian elements in their homes.[3] It's true that life in interfaith families involves intimate exposure to other religious and cultural expression. Thousands of children raised as Jews have Christian relatives and participate in their holiday celebrations. While this does not look like Jewish life when viewed from a traditional perspective, it does not make a child raised with Judaism "something else."

Many of the writers in InterfaithFamily's 2003 essay contest who were Jewish or the children of intermarried parents described participating in Christmas celebrations in varied ways.[4] Some had Christmas trees in their own home, others went to relatives' homes for the holiday. Some went to church, others didn't. But without exception, they did not experience Christmas as having religious significance—not even those who accompanied a spouse or parent to church:

> We observe Christmas, not as the birth of Christ but rather as a secularized, commercial experience.

> I dyed eggs and hunted candy on Easter Sunday. Mother never tried to bring Jesus or Christian theology into our house, only the fun memories she had of her childhood.

> The joy of Christmas for [my Jewish mother] is being able to give her children gifts she has purchased with care. It has nothing to do with the birth of the Christian savior, and everything to do with . . . love, giving, and sharing. That is the way I look at the Christian holidays we celebrate now, as well as a way to show respect for my father's faith.[5]

A Jewish educator whose child went to a Jewish day school explained in her contest entry that a Christmas tree is not "outright Christian," a statement that has stayed with me ever since. She had a tree in her home because her husband

> wanted our boys to appreciate the traditions from both sides of the family without necessarily identifying with anything outright Christian. . . . As we see it, our job is to make our family's Jewish identity so natural, so much a part of us, that it's not threatened by the presence of a Grand Fir in our living room for one month out of the year.[6]

It would be unreasonable to expect an interfaith family to cut off half of their family background. Participating in Christmas celebrations is a way of honoring, respecting, and caring for the tradition of the partner or parent from a different faith tradition. Perhaps paradoxically, it is an expression of the important Jewish value of *shalom bayit* (peace in the home). Sometimes Jews have to participate in something they are uncomfortable with in order for the partner from a different faith background to feel respected and heard.

In 2004, Fishman extended her earlier study into a full-length book, *Double or Nothing? Jewish Families and Mixed Marriage*. Her central assertion was that the vast majority of interfaith families who say they are raising their children as Jews "incorporate Christian holiday festivities" into their lives, which she describes as syncretism—combining Judaism and Christianity—such that Jewish identity is not transmitted to their children, even though they interpret these festivities as not having religious significance to them.[7] She suggested that "the presence of Christian symbols and activities in the home" amounts to "bringing the ideas [and] beliefs . . . of the Christian church into Jewish households."[8]

However, when intermarried couples explicitly deny that their conduct has religious significance, as Fishman acknowledges that at least some of her subjects did "emphatically,"[9] and when their children say they experience these holidays in a secular, commercial, cultural, nonreligious way, how can their behavior amount to an affirmation of a religious belief?

Because Fishman's conclusion was so inconsistent with our experience at InterfaithFamily, we decided to gather more information. Starting in 2004 and continuing for ten years, InterfaithFamily conducted an annual December Holidays survey.[10] The key results of the 2004 survey, in which 80 percent of the respondents were raising their children as Jews, were:

- 53 percent had Christmas trees in their homes.
- 75 percent said their Christmas celebrations were more secular than religious.
- 69 percent kept their Hanukkah and Christmas celebrations separate and did not blend them.[11]

Ten years later, the results of the 2013 survey were largely the same.[12]

The important *Millennial Children of Intermarriage* study in 2016 confirmed what InterfaithFamily's surveys showed: "Home observance of holidays from multiple faith traditions did not seem to confuse these children of intermarriage"; they recall holiday celebrations as "desacralized" family events without religious content, special as occasions for the gathering of extended family; "some indicated that celebration of major Christian holidays felt much more like an American tradition than tied to religion."[13]

InterfaithFamily's surveys consistently reported that a very low percentage of interfaith couples raising Jewish children "tell the Christmas story." The Christmas story, about the birth of Jesus as the divine savior, is fundamentally religious. The fact that in 2010, for example, only 1 percent were telling the Christmas story at home was a clear indicator of the nonreligious nature of these families' celebrations.[14]

In 2011, there was a back-and-forth in the Jewish media about interfaith families and Christmas. Some said that interfaith families who celebrate Hanukkah should not also celebrate Christmas because Hanukkah honors Jews who resisted practicing any religion other than Judaism.[15] Some went further to say the meaning of Hanukkah is antithetical to welcoming interfaith families because Hanukkah commemorates a rebellion by the Jews against assimilation into the Hellenistic Greek society that surrounded them. These arguments make the common mistake of seeing Christmas as a religious holiday for interfaith families and equating intermarriage with assimilation.

In a post on InterfaithFamily's blog, one writer responded:

> I simply fail to recognize how celebrating a secularized Christmas is a danger to me or my Judaism. . . . The idea that my childhood—being raised to respect and understand the traditions of my father—somehow damaged my Judaism is downright offensive. In fact, I think it would only be more offensive if my mother had insisted upon banishing my dad's traditions from our home entirely, despite his commitment to raising a Jewish child.
>
> Sadly, it's attitudes like these that lead interfaith couples and their children to feel alienated from, and unwelcomed by, the larger Jewish community—which is the exact opposite of their stated goal. If you ask me, that's a much bigger problem than the Christmas tree in my living room.[16]

When interfaith couples are willing to raise their children with Judaism but want to have a Christmas tree as a secular symbol of a family tradition, we should not criticize their decision. Rather, we should focus on and applaud their Jewish engagement.[17]

The antipathy that a decreasing but significant number of Jews still have for Christmas expresses a desire to hold tight to traditional behaviors without modification. However, the Talmud includes this well-known statement: "Go see what the people are doing" (Eruvin 14b). One of the main things Jewishly engaged interfaith families are doing is celebrating Christmas in a nonreligious way. Half of young Jewish adults have one Jewish parent, and almost all of them grew up celebrating Christmas in some fashion. When Elena Kagan was nominated to the Supreme Court in 2010, she was asked at her confirmation hearing where she was on Christmas Day. She joked, "Like all Jews, I was probably at a Chinese restaurant." It was funny, but if you think about it, we are way past the time when all Jews are at Chinese restaurants on Christmas. Probably half or more are having Christmas dinner with their relatives who aren't Jewish.[18]

The real question about whether Jewish traditions will be passed on to children in interfaith families is not what they do around Christian holidays but what they do the rest of the year. As my teacher Paula Brody emphasized, for interfaith families who celebrate Shabbat weekly and all the other special Jewish holidays, Christmas is not such a big deal. Or as one InterfaithFamily writer said:

> I am not worried that the sight of Santa will turn [my daughter] into an instant Christian. I have faith in the power of Judaism as a religion and as a way of life. Assimilation happens because what is outside, over there, looks better than what is inside. You don't guard against it by building a higher wall between you and the rest of the world. What you do is make sure the life you have is irresistibly worth leading.[19]

8

EXPRESSING SPIRITUALITY
IN JEWISH SETTINGS

Jewish traditions can help interfaith couples and their children fulfill their spiritual needs and thus feel connected to something greater than themselves. As Barry Shrage, former president of Combined Jewish Philanthropies, said, "In a time that lacks vision and prophecy and that yearns for meaning, our stories are carrying an ancient faith in an ancient God so that our children and grandchildren will have spiritual options to fill their lives with light and joy."[1]

Liberal Judaism, however, tends to downplay concepts of and belief in God, and Jews score low in surveys on measures described as religious. Many liberal Jews don't think of God as described in the prayer book, intervening in the world to reward good and punish evil. Some say God exists in the encounter and relationships between people, others that God is a force for good. Jewish secular humanists don't talk about God. Still, many people feel a need for a connection to something greater than themselves—and Jewish practices can foster and nurture that connection.

In *The Jew Within*, Steven M. Cohen and Arnold Eisen found that moderately affiliated, contemporary Jews had a strong desire to find direction and ultimate purpose and wished to do so in Jewish religious communities and through ritual practices that were "a meaning-making and interpretive structure through which they seek coherence in their lives."[2] Today there is a great deal of ongoing experimentation with and expansion of Jewish ritual and spiritual practices to address contemporary styles and interests, with examples including the emerging spiritual communities that are part of the Jewish Emergent Network, and the spread of meditation practices and Mussar, among others.[3]

Intermarried Jews and their partners from different faith traditions are just as interested in finding direction and ultimate purpose in their lives, many through religious communities and ritual practices. The question is whether they can and will be interested in Jewish communities and practices. With appropriate encouragement and adaptation, they can, and they will.

When *The Jew Within* was published in 2000, I wrote about the phenomenon of intermarried parents wanting to define the religious identity of their family as Jewish and to worship together as a family.[4] Partners from different faith traditions, instead of practicing their own or another religion, were seeking to have their religious and spiritual needs met in Judaism, attending Jewish religious services and feeling comfortable joining in the prayer and song.

In discussions at my own synagogue, one intermarried partner said, "For a lot of us, this is the only place we worship, and we worship as a family here." Another said:

> I was raised Catholic. I came here because we can worship here and be a Jewish family here. We couldn't have been a Christian family, but I could embrace much of what's here. At many times I've felt part of the "us" here.[5]

One lesson from InterfaithFamily's 2003 essay contest was that questioning, searching, and struggling for answers in a context of nondogmatic theology are aspects of Judaism that appeal to both partners in interfaith couples. As one said:

> I enjoyed the Jewish encouragement of asking and answering questions. I am still fascinated that through the guidance of texts, traditions, and teachers, I have the freedom to question my religion and search for answers.[6]

The more Jewish communities emphasize spirituality, the more interfaith families will be attracted to Jewish life. In *The Jew Within*, Cohen and Eisen suggest that in a context of declining ethnicity, the religious sphere can be seen as more acceptable than an ethnic conception of being Jewish.[7] Intermarried partners from different faith traditions can find the spiritual experience, peace, and reflection that moderately affiliated Jews find, along with the family, community, learning, and connection to Jewish tradition that religious communities provide. This necessarily entails some adaptation, especially balancing our prayers' emphasis on the particular relationship of the Jews to God with more emphasis on universal themes.

ARE INTERFAITH COUPLES LESS SPIRITUAL?

In 2009, Synagogue 3000 published "How Spiritual Are America's Jews? Narrowing the Spirituality Gap Between Jews and Other Americans," a study that found that on all scales, Jews are less spiritual than other Americans.[8] A key finding was that aside from the Orthodox, who scored highest on all spirituality scales, Jews with just one Jewish parent are more spiritual than Jews with two Jewish parents. Because parents from traditions other than Judaism tend to be more spiritual, children growing up with at least one parent from a different faith tradition are more likely to resonate with spirituality and be culturally predisposed to spiritual concerns.

The study's authors, Steven M. Cohen and Lawrence A. Hoffman, state that spirituality is growing in importance as a gateway into meaningful Jewish life. They say that synagogues need to become spiritual communities to attract the children of intermarried parents, a growth sector of the Jewish population. Significantly, they acknowledge that "accenting spirituality will especially broaden Judaism's appeal" to groups including the children of the intermarried "who sometimes feel marginalized among born Jews but find familiarity in spirituality."[9]

Around the same time, an analysis drawn from the 2008 American Religious Identification Survey (ARIS) reportedly found that the number of American Jews who adhered to Judaism as a religion had declined by more than 20 percent over the last two decades, while the number of Jews who consider themselves secular had risen from 20 percent to about 35 percent. The authors, Barry Kosmin and Ariela Keysar, reportedly attributed the increase in secularism in large part to high rates of intermarriage.[10]

The apparent conflict between growth in secularism reported in one study and growth in spirituality reported in another is a matter of definition. The people who Kosmin and Keysar say are less religious and more secular are not people who do indeed feel spiritual yet are uninspired by traditional forms of Jewish prayer. Clal's Rabbi Brad Hirschfield said that what the ARIS study "is saying is the way religiously identified Jews are practicing their Judaism is not working for a lot of people. It's an opportunity—the kind of opportunity that paved the way for the Protestant Reformation."[11]

A few years later, the 2013 Pew report, *A Portrait of American Jews,* indicated Jews' ongoing ambivalence about God and religion. Even among Jews by religion (those who said "Jewish" when asked their religion), just under 40 percent belong to a synagogue or believe in God with absolute certainty, and just under a third describe religion as very important in their lives or attend religious services at least once a month.[12] Those levels of identification do not sound very religious. Sociologist Theodore Sasson wrote, "I suspect that many respondents who answered 'Jewish' in response to the religion question would have also liked to indicate 'agnostic' or 'atheist' but the survey forced a choice."[13]

The Pew report found a major trend toward secularism, especially among young Jews, and found an association between intermarriage and Jews of no religion (those who said they consider themselves Jewish or partly Jewish aside from religion): intermarrieds represent more than three-quarters of married Jews of no religion but only a little more than a third of married Jews by religion.[14] But Sasson questioned the association between intermarriage and secularism, pointing out that basically half of the children of intermarrieds who identify as Jewish are Jews by religion.[15]

Should the intermarried be tarred with the brush of secularism? There is no reason to believe that interfaith couples are less spiritual, less interested in a relationship with the sublime, or less responsive to meaningful supportive ritual at times of sadness or joy, than inmarried couples. Rabbi Arthur Green, writing in 2013 about whether people are "religious," noted:

The question is not: "Do you believe that God created the world, and when?" but rather, "Do you encounter a divine presence in the natural world around you" and "What does that encounter call you to do?"[16]

Current forms of Jewish religious expression may not be satisfying the spiritual interests and needs of many Jews, especially young adult Jews, whether intermarried or not. A respondent who feels spiritual and expresses spirituality through meditation or in nature even within Jewish frameworks may well provide the survey answer "My religion is not Jewish." This is part of a larger trend of spirituality splitting off from religion, of more people in general not finding spiritual expression through religious traditions, as identified by Erika B. Seamon in her book, *Interfaith Marriage in America: The Transformation of Religion and Christianity.*[17]

EXPRESSING HOPES FOR JEWS OR FOR EVERYONE

Prayers that emphasize the particularism of Jews and their relationship to God, as opposed to more universal prayers that refer to all people, are a challenge for interfaith families who want to express their spirituality in Jewish settings. Cohen and Eisen found that while contemporary Jews wished to find direction and ultimate purpose in Jewish religious communities and through Jewish ritual practices, they had "left aside or rejected those parts of Judaism that claim a special relation between God and the Jewish people." They had become more universalist and moralist, wanting to remain integrally involved in secular society and tending to see Judaism as emphasizing ethical values shared by the larger society.[18]

Cohen and Eisen found, for example, that "the particularist opening of the Aleinu prayer . . . which praises God 'who has not made us like the nations of the earth,' does not resonate at all for our interviewees." That would be even more off-putting to intermarried partners seeking spiritual satisfaction in a Jewish worship service. They, like Cohen and Eisen's subjects, would "prefer the prayer's universalist conclusion, which looks forward to the day when God will be ruler of all the earth."[19]

Contemporary liberal Jews in general—and interfaith families in particular—would get more involved in the Jewish religious sphere if there were greater emphasis on universal themes. For example, the often-sung *Oseh Shalom* prayer traditionally asked God to make peace "for us and for all Israel" but in the most recent Reform prayer books adds in Hebrew and English "and for all who dwell on earth," making the prayer that much more appealing.[20] Instead of focusing just on the concerns of "our" Jewish people, we need to broaden our focus to include the universal concerns of all people.

Another example of a liturgical change specifically impacts interfaith couples. In 2000, I had a visceral reaction at Rosh Hashanah morning services when my least favorite prayer—more accurately, my least favorite *translation* of a prayer—was read aloud. Part of the series of *Birchot Ha'shachar* (morning blessings) that all begin with "Praised be You, Adonai our God, Sovereign of the Universe," this particular prayer had the Hebrew ending *"she'asani Yisrael,"* which was translated as "who made me a Jew."[21] Hearing that blessing while sitting next to Wendy, who lived Jewishly but was not yet "a Jew," made me feel as if I had been kicked in the stomach, as I later told my rabbi.

In a traditional Orthodox prayer book, the blessing that ends *"she'asani Yisrael"* does not appear. Instead, the blessing ends with *"she'lo asani goi,"* which is translated as "who did not make me a heathen."[22] By the late 1940s, the Conservative movement's prayer book had replaced *"she'lo asani goi"* with *"she'asani Yisrael,"* which it then translated as "who hast made me an Israelite."[23] Presumably the editors were not comfortable with a prayer that was negative about other religious groups and wanted to replace it with a positive statement of gratitude for Jewish identity.

By 1978, when the Reform movement published *Gates of Prayer*, the *she'asani Yisrael* language also appeared, but it was translated as "who made me a Jew." When the Conservative movement came out with a new prayer book at about the same time, it also used that translation.[24] That translation is inaccurate, as the Hebrew word *Yisrael* doesn't mean "Jew." It means "Israel" or "Israelite." Presumably, again, the editors felt that it was the best way to convey gratitude for Jewish identity. But the "who made me a Jew" translation presented a real obstacle to partners from different faith traditions seeking to have their spiritual needs fulfilled in Jewish worship services, as well as to their sympathetic Jewish partners.

Of course, a Jewish worship service should have particularistic references to Jewish identity. Jewish liturgy is filled with references to God's covenant with the Jewish people, for example, that do not have to be off-putting to partners from different faith traditions. Statements that express gratitude for Jewish identity, however, can be made in much more inclusive ways. The Reconstructionist movement translated *she'asani Yisrael* as "who made me of the people Israel"; in a commentary, the editor said that that language gives "thanks for our particular identity as Jews."[25] One of the prayer book's editors told me that while they did not choose that translation out of consideration of the feelings of others, he could see how a person who lived Jewishly but was not a Jew could feel that he or she was "of the people Israel."[26]

After my Rosh Hashanah experience, I contacted Rabbi Elyse Frishman, the coeditor of a project then underway to create a new Reform prayer book for Shabbat, weekdays, and festivals. Rabbi Frishman said she wrestled with the phrase, noting that, on the one hand, it was exclusive, yet on the other hand, it heightened the sense of being a Jew, "which is what we mark in our prayer." She said the challenge was to reword it "so that we celebrate being Jewish without alienating" others among us.[27] The new prayer book, published in 2007, retained the "who made me a Jew" translation, but in 2015, when a new Reform prayer book for the High Holidays was published, *she'asani Yisrael* was translated as "who made me Yisrael."[28] I viewed this as a positive change..

Prayer book editors and prayer leaders need to continue to take into account those partners from different faith traditions in our synagogues who are seeking spiritual fulfillment in Jewish worship services.[29] Avoiding language that tends to exclude partners from different faith traditions will increase the comfort level of interfaith couples and facilitate their finding spiritual satisfaction in Jewish worship. This will increase the chances of attracting interfaith families to synagogues and having them raise their children with Judaism.

Find Belonging in Jewish Community

Being social and living in community is a basic Jewish sensibility, as expressed by Hillel's "Do not separate yourself from the community" (Pirke Avot 2:4). As Barry Shrage, former president of Combined Jewish Philanthropies, says, "In a time of anomie and loneliness, our stories are imbued with a thirst, and we maintain a commitment to creating community and providing a sense of belonging."[1]

Most Jewish traditions in which interfaith families are or could be participating either involve or are enhanced by doing so with others who share similar values and interests. Community provides a sense of connection to other people with whom to share joy and sorrow, engage in collective action, and worship.

For interfaith families, however, finding a sense of belonging in Jewish communities can be difficult, raising complicated issues of peoplehood and identity, which can be addressed by widely varying strategies of conversion on the one hand and radical inclusion on the other. Chapter 9 addresses the two different perspectives on Judaism—*being* Jewish and *doing* Jewish—that underlie the issues of belonging, identity, and peoplehood that face interfaith couples. It explains why conversion is a wonderful personal choice but not an effective or appealing engagement strategy for the great majority of partners from different faith traditions. Chapter 10 explores how partners from different faith traditions can feel part of a Jewish community that includes both Jews and their partners, with some coming to identify as Jewish—and the positive impact that a strategy of radical inclusion can achieve.

9

BEING JEWISH—CONVERSION

Mordecai Kaplan, the founder of Reconstructionist Judaism, taught that there are three ways of identifying with a religious community: (1) behaving—engaging in holidays and life-cycle celebrations (discussed in chapter 6); (2) believing (discussed in chapter 8); and (3) belonging, "that intuitive sense of kinship that binds a Jew to every other Jew in history and in the contemporary world," which Kaplan defined as the primary form of Jewish identification:

> Whatever Jews believe, and however they behave as Jews, serves to shape and concretize that underlying sense of being bound to a people with a shared history and destiny. When that connection disappears, Judaism too will disappear.[1]

The concept of peoplehood, however, is particularly challenging for partners from different faith traditions, as is feeling attached to Israel, another traditional measure of Jewish engagement integrally related to peoplehood. If the Jewish people consists of people who are *in*—who identify as Jews—and if the partner is *out* or *other*—not a Jew—then the partner is not part of the Jewish people. If Judaism is a set of traditions for Jews, in which only Jewish people believe and/or do this and that, then the traditions are not for the partner. If Israel is the homeland of the Jewish people, then it's not for the partner.

In a 1999 conversation with Rabbi Carl Perkins, I came to understand that two different perspectives on Judaism underlie the issues of belonging, identity, and peoplehood that face interfaith couples.[2] I explained that my wife, who had not converted at the time, when asked her religion, would respond that she "lived Jewishly but was not a Jew." Rabbi Perkins countered with "I'm not sure what that means," or words to that effect.

In one view, Judaism is a system of and for Jews. What matters is who is a Jew and who is not. Jews engage in certain behaviors and attitudes, and others do not. In this view, it wouldn't make sense for someone such as Wendy to live Jewishly because she wasn't a Jew. In the second perspective, Judaism is a system where what matters is the engaging itself, not whether the person engaging (such as Wendy) is a Jew or not. In the first view, Jews are a people and the Jewish people consists of Jews. In the second, Jews and others—including their partners from different faith traditions—can engage in Jewish life, and a Jewish community consists of those people who do so.

For most of Jewish history, there was no division between being Jewish and doing Jewish; Jews identified as Jews and thought and acted in certain ways. The *others*—people from different faith traditions—didn't think or act in those ways. Or they weren't allowed to, either by Jews or by their own groups that excluded and oppressed Jews for centuries. As a result, Jews developed negative attitudes about the others and policies that excluded them. Intermarriage changes all of that.

The alternative perspective that emphasizes doing, not being, Jewish was expressed by Rabbi Noa Kushner in her essay "Judaism for Gen X: Get Your Jewish On." There she describes her approach as founder of San Francisco's emerging spiritual community, The Kitchen:

> There is a big distinction between somebody's religion by birth and what they are willing to do. We are careful to note: Anybody can do Jewish stuff. I am not interested in lineage and pedigree. I am only interested in what someone is willing to do right now, Jewishly speaking.
>
> Similar to yoga's metamorphosis, if we want people to grow Jewishly, we need to encourage them to do Jewish. I am not asking anyone to sign on the dotted line or join a group. There is no identity shift.[3]

Rabbi David Ellenson once referred to this emphasis on doing, not being, as leading to "a 'Judaism of meaning' as opposed to a 'Judaism of boundaries and borders.'"[4]

CONVERSION

Conversion can be an effective solution to the challenge of belonging. A convert becomes part of the Jewish people to whom Jewish traditions belong. Surveys have shown that households with conversionary marriages—between a Jew and a convert—are even more Jewishly engaged on traditional measures than inmarried households.[5] That is why when intermarriage can't be prevented, critics of intermarriage want to encourage the partner from a different faith tradition to convert.

People often asked me why I was opposed to conversion. Let me be clear: I am not. I believe deeply that conversion is a wonderful personal choice. As noted earlier, my wife converted after we had been married for thirty years. A therapist, she said people converted when they felt a dissonance between how they lived and how they identified. She was comfortable saying that she lived Jewishly but was not a Jew—until she began feeling that dissonance. Whenever we talked about it, I always said, "Whatever you want to do is fine with me, I love you just the way you are." This dissonance is different for everyone and is triggered by very diverse and personal events.

InterfaithFamily always provided resources for prospective converts. We were delighted if we helped anyone along the path to conversion. But our approach to conversion of partners from different faith traditions was very nuanced. We believed that more children will be raised with Judaism in interfaith families if interfaith couples are included as they are rather than if conversion is promoted too aggressively. Converting to become part of the Jewish people is not appealing to the great majority of partners in interfaith relationships, especially not at the outset of their relationships.

Many partners from different faith traditions live Jewishly, without converting, as Wendy did for a long time. Many hesitate to convert, for very personal reasons. Some have reason to believe that their own parents may feel a rejection of their identity. Others focus on the ethnic aspects of Judaism and believe that conversion would not make them feel part of the Jewish people when defined as an ethnic group. Some feel that conversion is simply not important or necessary for them. One person told InterfaithFamily:

> I was raised Catholic. My wife and I went through a painstaking process in deciding to raise our children as Jews. I didn't want to convert but would do what was necessary. I learned Hebrew, I joined the Brotherhood, to show my commitment and example. I think commitment through showing and doing is more important than conversion.[6]

Another said:

> Judaism can be adopted in a process without conversion, which is an act. Many people grow into the Jewish community. They adopt Judaism as their form of worship. People are on different points on a continuum, it's hard to pinpoint where they are.[7]

I often encountered Jews who said that if a partner from a different faith tradition wanted to be active in the synagogue, why didn't they just convert? Given that Jews have historically experienced persecution, and that the Spanish Inquisition involved the forced conversion of Jews to Christianity, one would think that Jews would understand that pushing conversion can be alienating. Moreover, many Jews, raised as I was, recoil at the notion of a Jew converting *out*, to another religion. Isn't it inconsistent to be cavalier about the significance of a decision by a partner from a different faith tradition to convert *in*?

One of my first contributions to the intermarriage debate was an op-ed in *Reform Judaism* magazine's spring 2000 issue that responded to a call by Rabbi Eric Yoffie, then president of the Reform movement, to encourage conversion. I argued instead for a policy of radical inclusion of unconverted partners from different faith backgrounds.[8] When a rabbi or a religious movement calls for conversion, those who are not interested or ready to convert will not hear a message of welcome but an implication that they are suboptimal—less valued, less worthy, deficient in some important respects. A call for conversion by Jewish leaders or organizations risks making partners from different faith traditions feel different and unwelcome.[9] It is not encouraging or supportive of the efforts of these parents to raise their children as Jews. As one parent who felt pressure to convert told InterfaithFamily:

> It's not easy to find the way. It took us a long time. Feeling "part of" has been really important. Our family grew up here, felt together here. Being "part of" and included is the most important aspect of the temple for us.[10]

If we state, suggest, or imply that conversion is the preferred option for responding to intermarriage, we risk pushing away people who might otherwise come in. We risk losing those interfaith families deciding to raise their children Jewish and looking to Jewish communities for support in that endeavor. Paradoxically, the less aggressively we promote conversion, the more likely that people who are intermarried eventually will choose it, if they experience a welcoming embrace and support from Jewish communities. Posting guards at the gates saying—or even implying—"If you have not converted you cannot enter" is a losing strategy.

At the Reform movement's 2005 biennial, Rabbi Yoffie gave a remarkable sermon on spouses from different faith traditions and conversion. First, he called the partners who commit to raise their children Jewish "heroes" and said they deserve celebration and gratitude. Second, he called for Reform temples to do more than just celebrate and thank them. He said they should "ask, but not pressure; encourage, but not insist" that the spouses convert to Judaism.[11]

Taken on its own, Rabbi Yoffie's idea of what I would call a "soft sell" on conversion was a worthy approach. Unfortunately, in the Reform movement's own publicity about the speech, and in the following major media coverage, the notion of gratitude was almost completely lost. A *New York Times* article was titled "Reform Jews Hope to Unmix Mixed Marriages" and focused exclusively on the call for conversion.[12] At the time we heard more than one story from partners in interfaith couples who had carefully negotiated a decision to create a Jewish home and now feared being pressured to convert. Anticipating pressure to convert was a setback to their plans. One Jewish friend told me about her daughter-in-law, who was not Jewish but had been married by a rabbi, joined a synagogue, and agreed to raise children as Jews. She had become very upset when her boss at work, who was not Jewish, said to her, "I hear the synagogues want people like you to convert."[13]

In a January 2006 op-ed in the *Jewish Week*, Steven Bayme and Jack Wertheimer responded to criticism regarding efforts to encourage conversion. They objected to the position of some interfaith engagement activists "that the very term 'interfaith family' be changed to 'Jewish family' when gentile spouses agree to raise their children as Jews." They also wrote, "Conversion offers the best hope to create 'wholly' Jewish homes as well as 'holy' Jewish homes."[14] I understood these statements to mean that interfaith families raising their children as Jews should not or cannot properly be called "Jewish families" and that inmarried and conversionary families have "holy" homes, but intermarried families do not. In a letter to the editor, I wrote:

> Steven Bayme and Jack Wertheimer apparently don't care that promoting conversion aggressively, as they propose. . . , distresses and pushes away people like [my friend's daughter-in-law]—not to mention her Jewish husband and in-laws. Do they think telling her that her family can't be called a Jewish family, or her home holy, will encourage her Jewish involvement? Whether intentional or not, their message is that unconverted non-Jews raising their children as Jews should not be included in the Jewish community, that such people and their Jewish behaviors just aren't good enough.[15]

Even Sylvia Barack Fishman, while arguing that advocating for conversion is effective, has acknowledged that research on young interfaith couples reveals that they have "strong anti-pressure feelings," "see pressure to convert as a negative," and "would be 'turned off to Judaism' if they were approached about conversion by clergy or even family friends."[16] InterfaithFamily heard similar comments in a series of surveys it conducted about what attracts interfaith families to Jewish organizations.[17] Twice as many respondents said they appreciated invitations to learn about Judaism as said they appreciated invitations to convert. Responses to open-ended questions mentioned the absence of pushing to convert as a helpful factor and perceived attempts to convert people as a barrier.

Let me restate that I am not opposed to conversion. It is a wonderful personal choice for many people. There are excellent programs to explore Judaism that result in not insubstantial numbers of people deciding to convert, even when they started the program not intending to do so.[18] My teacher, Dru Greenwood, has impressed on me the "sense of wonder, of homecoming, of not believing one's good fortune" that many converts experience, that conversion is "a discovery, a growing into."

It is important that those who might be interested in pursuing conversion know that paths are available to do so. But the Jewish community shoots itself in the foot every time it takes anything other than a very unpressured approach toward conversion with interfaith families.

10

Doing Jewish—Radical Inclusion

Since my first forays in 2000 into the intermarriage debate, I have consistently contended that if our goal is to perpetuate Judaism in an open society in which intermarriage is common, we should adopt a policy of radical inclusion of the intermarried.[1] Instead of insisting that partners from different faith traditions convert—in order to *be* Jewish or *in*, part of the Jewish people with a Jewish identity—we should include partners from different faith traditions who *do* Jewish as part of a more broadly defined Jewish community made up of Jews, their partners, and their children. Feeling part of a Jewish community—national, local, or organization-based—can be appealing to partners from different faith traditions, who are bound to Jewish communities through loving relationships with their Jewish partners. They can feel proud of—and even love for—the history and the accomplishments of the Jewish community, without identifying as Jewish themselves. Some may come to informally identify as partly Jewish, kind of Jewish, or Jew-*ish*. Eventually some may even decide to make that identification formal and convert.

For partners from different faith traditions, the most important thing is to do Jewish, not be Jewish. Welcoming and encouraging them to engage in Jewish life as members of Jewish communities can satisfy their desire for community, while Jewish traditions can enhance their lives. Whether they end up identifying as partly or formally Jewish, or think of themselves as part of or a member of one or more Jewish communities, is incidental. It's the feeling of belonging that is critical.

When children are involved, though, it's a different story. As will be discussed in chapter 12, the children of interfaith families benefit from being raised to identify at least partly, if not exclusively, as Jews.

IS A FUNDAMENTALLY DISTINCTIVE
JEWISH IDENTITY REQUIRED?

My conversation with Rabbi Carl Perkins about living Jewishly without being a Jew expanded into point-counterpoint essays.[2] My view was that the Jewish religious movements had not sufficiently addressed the phenomenon of intermarried spouses who actively participate in raising their children with Judaism, who don't practice another religion, and/or who attend Jewish services and observe Jewish holidays—people who are living Jewishly without converting. We should allow and encourage these partners from different faith traditions to live as Jewishly as they choose to, whether or not they are or become Jewish.

Rabbi Perkins disagreed. He referred to "the fundamental distinctiveness of a Jewish identity," which is taken on when a person converts and becomes a "full member of the Jewish people." Conversion makes a difference in a person's religious, spiritual, and cultural life. People who have decided not to convert understand that difference. They don't consider themselves to be Jewish or want to be treated as if they are. To respect their integrity, maturity, and sense of self, Rabbi Perkins said, we shouldn't "pretend" that people who are not Jewish are Jews; that would be condescending and disrespectful.[3]

I responded that if we are up front about saying that we encourage and allow partners from different faith traditions to live Jewishly—in other words, we treat them as if they were full members—even if they aren't or don't become Jewish, we aren't pretending. We aren't making believe that people have chosen not to convert, nor are we stating that they are in fact Jews. We are acting as the Torah instructs (Leviticus 19:34) and treating the *gerim toshavim* (strangers who reside with you, or in Everett Fox's translation, "sojourners that sojourn with you") as full members of the community.[4]

These are very different perspectives. While Rabbi Perkins emphasizes respecting a person's choice not to become Jewish, he interprets that choice as meaning that the person does not want to live Jewishly or be treated as if they were Jewish. My concern is with the partners from different faith traditions who live with the dissonance, who are not ready or willing to convert yet, who are interested in, learning about, and engaging in Jewish life; those who define their families as Jewish and perhaps seek to have their spiritual needs met in Judaism. These are people who want to feel unified with their Jewish families by participating fully in synagogue life and ritual. It is completely respectful of these individuals, and their integrity, maturity, and sense of self, to encourage and allow them to live as Jewishly as they choose, without becoming Jewish.

Having partners from different faith traditions live Jewishly is more important than having them become Jewish. A radically inclusive approach supporting and encouraging more interfaith families to engage more fully in Jewish life will ultimately result in more Jewish families raising children with Judaism.

These different perspectives have important consequences. Insisting that people formally commit to being Jewish in order to be included leads not only to policies to promote conversion but also to maintaining boundaries in terms of who can be married by a rabbi, who can participate in Jewish ritual, and more (see chapters 15 and 16). Prioritizing being Jewish risks alienating the very individuals we need to include—and makes the challenge of feeling a sense of belonging in Jewish communities even more difficult.

Indeed, much of the debate about intermarriage rests on the exclusivist perspective that Judaism is for Jews and Jews alone. The "stranger among us" is suboptimal, marriage with them is bad. An either/or identity is key to this perspective—one is either a Jew or not. Negative attitudes about the other flow from this in-versus-out perspective, support restrictive policies on what the other is allowed to do, and push interfaith couples away. Surveys then record that interfaith couples are disengaged, with the critics of intermarriage having supported the conditions that lead to that disengagement. Those critics want socially exclusivist, Jewish ethnic groupiness back, at a time when identities are fluid and "life in an open society means that group boundaries are weakened and transgressed."[5]

The alternative is an inclusivist perspective that sees Judaism as a system for all who want to engage in it, partners from different faith traditions as equals, and intermarriage as an opportunity with positive potential, leading to elimination of obstructions to engagement.

TRIBALISM AND ISRAEL

In *The Jew Within*, Steven M. Cohen and Arnold Eisen write that Jews think of their relationship to other Jews as a matter of belonging to a group that extends vertically through time and horizontally through space—a feeling of deep connection to previous and future generations and to Jews all over the world. They describe three elements that constitute Jewish tribalism: (1) Jews should be familiar with one another, (2) Jews should be responsible for one another, and (3) Jews should have a higher opinion of Jews and a lesser opinion of others.[6]

The great majority of partners from different faith traditions are not going to feel that they should be more familiar with other Jews than members of other groups, be responsible for them, or have higher opinions of Jews than others. Cohen and Eisen note that contemporary Jews disfavor particularist notions that Jews are special or require exclusivity or separation from others.[7] This would be even truer of interfaith couples.

Feeling connected to Israel has also been a traditionally important aspect of feeling part of the Jewish people. I consider myself to be a Zionist, which I define as supporting a Jewish state in Israel. Then again, Israel is a nuanced and challenging issue for interfaith couples, as it is for increasing numbers of liberal Jews.

On one hand, the fact that the ultra-Orthodox Chief Rabbinate in Israel controls questions of Jewish identity, conversion, marriage, and the like, and essentially completely disregards the Jewishness of anything other than its own ultra-Orthodox approach, serves to distance liberal Jews from Israel, and interfaith couples even more so. Differences about the Israeli-Palestinian conflict also serve to distance liberal Jews and interfaith families.[8]

On the other hand, the creation of the State of Israel after the Holocaust—with its democratic ideals, stunning economic development, and astounding technological advances—is a source of deserved pride in Jewish accomplishment. Many Jewish partners and partners from different faith traditions report developing strong emotional connections to Israel. InterfaithFamily reported these connections—for example, in a story about a Birthright Israel participant who has one Jewish parent[9] and a story about an intermarried parent taking his family to Israel.[10] We encouraged interfaith couples and families to travel to Israel because all experience shows that doing so leads to the ultimate goal: further Jewish engagement. This increased Jewish engagement can include increased feelings of attachment to and support for Israel—in not only the Jewish partner but the partner of another faith background as well.

JEWISH PEOPLE OR JEWISH COMMUNITY?

Can intermarried partners from different faith traditions who do not convert be considered part of the Jewish *group*? It depends on how the group is defined. A better word for the Jewish group than *peoplehood* is *community*. Partners from different faith traditions who engage in Jewish life could very well say, "I do feel that I'm part of the Jewish community." They might even say, "I'm doing something very important to support it." The term *community* would be a good way to broaden the definition of Jewish peoplehood to include both Jews and their partners.

Partners from different faith backgrounds have always had a recognized place within the Jewish community. The Torah itself, as noted previously, refers to *gerim toshavim* (sojourners that sojourn with you) (Leviticus 25:6). The Torah portion read in Reform synagogues on Yom Kippur morning suggests that the sojourners were included among the people who entered into God's covenant: "You stand this day, all of you, . . . every man, woman, and child of Israel; and the stranger in the midst of your camp; . . . to enter into the covenant of Adonai your God, . . . to establish you as God's people" (Deuteronomy 29:9–12).[11] Elsewhere the

Torah refers to *kol adat b'nai Yisrael*—translated by Everett Fox as "the entire community of the Children of Israel" (Leviticus 19:2).[12]

If intermarried partners from different faith backgrounds were allowed to choose complete participation in Jewish life, and Jewish *people* meant a broader Jewish *community* made up of both Jews and the sojourners among us, then both Jews and their partners could feel that they belong, that they are members of the Jewish community, and even identify as such. This radical inclusion would help eliminate the feelings of being different, and excluded, that inhibit their Jewish living and child raising.

Under a radically inclusive approach, conversion would be an option for those who chose it, but those who have not and may never convert would get the message that they are welcomed and accepted just as they are. Unconverted partners from different faith backgrounds would be allowed to choose to participate in all rituals. They would be considered part of the *us* entitled to join in all prayers. Feeling included would advance and reinforce their efforts to live Jewishly and raise children with Judaism.

Like prayers about the Jewish people only, the concept of Jewish peoplehood and conversion to become part of the Jewish people are particularistic notions that are not appealing to many interfaith families. Feeling part of or a member of the Jewish community is a more universal approach that appeals to people who are uncomfortable with tribalism, chosenness, and particularism.

In 2015, Steven M. Cohen and Rabbi Joy Levitt, executive director of the JCC Manhattan, wrote an important op-ed for the Jewish Telegraphic Agency: "If You Marry a Jew, You're One of Us." They present a way to "create more households where both partners see themselves as part of the Jewish people." Note their use of the term *community*:

> One answer is for all of us to change the way we think of, and treat, those who love and marry our children, family members and friends. Basically we should agree and fully internalize the idea: If

you marry a Jew, you're fully part of our community until proven otherwise.

Born Jews would undergo a subtle but critical shift in the way they relate to family members and friends not born Jewish. It would mean fully including them in holiday practices, life-cycle ceremonies, and Jewishly centered social action and political activities.

[F]or those who choose to be part of our community without formal conversion—who come to the Passover Seder and drive their children to Hebrew school, who sit *shiva* with us, or who bring their sons into the community at a *brit milah*, who *shep naches* [derive pleasure] at their daughters' bat mitzvah and who go to Israel on vacation—we say welcome. It's a pleasure to know you. Come learn. You're one of us if you want to be.[13]

I couldn't have said it better myself.[14]

IDENTITY IN AN INCLUSIVE COMMUNITY

When partners from different faith traditions engage in Jewish communities, there will be a range of Jewish identities in those communities. People with Jewish ancestry may identify as Jews. Cohen and Eisen noted in *The Jew Within* that their intermarried interviewees felt that Jewishness is unalienable, an absolute that can't be increased or lessened by inmarriage or intermarriage; they are "confident of [their] unalterable Jewish identity by reason of birth to at least one Jewish parent" and "the children of an intermarriage will automatically be Jewish for the same reason, as will their children."[15]

Some partners from different faith traditions who engage in Jewish life with Jews will identify their partner and their family but not themselves as Jewish. One InterfaithFamily writer said that although her husband never converted to Judaism, he "no longer refers to us as an interfaith family; he calls us a 'Jewish family in which one parent is not Jewish.'"[16] Some partners from different faith traditions may identify as part of or a member of a Jewish family or Jewish community. They may feel that Jewish history and traditions have a claim on them through their relationship with their partner and are compelling and valuable to them. They may come to identify in some fashion as Jewish themselves: partly Jewish, kind of Jewish, Jew-*ish*.

At InterfaithFamily, we heard many comments, usually from parents from different faith traditions who were raising their children as Jews, along the lines of "I feel a little bit Jewish" or "I feel more and more Jewish as time goes by" or "I'm sort of Jewish, aren't I?" Rabbi Kerry Olitzky wrote a wonderful article for InterfaithFamily, "Doing the Conversion Two-Step" in which he explains how many people experience a "conversion of the heart" long before they formally convert, if indeed they ever do.[17] As Rabbi Susan Fendrick said:

> We gain nothing by ignoring or failing to name the ways that an individual's Jewishness "counts"—whether they live a Jewish life and identify as a Jew, come from a Jewish family or are "half-Jewish," or are simply identified by other Jews as being "one of us. . . ." Simple yes/no definitions of Jewishness are inadequate to the task of naming reality. We need to make room for descriptions that tell us about Jewishness as it is, not obscure its realities and complexities.[18]

A fascinating incident in 2015 sheds light on shifting and multiple identities. Rachel Dolezal resigned as president of a chapter of the National Association for the Advancement of Colored People after it was revealed that she identified as African American while her parents are white. She claimed to be "transracial." In "What My Black Jewish Son Teaches Me about Rachel Dolezal," Alina Adams, a Jewish woman married to an African American man, wrote that her three children "are being raised Jewish, and they identify as 100 percent Jewish, not 'half,'" while her husband "didn't convert, and he doesn't self-identify as Jewish. But he does identify with the Jewish people via his children."[19]

Adams writes:

As the wife of an African-American man and the mother of three biracial children, I feel much more personally connected to cases of police shootings, racial profiling and the academic achievement gap for minority children than I ever did before my marriage.

Would I self-identify as black? No. Never. That would be insulting, in my opinion. (I believe even wearing ceremonial clothes of another culture is pretentious, though many would disagree with me.)

But do I feel black?

Sort of.[20]

Then, about her husband, she says:

The same way my husband sometimes says "us" or "we" or "our" when he's talking about Jews. I honestly can't imagine how you can love a person and not feel like a part of their struggle. Which is a part of them. Which becomes a part of you.[21]

Alina Adams doesn't "self-identify as black" but she "sort of" "feels black" while her husband sometimes includes himself when talking about Jews, and his wife's and their children's Jewishness has become a part of him. Similarly, in a letter to the editor about the Dolezal incident, a Christian married to a Jewish woman for thirty years, with adult children who identify as Jewish, writes:

Over time, I have grown to "feel" Jewish myself. I even feel a bit insulted and left out when I am singled out as the only one in the family who is Christian. I can understand feeling so identified with a certain group that you wish you were born into that group, so identified that even a reminder that you are separate from that group hurts. I can understand Rachel Dolezal.[22]

The notion of a person who is born with and/or raised with one identity who feels an affinity with and eventually adopts in some fashion a different identity strikes close to home where interfaith families are concerned.

Many people who were not born or raised Jewish who are married or partnered with Jews feel an affinity with Jews and Jewish traditions and in some fashion adopt a Jewish identity, the way Alina Adams's husband has. The increasing understanding that that kind of identity shifting happens is the positive implication of the Dolezal incident for those interested in engaging interfaith families Jewishly.

I agree with Adams's conclusion and its applicability to interfaith families:

> My primary takeaway from the incident and my family's own experience is that, apparently, identity is much more complicated than my husband and I ever imagined it would be before our kids were born. And that instead of having all the answers, we're going to be learning right alongside with them—and the rest of America.[23]

Finally and paradoxically, a policy of radical inclusion might well lead to more conversion. In 1999, Gary Tobin wrote a book about what he called "proactive conversion"—not proselytizing but simply welcoming people to become Jews, and having a positive attitude about conversion and converts.[24] Tobin's book included an excellent discussion of conversion as a transformation of identity through experience and understanding—a process of becoming that begins prior to a formal conversion ceremony and continues thereafter, and shouldn't be expected to occur prior to marriage. Psychotherapist Esther Perel takes a similar view of conversion as a process of becoming after experiencing traditions:

> It can happen that one partner (usually the Gentile partner) experiences a gradual shift of allegiance and a change in religious beliefs, thereby incorporating a new world view. This process is similar to a resident alien who, after years of residing in a foreign country, sharing its customs, and identifying with its cultural heroes and institutions, decides to adopt the nationality of that country. . . . This type of conversion is quite different from a conversion that takes place under pressure, coercion, and anxiety.[25]

Radical inclusion is key to both Jewish partners and partners from different faith traditions feeling that they belong in Jewish communities. It supports Jewish partners continuing to identify as Jewish, and it fosters partners from different faith traditions feeling that they belong, identifying either as members of Jewish communities or perhaps as Jewish in some fashion. This feeling of belonging will motivate their engagement in Jewish traditions.

Raise Children with Judaism

Interfaith couples who identify with the Jewish community by behaving, believing, and/or belonging—finding value and meaning in Jewish traditions, finding spiritual connection in Jewish settings, and/or finding community with other Jewishly engaged people—are likely to want to raise their children with Judaism, that is, engaging in Jewish traditions and identifying partly if not exclusively as Jewish. As discussed in chapter 3, how children are raised religiously is the biggest area of concern from a Jewish communal perspective in which it is important that Jews and Jewish traditions continue. That coincides with being the most challenging issue for interfaith couples.

With respect to Judaism, interfaith couples have a range of options: raising children to identify as Jews; raising children to identify as Jews and also with another culture or religion; or raising children with Jewish traditions but not with one or more religious identities. These options, and the reasons supporting the various decision that can be made, are the subject of chapter 12, with particular attention to the choice between raising children with one religious identity, or both—meaning Jewish and something else.

Some couples decide about these options before they get married. Others decide when a child reaches school age and choices about religious education become important. Still others decide when a child reaches the age of bar or bat mitzvah, confirmation, or other coming-of-age ceremony. Often, however, compromise and negotiation over the religious identity of children begin when a child is born and the question of having a baby welcoming ceremony is presented. That is the subject of chapter 11.

11

Welcoming a Baby

Both of my children, who are now parents themselves, are Jewishly engaged. From the way we marked their births, it might not have looked like that would be the result. They actually each received their Hebrew names twice. When Emily was born, I knew it was a Jewish tradition to name a child after a deceased relative, but we hadn't done that. It didn't occur to us to give her a Hebrew name or have a naming ceremony. When she was three or four, we were at a fair at the Boston Children's Museum where one of the activities was getting your name calligraphically written in Hebrew letters. Emily said her English name. The attendant looked in a book and found that the name Emily meant "industrious"; then she looked in another book and found that Tirzah is the Hebrew name that means "industrious." Thus Tirzah became her Hebrew name.

Baby boys are more of a challenge because it is traditional to have a bris, or *brit milah* (ritual circumcision), eight days after their birth. When our son, Adam, was born, we used a middle name that started with the same letter as the name of my father's mother, so we at least followed that tradition. I remember thinking that his Hebrew name would be the same as his English name. But it didn't occur to me to have a bris. He was circumcised by a doctor while I watched from behind a thick glass window. I remember feeling vaguely uncomfortable and expressing a silent hope that this would be a sign that he was a Jew.

Before Emily started school, Wendy and I had agreed it was important for our children to have a religion. We didn't have any disagreement that theirs would be Jewish. By the time Emily was about ten and Adam was six, we had become active in our Reform synagogue. The kids had started religious school, and the question had come up whether they had Hebrew names. Looking ahead we also knew Emily would need a Hebrew name for her bat mitzvah. We decided that we should formalize our impromptu choices of Tirzah and Adam. Our rabbi came to our house, and we had a private naming ceremony, complete with an official certificates.

Looking back, I wouldn't have done anything differently. It must not have felt right to me to want a naming ceremony when they were born. That may have to do with the dynamics of my relationship with Wendy and her parents. Perhaps I felt that pushing the children's religious identity from the moment of birth might be counterproductive, leading to negative feelings from them. Possibly I subconsciously felt that we needed to learn to trust each other as parents together for a while before addressing the religious identity issue. I never felt that a naming ceremony was essential to making a person a Jew. For us, I think it was better that the official naming came much later, when the kids could be aware of what was happening and they were already clearly on the road of their Jewish education.

I've been at Jewish baby naming ceremonies that are very meaningful for families. If intermarried parents can agree to have one, they're a great way to mark the start of a Jewish life. From a grandparent's perspective, a naming ceremony is an indicator of continuity. In many cases, the new parent is saying to his or her parent, "I'm doing for my child what you did for me." Then again, my own experience shows that for some intermarried families, having a naming ceremony isn't that important, and they choose not to have one. This should not be viewed as their decision about the child's religious identity. Many interfaith parents, while foregoing this ritual, go on to raise their children with Judaism. There are many different pathways that can lead to that result.

Since the time of Abraham in the Torah, circumcision has been a very strong Jewish tradition, serving as a clear indicator of Jewish identity for thousands of years. Newborn circumcision is very common in the United States, although declining, from 83 percent in the 1960s to 77 percent in 2010.[1] For many interfaith couples, circumcision may not be a difficult issue. They may, for example, want a son to look like his father. For many partners from different faith backgrounds, though, either the circumcision itself and/or the ritual circumcision at a bris can be the most challenging Jewish life-cycle observances.

With respect to the ritual, a boy does not have to have a bris to be Jewish. My son, Adam, chose not to have one for his own son, who was circumcised by a doctor in the hospital. If I were asked for advice, I would encourage interfaith couples to consider having a bris. The home-based ceremony can be a very meaningful occasion for everyone, and it can serve as a marker that the child will be raised with Judaism. Many interfaith couples do have a bris for a boy, and there are ways to make the ceremony welcoming and inclusive to relatives from different faith traditions.[2]

With respect to circumcision itself, there are sincere Jews who oppose it as inhumane and unfair to the child.[3] People argue back and forth about whether there are health benefits of circumcision; that issue may be persuasive to some, but not others. Ultimately the religion-related reason for an interfaith couple to circumcise a son is, again, to mark that the child will be raised with Judaism. If asked, I would encourage interfaith couples to circumcise for that reason.

When Emily was pregnant the first time, she approached me a few months before her due date to say, "If we have a boy, we are not sure we will circumcise him." I told her that she might be surprised by my reaction, but I would not push her and her husband on the issue, I would respect their decision, and I added that I thought that in the future there will be a lot of men who identify as Jewish who are not circumcised. They ended up having a bris for their first and again for their second son. They were deeply moving experiences for everyone, and I'm glad they made those decisions. But it would be counterproductive to suggest to interfaith couples that if they don't circumcise, that's the end of Jewish engagement for their children.

In one of the most important articles ever published by Interfaith-Family, "Is Heaven Denied to an Unbaptized Child?," Father Walter Cuenin explained that under modern Catholic theology, salvation is not denied to unbaptized people. Father Cuenin wrote that the importance of baptism is that, like a bris, it is a marker—a ritual to mark the child's entrance into a religious community.[4] These markers raise the critically important longer-range question interfaith couples need to resolve: the religious identity of their children.

12

RAISING CHILDREN—JEWISH OR BOTH?

All interfaith couples who are serious about having religious traditions together confront certain issues. Resolving these issues, such as what kind of wedding to have or how to celebrate in December, requires negotiation and compromise. By far the largest arena for negotiation and compromise is what to do with the religious upbringing of children. As Esther Perel says, "Because children symbolize the continuity of the family, its values, and tradition, they bring into focus the differences of the partners' background."[1]

Every couple is unique, but there are patterns of partners' attachments to their traditions and interactions that are associated with the likelihood of their children being raised with Judaism. The key factors in these patterns are the strength of the partners' attachments to their own traditions, the strength of the partners' interests in having religious traditions for their children, and the openness of the partners to learning about and experiencing each other's traditions.

In one typical pattern that is likely to result in children raised with Judaism, the Jewish partner has a stronger connection to Judaism than the partner from a different faith tradition has to his or her tradition, and the partner from a different faith tradition is open to learning about and experiencing Jewish traditions. In another representative pattern that often results in children raised with Judaism, the partner from a different faith tradition may have a stronger connection to that tradition than the Jewish partner has to Judaism, as well as a stronger interest in having religious traditions in the family. However, the couple may still mutually decide that raising children with Jewish traditions is the approach most comfortable to them. Lastly, neither partner may have a strong connection, but they may decide that their children would benefit from religious traditions and mutually decide that Jewish traditions are more comfortable.

When each partner has strong connections to their own tradition and wants to practice them individually, they may decide to raise children as one or the other. They may, however, want to raise children exposed to both traditions in the family or as both—partly Jewish and partly another religion.

It's important to remember that parents' ideas about how to raise their children with religion may change over time. Decisions made before real children are on the scene may be reevaluated when a baby arrives or a child comes of school age.

RAISING CHILDREN JEWISH

Many interfaith families choose to raise their children to identify as Jews. InterfaithFamily always recommended that interfaith couples who make that decision should also honor the other parent's and grandparents' religious tradition, not hide or disregard it. In my own case, we were as close to my wife's parents as we were to mine, and our children clearly knew that their mother and her parents came from a different faith tradition. We spent every Christmas at my in-laws. But our children weren't confused about being Jewish themselves—at least not for long.

My daughter, Emily, remembers feeling, when she was little, that she was "half and half." She remembers that while she and I were walking hand in hand one day, I told her that she wasn't half and half, that her Mom and I had decided that she was all Jewish. She says that from that point on, that's what she felt. It's hard to believe it was that simple, but children do pay attention to what parents say, and at least some of the time it has a real impact.

I learned that it's important for parents to make sure to communicate their thoughts on religious identity to their children. When Emily's bat mitzvah approached, she asked, "Why is it so important to you, anyway?" (By then she had stopped accepting everything I said.) I was taken aback because I assumed that she knew why it was so important to me—but I hadn't told her. I ended up writing a long letter to her, about how I loved my immigrant grandparents, how I experienced some anti-Semitism growing up, how I was one of the rare people who enjoyed Hebrew school and Jewish learning, how I felt about Israel, and more. Parents can't expect their children to know what's in their heads if they don't express it to them explicitly.

I also learned at InterfaithFamily that many parents recognize the importance of giving children one religious identity. One parent emphasized that not choosing led to confusion: "By not choosing we were treading water in a swirling current of religions, without a boat to claim our own."[2] In one of my favorite stories, another said:

> Religion is like clothing. It is the parents' responsibility to dress the very young child appropriately. ("Here is your red coat.") As the child gets older, explanations may be added, but the clothing decision is still ultimately the parents'. ("You need your red coat because it is very cold today.") Eventually the child will be able to choose between a red coat, a blue coat, or even no coat at all. Undoubtedly, if my husband and I had only spoken of religion in the theoretical sense, our children would have been running in the snow with shorts on and wondering why they were cold.[3]

Several committed Christians said they were comfortable choosing Judaism for their children and family because Jewish theology is not inconsistent with their beliefs. At the same time, they recognized that Christian theology is inconsistent with Jewish beliefs. One said that the question came down to how they could best worship as a family.[4]

Interfaith couples who want to raise their children with Judaism need to take action to make that happen. Critics who say that the children of intermarriage inevitably won't be Jewishly engaged are wrong. It's not the fact of intermarriage but what the intermarried couple does that determines their children's Jewish engagement.[5] That makes what intermarried parents are doing around Jewish education a key issue and highlights the importance of Jewish leaders taking action to make Jewish education more attractive and more accessible to interfaith families.[6]

RAISING CHILDREN BOTH

The phenomenon of interfaith couples saying they are raising their children in or with more than one religion—both, or partly Jewish and partly something else—is real: the Pew report, *A Portrait of American Jews*, said that 25 percent of intermarried families were doing so, which means over 140,000 children.[7] But what interfaith families who say they are "doing both" are actually doing is not at all clear. There's no research or study of that population.

At one end of the spectrum, a number of families are very serious about providing religious education for their children about both (or more) of the religious traditions of the parents. These families are served by organizations such as the Interfaith Community, the Interfaith Families Project of Washington, DC, and the Chicago Interfaith Family School, which in addition to religious schools offer holiday celebrations and religious services from multiple traditions. Proponents of this approach, including Sheila Gordon, founder of the Interfaith Community, and Susan Katz Miller, author of *Being Both: Embracing Two Religions in One Interfaith Family*, say that they are not blending together or merging religions (which is the definition of syncretism) but respecting the integrity of each and teaching about and celebrating both.[8] They are distinct from and opposed to Messianic Judaism, which believes that Jesus was the messiah and includes Jewish practices in its rituals; I don't consider Messianic Judaism to be Jewish at all because its core beliefs are theologically incompatible with Judaism.[9]

At the other end of the spectrum, some interfaith families say that their family is Jewish and their children are Jewish, but they teach their children about the other religious traditions of their family. Or they celebrate Christmas (and/or Easter) in a nonreligious way and view their children as having two cultural identities but one religious identity. Some of these couples may respond to a survey question by saying they are "doing both" or raising their children Jewish "and something else." In between those endpoints there are many possible permutations of what doing both or being raised partly Jewish means.

In 2010, Kate Fridkis asked the provocative question "Can someone identify as a Jew and a Christian simultaneously?" Fridkis thought that people involved with the Interfaith Community were doing that by educating children of interfaith marriages in both Jewish and Christian traditions. She wrote that "a growing number of people are unwilling to give up their religious tradition just because their partner has a different one."[10] However, it's still not clear what "giving up their religious tradition" means in this context. Many Christian parents are unwilling to give up their celebrations of Christmas, but that doesn't mean they are raising their children to identify as both Jewish and Christian.

IS IT POSSIBLE TO BE BOTH? IS IT A GOOD IDEA?

There are compelling reasons for intermarried parents to choose to raise their children in one religion while still honoring the other parent's religion. The first reason questions whether it is even possible to be both. In "You Can't Be Both (Jewish and Not)," Jane Larkin writes:

> How could our family be "really Jewish" if we recognized Jesus as the Messiah? How could we be "really Christian" if we didn't? It seemed that by choosing a hybrid path, our family would simply be on the threshold of both faiths but not be truly part of either.[11]

It is difficult to understand how someone can consider themselves to be both Jewish and Christian when a fundamental dividing line between Judaism and Christianity is the belief that Jesus was divine. Apparently, though, even that isn't clear-cut. Susan Katz Miller says that "many adults raised as Christians believe that Jesus was a great leader, a teacher, a political renegade, a rebel rabbi. Some do not believe in the Virgin Birth." She cites a 2000 poll that showed that one-third of Protestant clergy did not believe in the physical resurrection of Jesus. She says that "teens and young adults who have gone through [dual education] programs tend to express consistently positive views of Jesus, although few claim him as the Messiah or as the only son of God"; most "see Jesus as a teacher, not as a personal savior."[12]

In an interfaith education program, children are offered a whole spectrum of ways of looking at Jesus: as literary fiction, as an important historical figure, as a mysterious inspiration, or as the literal son of God. Miller quotes one such child as saying, "Whether Jesus was the Messiah or not doesn't affect my relationship with God. The reason I practice both religions is that both have ceremonies and rituals and values that get me closer to God and allow me to have a stronger faith."[13]

Miller quotes another teen as saying, "I don't know if I see Jesus as the son of God. I see him as a role model. I don't see him as a deity but as a person, a great person. Part of why he has been made into a godlike figure is that what he represents isn't really attainable by a normal human."[14]

Miller says that such a child could be categorized as a liberal, progressive Christian with a deep appreciation for Judaism. But if believing in the divinity of Jesus is what defines a Christian, this sounds to me like a Jewish child who is educated about and admires the historical Jesus, but not a Christian.

It's too easy, or avoids the difficult question, when Miller says:

> I believe that Jesus was the son of God, in the sense that we are all children of God—meaning that all human beings should aspire to tap into the goodness within themselves. . . . I am comfortable discussing the "godliness" and goodness of Jesus, even if I don't believe he is my personal savior.[15]

As mentioned in chapter 7, few interfaith couples who are raising their children as Jews and who celebrate Christmas tell the story of the birth of Jesus as the divine savior. However, the children of interfaith couples being raised as Jews could learn about Jesus if their parents want them to. In "Jesus and the Promise of Christmas," author James Carroll writes that "acting in his Jewish tradition," Jesus confronted and rejected violence and proposed peace and justice to counter it. He continues, "The great religions of the world—Judaism, Islam, Buddhism, Hinduism, Confucianism—and the no-religion of rationalism have all countered the normalcy of violence with assertions of compassion and loving kindness." As a figure representing the ideal of peace and justice, Carrol concludes, Jesus has survived even for those who regard him in purely worldly terms as an image of a hope that cannot be fully articulated and that can never be exclusively claimed by any group, including Christians. In that sense, he says, Christmas observances can belong to everyone who chooses to enjoy them.[16] Perhaps that's a way for interfaith couples raising their children with Judaism to include Jesus in their Christmas celebrations.

As to whether it is advisable to raise children as both, the other compelling reason to choose one religion is to avoid making children feel confused or torn. Jane Larkin writes that she and her husband did not want to put their children in the position of choosing between mother or father.[17] Choosing one religious identity provides a framework for imparting values that parents want to instill. Having one faith does not deprive or shield children from having full knowledge of their religious background but provides a foundation and strong basis from which to discuss commonalities and differences and build knowledge of other religions.

One young adult at a conference expressed the great sadness she felt when her parents left her to pick a religious identity and community. She felt as if she was choosing not between her mother and her father but between her two grandmothers. There are numerous personal narratives and professional opinions on the InterfaithFamily website to the effect that being grounded in one religious identity and feeling part of one religious community is important for children and young adults.

On the other hand, some argue that educating children in both traditions better prepares them to make their own future choices.[18] Miller quotes a minister from the Interfaith Families Project as saying that dual education makes Judaism very attractive because no one is trying to force the kids to stay Jewish—rather, it's a choice.[19]

IT'S IMPORTANT FOR CHILDREN TO HAVE AN IDENTITY

From a Jewish communal perspective, the idea of people raising their children as both is very challenging. It matters a lot whether the child of an interfaith couple identifies as a liberal Jew who is educated about and respects Jesus but doesn't believe in his divinity or as a progressive Christian who also doesn't believe in Jesus's divinity but is educated about and engages in Jewish traditions. It matters because belonging—identifying as a Jew or part of the Jewish community—motivates people to engage in Jewish life and because engaging in community with other Jewishly engaged people is so rewarding.

I asked about the interplay between identity and engagement in an interview with Cokie and Steve Roberts in 2011 when their book *Our Haggadah: Uniting Traditions for Interfaith Families* was published. Cokie, the well-known political analyst, is Catholic, while Steve, the well-known journalist, is Jewish. They observed both religions in their home, exposed their children (now grown) to both, and did not raise them to identify with one or the other. I asked whether they thought that interfaith couples would still be having Seders twenty or thirty years in the future, and both were quite certain that they would. Cokie's answer was that what children will do in terms of Jewish practices is always a question—and she aptly added that it is a question about children of two Jewish parents too. They told me that their family has more "Jewish content" than the families of Jewish relatives of Steve who are inmarried. Cokie added that given the reality of intermarriage, a good solution is to celebrate Jewish traditions as "a major part of the family."[20]

It sounds as if the Seders that Cokie and Steve Roberts lead are so wonderful that their children, raised exposed to both religious traditions, would want to continue to have Seders for their families. But if interfaith couples don't identify their families or their children as Jewish, then in another generation, will the children of those families—themselves married, perhaps intermarried—still be interested in having Seders? If most children of interfaith couples end up identifying as progressive Christians who engage in Jewish traditions, will those traditions continue for long into the future, detached from people who identify as Jewish or as members of communities of Jewishly engaged people? Most likely not. For Jewish traditions to continue, it's best for the children of interfaith families to be raised as Jews.

Moreover, I am persuaded by the theological complications that it's hard for someone to identify as Jewish and something else. I'm also persuaded that the "better prepared to choose" argument is outweighed by the confusion and choice arguments. For those reasons, it's best for interfaith couples to choose one religious identity for their children while exposing them to the traditions of their other parent and grandparents. Children being raised both can and do identify as Jewish in part and may choose to identify as Jews as adults. But the chances of children identifying as Jewish when they are adults are greater if they are raised as Jews than if raised as both.

However, if raising children as both is what interfaith couples want to do, they will and they should. That's why I have referred throughout this book to children being raised "with Judaism," which I define as meaning engaging in Jewish traditions and identifying partly, if not exclusively, as Jewish. We don't have to view being raised as both as inevitably leading to loss of Jewish engagement. While we may prefer that young adults with one Jewish parent identify as Jewish, it's not wrong for them to identify as "half Jewish" if they so choose. There was a group at Brown University called the "half-Jew crew"; there has been a "Half-Jewish Network"; and there are books about being half.[21] There is always potential for greater involvement with people who are engaged already and identify to some degree as Jewish.

The reasons Susan Katz Miller advocates for doing both, while they merit respect, demonstrate how radically inclusive attitudes and policies, the subject of part 3, might influence couples to decide to choose one religious identity for their children.

- Miller asserts that children appreciate that couples who do both don't suppress either parent or religion. The counterargument is that parents from different faith traditions, if radically included, may not feel that they or their religion are suppressed.
- She says doing both gives grandparents equal weight, free to transmit their traditions. The counter is that partners from different

faith traditions, if radically included, may choose to have their parents share their cultural but not religious traditions with their grandchildren.

- Miller asserts that choosing one religion clashes with societal assumptions, referring to Jews who say the children are "not really" or "don't look" Jewish. Those assumptions will disappear when radically inclusive attitudes are adopted.

- She says that choosing one religion makes family unity not possible without conversion, while doing both allows each partner to do everything. Those kinds of restrictions also will disappear when radically inclusive policies are adopted.[22]

If Jewish leaders and institutions presented the value of Jewish life in compelling ways and adopted radically inclusive attitudes and policies, more of the folks who are attracted to the idea of doing both might decide to identify their children as Jewish.

PART THREE

THREE ROAD MAPS FOR ENGAGING INTERFAITH FAMILIES

Invitations to interfaith families to engage in Jewish life will succeed when Jews, Jewish leaders, and Jewish organizations genuinely include them and support their engagement. It's a virtuous circle—invitations fall on receptive ears, couples get interested, they stay because they feel included. When they expect inclusion, they are more likely to come. When they experience inclusion, they are more likely to stay.

Interfaith couples who have chosen love can also choose Jewish tradition. By the same token, Jews engaged in Jewish tradition can also choose to love interfaith couples and especially the partners from different faith backgrounds.

The three arenas in which Jews, Jewish leaders, and Jewish organizations can encourage more interfaith couples and families to engage in Jewish life and community are attitudes, policies, and programs. But everything flows from attitudes. When Jews, Jewish leaders, and Jewish organizations adapt their thinking to radically inclusive attitudes about intermarriage and about partners from different faith traditions, radically inclusive policies, and a serious programmatic campaign to attract interfaith couples and families, will naturally follow.

Attitudes

It's the job of leadership to move people to adapt their attitudes.[1] When Steven M. Cohen and Joy Levitt proposed that partners from different faith traditions be considered members of the Jewish community, they said this would require that Jews "undergo a subtle but critical shift in the way they relate to family members and friends not born Jewish. It would mean fully including them."[2] A critical shift is definitely needed, but it's not a subtle one. The negative to ambivalent attitudes Jews have toward intermarriage and the exclusivist attitudes Jews have toward partners from different faith traditions need to shift substantially toward the positive. Chapter 13 reviews prominent examples of the discouraging messages interfaith couples and families continue to get from Jews; unfortunately, an entire book could be filled with more examples. Fortunately, however, more and more Jews and Jewish leaders are seeing intermarriage as an opportunity and understanding the need to be radically inclusive of partners from different faith traditions—treating them as equals—the subject of chapter 14.

13

THE DISCOURAGING ATTITUDES THAT NEED TO CHANGE

In April 2009, the rabbi in the rabbi-priest pair that formed the popular "God Squad" in newspaper columns and on TV responded to a young Jewish woman who wrote seeking advice. Her parents had rejected her Catholic boyfriend, even though she and her boyfriend intended to raise their children with the same connection to Judaism that she had. Speaking on behalf of her parents, the rabbi said she could not have both love and tradition:

> Our task in life is not merely to find love for ourselves but also to honor and preserve the spiritual legacy and traditions bequeathed to us. Hundreds of generations of Jews before you have lived as Jews and sacrificed as Jews, even in the face of terrible oppression and death. If they could preserve their faith through times of hell, why can't you preserve your faith in times of freedom? The idea that Judaism will end in our family with you for no other reason than that you met a nice Catholic guy is devastating to us.[1]

Guilting young Jews with the notion that their ancestors preserved Judaism through persecution and that they must choose their Jewish heritage over their personal happiness, as the rabbi did here, is alienating. Having Jewish leaders make them feel terrible about who they love is most likely to push them and their partners away from any Jewish involvement.

It's a simple, obvious truth that most people will hesitate to go where they are made to feel unwanted or where their decisions are disrespected. But the dominant Jewish communal response to intermarriage since the 1990s continues to make many interfaith couples feel that way.

When Jewish leaders say that inmarriage is a fundamental norm of Jewish life, their message, implicitly if not explicitly, is that intermarrying is wrong and not what Jews are supposed to do. When no further reason is given for their stance, this amounts simply to tribalism.

When Jewish leaders make statements such as "Intermarriage is a bad thing for the Jewish people," they are sending a message that interfaith families do not and cannot live Jewishly or raise their children with Judaism. A variant is to question "how Jewish" interfaith families who say they are living Jewishly really are by suggesting that their children are Jewish "and something else."[2]

Disapproval of intermarriage necessarily conveys a message of disapproval of the partner from a different faith tradition. What the interfaith couple and their families hear is that the partner from a different faith tradition is suboptimal, not worthy or desirable. Too many Jews continue to adhere to this negative narrative.

HOW WE TALK ABOUT INTERFAITH MARRIAGE

For better or worse, we live in a culture that is obsessed with celebrities. How Jewish leaders and journalists talk about celebrities who are intermarrying is significant. A prime example of this is the 2010 marriage of Chelsea Clinton to Marc Mezvinsky, which was a subject of fascination throughout the world. In November 2009, the week the engagement was announced, InterfaithFamily blogged about whether a rabbi might officiate at the wedding. The traffic to the website was the highest ever to that point.[3]

Hillary Clinton's reaction to the engagement was positive and affirming. Asked how she felt about Chelsea marrying "in an interfaith context," she said:

> I think it says a lot about not only the two young people involved
> and their strong love but also their deep faith, both of them. But it
> says a lot about the United States, it says a lot about this wonderful
> experiment known as America, where we recognize the right that

every single person has to life, liberty, and the pursuit of happiness. And over the years so many of the barriers that prevented people from getting married, crossing lines of faith, or color or ethnicity, have just disappeared. Because what's important is, are you making a responsible decision, have you thought it through, do you understand the consequences?[4]

Jewish leaders, however, reacted with clear expressions that intermarriage is wrong. Before the wedding, the *Washington Post's* On Faith column ran a series of articles[5] and assembled a panel of rabbis whose comments expressed a great deal of ambivalence toward intermarriage. This was typified by one rabbi who expressed the common attitude that "I oppose intermarriage before the fact. After the fact, I support marriage."[6]

The news finally emerged that, while the wedding took place before sundown on the Sabbath, a rabbi had co-officiated; Mezvinsky wore a *kippah* and *tallis*; and the couple incorporated several elements of a traditional Jewish wedding ceremony, including a ketubah (Jewish marriage contract), a chuppah (wedding canopy), and reading of the "seven blessings." Jewish leaders had a singular opportunity to congratulate the couple, welcome them to the Jewish community, and focus on what might be next for them in terms of Jewish engagement.

Instead, the Jewish Telegraphic Agency's story was titled "Clinton-Mezvinsky Wedding Raises Questions about Intermarriage." In it, Rabbi Eric Yoffie said, "The Reform movement frowns upon its rabbis conducting weddings on the Sabbath"; Rabbi Steven Wernick, head of the United Synagogue of Conservative Judaism, said, "Intermarriage is certainly 'not ideal,' but ... the Conservative movement in 2008 decided that it must welcome interfaith families and 'help their spouses along their spiritual journeys.'"[7] The *Forward* summed up the Jewish reaction: "Top leaders from all the major streams of Judaism—Reform, Conservative, Orthodox, and Reconstructionist—were at pains to stress that the Sabbath day nuptials of Chelsea Clinton and Marc Mezvinsky were not a Jewish event."[8]

When celebrity interfaith couples engage Jewishly, the interest of other interfaith couples in doing so may increase. There was an opportunity here to inspire those couples to seriously consider incorporating Jewish practices in their weddings—as Chelsea and Marc did so prominently—and hopefully in their lives together after their weddings.

Pronouncing the wedding as "not a Jewish event" was the worst possible response because it could only serve to discourage and push away not just Chelsea Clinton and Marc Mezvinsky but also the thousands of other interfaith couples who were watching. If you were in an interfaith relationship, considering whether to get more involved in Jewish life, how would you feel reading statements from Jewish leaders such as "Intermarriage is not ideal"? The *Forward* captured the lost opportunity perfectly with the title it gave to my op-ed on the subject: "The Missing 'Mazel Tov.'"[9]

The negativity about intermarriage expressed around the Chelsea Clinton wedding is far from isolated.[10] Consider another celebrity interfaith relationship, that of Mark Zuckerberg and Priscilla Chan. Here the reaction of Jewish leaders was not only that intermarriage is wrong but also that the children of intermarriage won't be Jewish. In 2010, journalist Danielle Berrin said that a profile of Zuckerberg in the *New Yorker* gave "the Jewish world yet another reason to fret over its future by suggesting Zuckerberg is on the road to intermarriage."[11] After Zuckerberg did intermarry in 2012, an "expert" pronounced that "the children of another successful Jewish man will not be counted as Jews."[12] But in 2017, Zuckerberg posted on Facebook that he had given his great-grandfather's Kiddush cup to his daughter, accompanied by photos with the Kiddush cup, Shabbat candles, and challah. That was after he said in the commencement speech at Harvard that he sings an adaptation of the *Mi Shebeirach* prayer for healing to his daughter at night.[13]

At one time I thought about starting a "Razzie Award" for Jewish journalists whose comments were not conducive to attracting interfaith couples to Jewish life. Consider these comments from senior editors of the *Forward*:

- Editor in chief Jane Eisner, in a thoughtful discussion of marriage and birth rates, added she was "haunted" by whether marriage-age children will marry other Jews, not mentioning the potential for positive Jewish engagement that could result.[14]
- Editor-at-large J. J. Goldberg, in a discussion of Jewish population estimates, mentioned that "there's a growing, still unmeasured tendency among children of intermarriage to identify as Jewish, perhaps because it's fashionable in Washington and Hollywood."[15]
- The *Forward* editors, in an article that referred to intermarried individuals choosing to live lives of Jewish depth and meaning, questioned "however Jewish" they "actually are" and characterized intermarriage as "diminishment" and inmarriage as "essential."[16]

Pretty much any statement about intermarriage coming out of Israel is negative and essentially says that those who intermarry are lost to Judaism. This was true in 2009, when MASA, an Israeli organization that provided Israel programs for young adults, "launched a 'scare-tactic' campaign" that urged Israelis to combat assimilation in North America by working to prevent the "loss" through intermarriage of their own Jewish acquaintances.[17] It was equally true in 2018, when the new chair of the Jewish Agency for Israel referred to intermarriage as a "plague" and Israeli politicians condemned the celebrity wedding of a Jewish actor and an Israeli Arab news anchor as a "disgrace."[18]

These statements are important because they have an impact on Jews and interfaith couples in North America. Equating intermarriage with assimilation is a classic mistake repeatedly made by Israeli leaders.[19] Israelis don't understand that many intermarried families are engaged in Jewish life or that many more would engage if they were not described as a "strategic threat" by the community in which they want to participate.[20] As Paul Golin, then a leader at the Jewish Outreach Institute, aptly wrote in 2009:

> The suggestion that intermarriage also represents absorption beyond recognition into the larger culture is an affront to the literally hundreds of thousands of households where one parent

happens to be Jewish that are currently raising Jewish children. If intermarriage means the same thing as assimilation, there wouldn't be intermarried members of synagogues, children of intermarriage on Birthright Israel trips, or intermarried leaders of Jewish communal organizations.[21]

WELCOMING ENOUGH?

Critics of intermarriage have argued that Jews and Jewish organizations are already sufficiently welcoming and that further efforts are not necessary. They contend that interfaith couples are not deterred from engaging in Jewish life because they don't feel welcomed. In 2010, discussing a report about Jewish camps, Steven M. Cohen was quoted as finding that most interfaith couples feel as if they have an open invitation to be part of Jewish life and that outreach "has been misguided by focusing simply on being welcoming." He went on to say that "the response of welcoming, making personnel more sensitive to the intermarried, and watching your language and having smiling ushers is not going to be effective."[22]

These assertions demonstrate a deep lack of understanding of the impact that disparaging messages have on interfaith couples. After the camp report was publicized, InterfaithFamily received several emails from partners from different faith traditions who were actively engaged in Judaism, raising children Jewish, and yet felt "second class" and insulted. One said she was "the ideal interfaith partner" who gave up all her religious traditions and "accepted that I was always going to be fundamentally different and separate from my children." And yet, she continued:

> [T]he message that I get is that it is never enough, that I am simply wrong for not being Jewish, and I am a threat and a second-class citizen. When I hear rabbis stress the evils of interfaith marriage in synagogue, how does Dr. Cohen think I feel? How do my children feel, knowing that their father was considered wrong, and that he married an unacceptable person? Is it so much to ask that yes, they soft pedal the admonitions and prejudice against intermarriage, given that we are advocating and living Jewish choices?[23]

Another comment illustrated the difference between being welcomed and being truly included. One woman, who said she and her husband "sat through too many lectures" where the speaker "put in their two cents about intermarriage . . . being bad bad bad," said, "So, on one hand, we're welcomed into the event, but please put up with the insults we'll be throwing your way about your marriage."[24]

Another comment, in addition to mentioning speakers who "describe your marriage as the greatest threat to Jewish continuity," noted the impact of Internet postings:

> [I]magine you are researching about intermarriage on the Internet and see the negative comments posted on many blogs. Would you feel welcome? Would you be inclined to raise your children as Jews, or would you wonder if there might be a more welcoming community for you elsewhere?[25]

Arnold Eisen has acknowledged that Jews "sometimes" "pass judgment on the value of individual . . . marriages . . . [and] Jews married to non-Jews, insulted more than once, often hear such criticism, even when it is not intended." In researching *The Jew Within*, Eisen said, "Our interviewees told us with virtual unanimity that the thing they like least about Jews and Judaism is being told by other Jews that they are not real Jews, or good Jews."[26]

Between 2009 and 2012, InterfaithFamily conducted a series of surveys with questions that national and local community studies had never asked—namely, what factors contribute to interfaith families joining Jewish organizations and synagogues, and what do they experience as barriers? The primary reason why interfaith families do not participate in the Jewish community is that they do not receive explicit expressions of welcome, but rather have unwelcoming experiences. Seventy-nine percent of the respondents said an explicit welcome by organization professionals mattered "a lot" to them. Statements of welcome by the organization itself in membership materials, bulletins, and websites also attracted them "a lot" (70 percent). Welcome communicated in public and openly talking about interfaith family issues were specifically identified as helpful. Being vague about the approach to interfaith families was seen as a barrier. In comments on the surveys, one respondent said, "I feel that deep down the clergy . . . would prefer I be Jewish." Another said that the "Neanderthal attitude of some members to non-Jews . . . offended my wife royally." One summed up the importance of a welcoming attitude this way: "As long as being an interfaith family is considered a problem, we will never be reached."[27]

In a focus group conducted for InterfaithFamily in 2010, people said they didn't feel welcomed when they heard "don't intermarry" messages, when they felt subtle pressure to convert, or when the first reaction they experienced was suspicion. The issue of rabbinic officiation at weddings of interfaith couples, the subject of chapter 15, came up often. One person said, "Rejection stays with you. It turns you off to the synagogue and it turns you off to Judaism."[28]

A good friend in the San Francisco Bay Area, not Jewish herself but active in her Reform synagogue, told me in 2015 that a woman at the synagogue said, in her presence, "We Jews are dumbing ourselves down by intermarrying." My friend—herself at the highest level of anyone's intelligence scale—was so shocked at how insulting the comment was that she couldn't immediately respond. I once read a comment to another survey in which a couple said that at a Reform synagogue, someone who learned they were interfaith said, "Maybe people like you would be more comfortable" at some other synagogue.

A 2018 study of Washington, DC, notes that respondents in interfaith relationships "reported ways that the community made them feel unwelcome" and includes several comments from those people, including "I just want to be comfortable bringing my interfaith partner to events without him feeling pressured," and the following:

> As someone from an interfaith household, it's hard to engage with the community if I have to convince my spouse, "Don't worry, you'll feel comfortable and welcome." She often feels like the Jewish community is insular and skeptical of non-Jews, and that makes it hard for me to find ways to engage in the community as well.[29]

The 2011 New York study reports that the vast majority of the inter-married say they do not feel uncomfortable attending most Jewish events and activities; only 14 percent feel uncomfortable, compared to 10 per-cent of the inmarried. But a related finding exposed widespread negative attitudes about intermarriage. High percentages of parents—56 percent of non-Orthodox inmarried Jews—said they would be upset if their adult child married someone not Jewish who did not convert, compared to 12 percent of converts who would be upset, or 6 percent of intermarrieds.[30]

When a UJA-Federation of New York task force recommended strong efforts to engage interfaith families, Jack Wertheimer referred to "the reli-gious and communal imperative to perpetuate Jewish life through endog-amy" and suggested that the federation should assert that "intermarriage is bad for the Jewish people and the perpetuation of Judaism."[31] Interfaith couples may feel comfortable or welcomed at Jewish events and activities, but if they experience expressions of prejudice against intermarriage, they will not feel genuinely included.

Around the time that the Pew report, *A Portrait of American Jews*, found that 89 percent of intermarried Jews are proud to be Jewish but only 59 percent have a strong sense of belonging to the Jewish people,[32] the Jewish Outreach Institute published *Listening to the Adult Children of Intermarriage*. This study's key finding was that young adults with one Jewish parent are just as interested in many Jewish activities as those with two Jewish parents, but they participate in such activities less frequently when the programs are offered by Jewish institutions and prefer explor-atory, self-guided activities.[33] Why would intermarried Jews feel proud to be Jewish but not feel like they belong? Why would young adults with one Jewish parent be interested in Jewish activities but not participate?

Given the negative attitudes toward intermarriage they encounter, it shouldn't be surprising that interfaith families have relatively infrequently joined Jewish institutions, engaged in Jewish learning, or practiced Jewish ritual. It is equally simple and clear that adapting to positive attitudes will lead to increased engagement.

Edgar Bronfman, the former CEO of Seagram, leading Jewish philanthropist, and early supporter of InterfaithFamily, said intermarriage is "here to stay. Let's make it work for us, rather than against us."[34] Bronfman's 2008 book *Hope, Not Fear: A Path to Jewish Renaissance* is a model for the positive attitudes about intermarriage that are needed. He realized that the first essential step to inclusivity is to stop speaking negatively about intermarriage:

> If we speak about intermarriage as a disaster for the Jewish people, we send a message to intermarried families that is mixed at best. How can you welcome people in while at the same time telling them that their loving relationship is in part responsible for the destruction of the Jewish people?[35]

14

RADICALLY INCLUSIVE ATTITUDES

Jewish philanthropist Edgar Bronfman realized that partners from different faith traditions needed to be welcomed unconditionally and treated as honored guests:

> No one should be made to feel our welcome is conditional or begrudging. The many non-Jews who marry Jews must not be regarded as a threat to Jewish survival but as honored guests in a house of joy, learning, and pride.[1]

Bronfman realized that if the Jewish community was more welcoming, the numbers of children of intermarriage raised Jewish "could grow dramatically."[2]

Adam Bronfman, Edgar's son, has urged Jewish leaders to consider the potential for positive Jewish involvement by interfaith families if Jews and Jewish institutions welcome them. At the 2008 General Assembly of what is now the Jewish Federations of North America, he said that interfaith couples were in fact living Jewishly. He affirmed that Judaism was never meant to exist in a "gated community" but was always meant to be open. He expressed confidence in Judaism's value by saying that its central ideas will remain but be surrounded by evolving new ideas. If something is of value, people will be attracted to it and will not leave.[3]

In a Passover message to Combined Jewish Philanthropies donors, Barry Shrage explicitly brought the issue of engaging interfaith families directly into the spotlight:

> How will this year's Seder be different from all others? Who will sit at our Seder? What questions will they ask and what stories will we tell? As we gather our families and friends around the table, many of us will be sitting with children raised in interfaith households

and young adults who have returned from Taglit-Birthright Israel trips to Israel. Those children and grandchildren may be asking surprisingly spiritual questions. (A recent study found that the next generation of Jews is actually more spiritual than the last and that the children of intermarriage are the most spiritual of all.)[4]

These are the kinds of statements from Jewish leaders that recognize and speak positively about the reality and presence of people from interfaith relationships in the Jewish community.

Forward editor J. J. Goldberg described a transformation in his attitudes about partners from different faith traditions in "Generation to Generation, Our Changing Judaism."[5] At a family bar mitzvah at a Conservative synagogue, the bar mitzvah boy said about his Torah portion that "a religion can change and grow." To Goldberg, the parents' role in the ceremony was "downright astonishing." The boy's father was not Jewish but was called to the bimah—by his English name; he didn't have a Hebrew name—to join in an *aliyah*, reciting the blessing for reading the Torah:

> I've never before seen a traditional, old-fashioned Hebrew davening in which a non-Jewish parent was welcomed as a participant, honored like any other parent who brings a Jewish child into the covenant—perhaps even more so, since he was bringing his child into a covenant he had not taken as his own. . . . The inclusiveness didn't stop there. Both parents stood before the open ark and offered blessings to their son—Anne in Hebrew, Geoff in English.

Goldberg describes his reaction: "At first it was a shock to watch. Almost immediately, though, it felt completely natural. Now I can't get over the shock that this is still unusual."[6]

Goldberg's two conclusions were heartening. First, the father was "one-half of the couple that raised this Jewish child. How could he not be part of the celebration, not share his joy with the community as his child becomes a man?" Second, "how many other parents don't bring their children into the covenant because they think—correctly, all too often—they won't be welcomed?" So was his praise for the rabbi, who "dared to open [his community's] gates as few other rabbis have done."[7]

There have even been positive comments about intermarriage coming out of Israel. In a 2011 article, authors Rabbi Naamah Kelman, the dean of Hebrew Union College in Jerusalem, and her husband, Dr. Elan Ezrachi, an educational consultant, challenged "the "dominant line . . . that mixed marriages were a disaster that would lead to a decline in the number of Jews" and referred to another view that sees "a possibility for expanding the definitions of identity and enlarging the ranks. . . . [I]n American Judaism a dynamic of acceptance, embrace, and widening circles is developing."[8]

Gary Rosenblatt, publisher of the *New York Jewish Week*, wrote about new Jewish startups in Europe that "deal with intermarriage by, in a sense, ignoring it. Their programs tend to be open to everyone."[9] Contrary to the typical view of Europe as "an ageing demographic threatened by intermarriage and assimilation," Barbara Spectre, the director of Paideia, an academic institute dedicated to the revival of Jewish culture in Europe, says what is happening is "the dis-assimilation" of Jewish life, with even young people who are intermarried or not considered Jewish by halachic standards asserting their identity and exploring Jewish roots and culture. Spectre calls for a change in "rhetoric and attitude" among Israeli and American Jewish leaders who refuse to "hear good news" about what she sees as "a great transformation taking place."[10]

In 2010, journalist Julie Wiener reported a growing acceptance of interdating among Jews:

> Whereas ending up with a Jewish partner, regardless of his or her level of observance or commitment, used to be non-negotiable for those who wanted to live a Jewish life, the new priority increasingly seems to be finding someone, Jewish or not, who is supportive of one's Jewish pursuits.[11]

Actor Natalie Portman is a prominent example of this approach. In 2005, she said she was not necessarily looking for a Jewish husband: "A priority for me is definitely that I'd like to raise my kids Jewish, but the ultimate thing is just to have someone who is a good person and who is a partner."[12]

Jewish parents are also more accepting. A case in point: the popular *The Bachelor* and *The Bachelorette* TV shows. When bachelorette Ashley Hebert visited the families of the few remaining contenders, J. P. Rosenbaum's mother on Long Island came across as a stereotypical Jewish mother: warm, loving, but a little intrusive. In an interview, Ashley says she was nervous at first that his family would not be accepting of her. However, J. P. says he was never worried his family would wish she were Jewish. They would be accepting of whoever he brought home. Ashley expresses being open to raising their future children Jewish: "Whatever makes him happy makes me happy."[13]

In InterfaithFamily's essay contest, many writers told powerful stories of welcome and embrace by relatives who chose love and enabled tradition to be maintained. That includes grandparents. One writer tells how her Holocaust-survivor grandfather ended his first meeting with her boyfriend who was not Jewish by "giving him the same good-bye kiss he usually reserves for his grandchildren":

> There are few moments in my life that have been as meaningful
> as that kiss on the cheek. My courageous grandfather chose to
> show affection to a boy who likely represents some of his greatest
> fears, rather than make his granddaughter feel bad about who she
> loves.[14]

Additionally, many writers told powerful stories of welcome and embrace by rabbis who also chose love and enabled tradition to be maintained, especially those who expressed gratitude to the partners from different faith backgrounds. One wrote, "The rabbi said that non-Jews raising their children Jewish are making the ultimate generous gift to the world. My non-Jewish husband listened and lovingly said he understood." They also responded to rabbis who acknowledged the "Jewishness" of the lives of the partners who are not Jewish. One wrote, "Our rabbi said something that proved to be a defining moment in my spiritual journey: 'You may not have converted, but you do realize that you are living as a Jew, don't you?' Imagine that, being told by a rabbi that you act like a Jew!"[15]

InterfaithFamily's survey respondents emphatically acknowledged that they are heavily influenced by expressions of welcoming attitudes. One said, "My spouse was welcomed as a genuine part of the congregation family in all aspects, as was my son. This allowed me, as the Jewish partner, to comfortably express my Jewish identity without my spouse feeling alienated." Another said, "They treat me like an important part of the Jewish community, even though I am not Jewish."[16]

In 2009 I observed another sign of positive change: programs such as day schools, summer camps, and Birthright Israel trips, which had in the past been promoted by touting that fewer participants in those programs intermarry, had scaled back that message.[17] Children of one Jewish parent, who represent 50 percent of young Jewish adults, are underrepresented in those programs; for example, the percentage of Birthright Israel trip participants with one Jewish parent was 35 percent in 2017, up from 20 percent in previous years.[18] The leaders and funders of those programs must have realized that most interfaith couples and their children will not want to participate in programs that describe their type of family as something to be prevented. All of these programs are worthwhile because they promote Jewish engagement—regardless of whom people marry—and could and should be encouraged for that reason.

When attitudes shift, Jewish organizations can make engaging interfaith families a priority in their strategic planning, as Boston's Combined Jewish Philanthropies (CJP) did in 1998:

> To fulfill the biblical imperative to welcome the stranger and newcomer, we must reinforce and increase our efforts to be open and welcoming to interfaith families, to help and support them in the hope that they will find meaning in Jewish life, choose to create Jewish families, participate in Jewish communal activities and support Jewish institutions.[19]

Jewish organizations could expressly invite interfaith families to their programs and events. Since 1998, every invitation to a CJP program has included: "CJP welcomes those who would like to connect with the Jewish community and encourages the participation of interfaith families, couples and significant others in all its activities."[20] Every Jewish organization could have the equivalent of a sign on its doors that says Interfaith Families Welcome Here.

Rabbis in particular would do well to follow the example of my own rabbi, Allison Berry. In a stunning Rosh Hashanah 2017 sermon on inclusivity, Rabbi Berry said that at Mt. Sinai, "we stood there, those of us born Jewish, those who had chosen Judaism and those who were there because they loved someone Jewish."[21] Mentioning several members of the congregation by name, including an interfaith family, the rabbi quoted a teaching of the Baal Shem Tov that "'the Jewish people is a living Sefer Torah, and each of us is one of its letters.'. . . Somewhere embedded on the scrolls behind me, in our ark, is the letter containing" the story of that interfaith family. She went on to say:

> Together these letters of Torah construct our history and our future. They are an expression of our joys, sorrows, and moments of transcendence. When we leave people out or do not see those asking to be allowed in, we lose letters vital to the integrity of our Torah. When we build sacred, inclusive community we stand together as envisioned at Sinai.[22]

We need more rabbis who share Rabbi Berry's radically inclusive attitude that there are letters in the Torah not just for every Jew but for every Jewishly engaged person.

We need to believe in the possibility of and embrace the potential for positive Jewish outcomes. Instead of the silence that too often surrounds intermarriage, we need to talk about the positive outcomes that are already happening. We need to hear the people who say that because of their interfaith marriage, they live a more Jewish life, and have educated themselves and their children about Jewish practice to a far greater extent than they would have otherwise. We need to hear from the increasing numbers of people who are intermarried and yet are Jewish professionals and lay leaders. We need to recognize the active, involved partners who take on primary responsibility for their family's Jewish life—and who are not Jewish themselves. We need to recognize that J. J. Goldberg's cousin's family—with an unconverted parent from a different faith background participating in raising a Jewish child—is a positive Jewish outcome equal to any other. Then we will have a truly "changing Judaism." Most important, we need to embrace the idea that our children's partners can come from different faith backgrounds and still support our children and our grandchildren living Jewishly.

CAN WE PREFER INMARRIAGE AND WELCOME INTERFAITH FAMILIES?

I once saw a morning TV show segment about new Barbie dolls with different skin tones and eye colors. One of the correspondents said that her young children "don't see color," meaning they don't distinguish other children based on race. I asked my then seven-year-old grandson, who had a very diverse class, if he noticed the black and Asian kids in his class as being black or Asian. He said he didn't. When that grandson was five, I had asked if it was true that one of his friend's two mothers was a police officer. There was no sign that he needed to think twice about his classmates who have two mothers, two fathers, or one of each. Based on this limited sample of one, I'm pretty sure that young children see different constellations of parents as "normal."

This made me wonder if Jews will ever see Jews marrying "non-Jews" as "normal." As I mentioned at the outset, I try very hard not to use the term *non-Jew*, which is why I put it in quotes here. It's off-putting and people don't identify as "non-" anything. Nevertheless, people keep on saying *non-Jew*, and the very use of the term appears to support viewing the other as not "normal."

Adapting Jewish attitudes about intermarriage to the point that Jews marrying partners from different faith traditions is viewed as normal requires addressing a key conundrum: Is it possible to prefer or privilege inmarriage over intermarriage in any way while at the same time being genuinely inclusive of interfaith couples? I've come to the view that it's not possible because being genuinely inclusive means treating the parties concerned as equal.

In an article for InterfaithFamily in 2000, Arnold Eisen took the position that we could do both:

> I believe that we can say simultaneously to both spouses in inter-
> married families: we are glad you are both here with us, we hope
> you will help us build our communities and enrich our tradition;
> we think Judaism has important things to say to Jews and non-Jews
> alike, and we know we have much to learn from you as from all the
> members of our community, Jews and non-Jews alike. But we also
> hope that you can understand our desire that Jewish homes now
> as in the past inculcate one religious tradition and not two; that
> Jewish spouses now as in the past go deeply into life over the years
> side by side with a person committed to doing so in the same tra-
> dition; that Jewish children have the advantage of two Jewish role
> models, if two parents are present, rather than one; that we do not
> have to sacrifice the wonderfully "particular" in our tradition to
> the no less profound "universal."[23]

I originally thought that inmarriage could be promoted without expressing value judgments implying that intermarriage is wrong or bad, based on utilitarian grounds that it increased the chances that people will live Jewishly and raise Jewish children. I thought that approach would not burn bridges to those who would still intermarry regardless of what Jewish leaders said. I recommended that Jewish leaders take the same approach that I suggested for parents talking to their children:

> We would like to see you live Jewishly because we have found
> doing so to be a source of meaning and purpose in our own lives,
> although we recognize that you will have to decide for yourselves.

If you want to have a Jewish family and a Jewish life, your chances of doing so are far greater if you marry someone who is Jewish. . . . We're not saying that intermarriage is bad, but intermarried parents will tell you that while it is possible, it isn't so easy to have a Jewish family and to raise Jewish children in an intermarriage. So, we hope you marry someone who is Jewish—but if you don't, we'll do everything we can to welcome your partner and to support any effort you make to live Jewishly and raise Jewish children together.[24]

By 2010, my views were shifting. Paul Golin wrote an important essay asserting that "preference for one type of family over another inevitably must lead to a lesser welcoming for intermarried families. . . . You simply cannot say, 'We welcome everybody equally, but we prefer one kind over another.' Maybe the difference in the way people are treated doesn't always manifest on the surface level, but it bubbles up."[25]

Jews wanting their children to marry other Jews is a very deep-seated, almost subconscious attitude. I have my own experience being insensitive on this score. My entire family was at a wedding reception for the son of a close family friend. That friend pointed out a young woman at the reception and said that my son, who was then unattached, should meet her. Within earshot of my daughter's then boyfriend and now husband, Brett, I asked, "Is she Jewish?" Brett said, "Hey!" indicating offense. I believe I turned it to an advantage, as it gave me the opportunity to explicitly tell Brett that I loved him just the way he was. However, I'm sure that many Jews have on similar occasions asked whether a prospective date (or mate) for a child is Jewish.

By comparison, while I was making a few remarks at the bris of Brett's son, my oldest grandchild, I noticed a young adult guest starting to cry. She came up to me afterward and said that as a lesbian she had been overcome by my choice of pronouns in my remarks. All I had said was the following, directed to my son-in-law and daughter: "We just said a prayer that we hoped that Jonah had chuppah, a loving partner, in his life. I hope that twenty-five or thirty years from now the two of you are talking to each other about who Jonah is going out with, do you like the person, is the person good for him, is the person 'the one.'" It would have been easy for me to have said "if she was the one." I did choose my words carefully, but I was quite taken aback that what I said had such an impact. It left me wondering how many times the young woman had experienced expressed assumptions of sexual preference that left her feeling different and disfavored. How many times have people like my own son-in-law experienced an expressed preference for Jews that left him feeling disfavored?

Later in 2010, I gave a speech on the issue of preferring inmarriage. In my remarks, I said:

> So when we talk to our young people about marriage, we should not promote inmarriage, we should promote engagement in Jewish life, with a supportive partner, whether or not that partner is a Jew.
>
> Most Jews would say they want their children to marry Jews. But what we really want is for our grandchildren to be Jewish. We will collectively have a better chance of having more Jewish grandchildren if the community's message to our young people is this: living Jewishly has been a great source of meaning and value to us; we hope you will want it for yourself and your family and children; if you do we hope you will choose a partner who will support your family's Jewish engagement; you, your partner and children will always be welcome, will always be part of our family, and we will always support the Jewish choices you decide to make.[26]

Years later in 2016, a Jewish philanthropist who was very supportive of engaging interfaith families said to me, "I'm not interested in having someone tell me that I shouldn't tell my kids I want them to marry Jews." She didn't want to be told that what she really wanted was for her grandchildren to be Jewish. Nonetheless, the 2015 Boston Jewish Community study reported that the percentage of Jews who feel it is very important that their grandchildren are raised Jewish is 46 percent, higher than the

31 percent who feel it is very important that their children marry someone Jewish.[27]

It seems paradoxical, but liberal Jews have a better chance of having grandchildren be Jewish if they stop expressing a preference that their children marry Jews. Expressing that preference risks alienating their children if they do intermarry, as so many will. Young people want to be, and will insist on being, part of a community that is radically inclusive.

Policies

Referring to interfaith marriage, Rabbi David Wolpe, routinely identified as one of America's leading rabbis, once said:

> Love vaults over boundaries and that is often both beautiful and compelling. Much can be lost along the way however, and it is difficult to keep both the integrity of a tradition and its universal messages. As with all great blessings, the blessings of America exact a considerable cost.[1]

Radical inclusion of interfaith families in Jewish life and community raises many boundary issues of who is allowed to do what or who is entitled to what. For a long time, the Jewish community's stance has been to monitor and maintain its boundaries. That approach allows only Jews to engage in key rituals, including being married by a rabbi or buried in a Jewish cemetery, and questions whether a person who might engage in Jewish life and community would be recognized as a Jew or not. Different positions on these boundary issues rest on different views about who Judaism is for: Is it a system for Jews or a system for all who want to engage in it?

The key question going forward is: How open are our gates going to be? Radical inclusion—wide-open gates—means focusing not on who is included but on who wants to engage and participate, and all that follows from that starting point. Mamie Kanfer Stewart, InterfaithFamily's former board chair, says:

> [W]e have an opportunity to reframe the question, "Who is a Jew?" into "Who is part of the Jewish community?" Rather

than focusing on Jewish status, we can honor everyone, Jewish or not, who is bringing the riches of Jewish traditions and sensibilities to our lives.[2]

Or as Edgar Bronfman said, "Our concern as a community now should be to welcome people into our community, not to build boundaries around it."[3]

The next chapters will examine some of these boundaries and what is being and can be done to open the gates. Chapter 15 addresses rabbinic officiation at intermarriages. Chapter 16 looks at issues of recognition and ritual participation, including at the end of life. The issue of intermarried rabbis is addressed in chapter 17. Chapter 18 discusses welcoming families who say they are "doing both" into Jewish organizations.

15

RADICAL INCLUSION STARTS
AT THE WEDDING

In October 2016, the Cohen Center for Modern Jewish Studies at Brandeis University published *Under the Chuppah: Rabbinic Officiation and Intermarriage*, an important, in fact game-changing, study.[1] When first presented at the Interfaith Opportunity Summit, a conference on engaging interfaith families Jewishly, sponsored by InterfaithFamily in October 2016, the following data generated an audible gasp among the attendees:

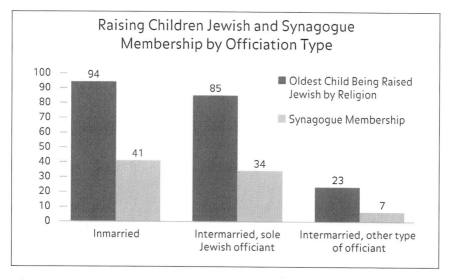

The study reported that 85 percent of intermarried couples who had only Jewish clergy officiate at their wedding are raising their children Jewish! That is close to the 94 percent of inmarried couples who have Jewish clergy officiate and much greater than the 23 percent of intermarried couples who have other officiants. In addition, 34 percent of intermarried couples with sole Jewish clergy officiants are synagogue members, not far from the 41 percent of inmarried couples and much more than the 7 percent of intermarrieds with other officiants.[2]

As careful researchers, the Cohen Center team will not claim causation. Nevertheless, the association between officiation and later Jewish engagement is significant—indeed, gasp worthy. They said:

> Interactions with Jewish clergy in preparation for the wedding may serve to welcome the non-Jewish partner into Judaism, establish the groundwork for a continuing relationship, and affirm the couple's prior decision to raise a Jewish family. However, the opposite may also be true. Rejection by Jewish clergy may serve to dissuade couples from pursuing other Jewish commitments and connections.[3]

Addressing the issue of rabbinic officiation at intermarriages has been a major priority of InterfaithFamily's work from the outset. In the early years, InterfaithFamily published many first-person accounts of the hurt and rejection couples experienced, with the impact of one of the most striking, an article from 2002, summarized in its title, "Why I Am a Unitarian."[4]

These were couples who wanted to have a rabbi officiate, surely a sign of at least potential interest in future engagement. They were the prospective parents of future Jewish children. No matter how nicely it was explained, those couples experienced rejection when rabbis said no and felt disapproval from Judaism's religious leaders. The result: fewer children raised with Judaism.

Rabbis' decisions not to officiate implicitly demonstrated negative attitudes about intermarriage and partners from different faith traditions, as well as the view that Judaism is a system just for Jews. A profound disconnect exists between rabbis who feel they can decline to officiate without offending interfaith couples and the couples' experiences interacting with those rabbis. I once met with the senior rabbi of a large Reform synagogue and his temple administrator. The rabbi said he explained to couples why he could not officiate in a way that did not alienate them. When the rabbi left the office, the administrator said, "I see those couples when they leave. They are never coming back."

InterfaithFamily routinely got comments like this: "Unfortunately, we had no success in finding someone willing to participate in our son's wedding. . . . I am saddened to see our son pushed away from our family's religion."[5] Raising the issue was a consistent focus of InterfaithFamily's advocacy speaking and writing.

Over the fifteen years between 2002 and 2017, increasing numbers of rabbis decided to officiate. Most estimates during the period suggested that "about half" of Reform rabbis would officiate for interfaith couples. In 2017, InterfaithFamily surveyed Reform and Reconstructionist rabbis and found that 85 percent would officiate.[6] While there is still progress to be made, especially on the frontier issue of co-officiating with clergy from other faiths, this development itself demonstrates that progress toward radically inclusive policies is possible.

HOW MORE RABBIS CAME TO OFFICIATE

Rabbis have relied on two main reasons to explain their decisions not to officiate at weddings of interfaith couples: (1) their view of, or their relationship to, Jewish law, and (2) their view of the impact of intermarriage on Jewish life.

Rabbis who regard Jewish law as binding, including Conservative and Orthodox rabbis, explain that they cannot officiate Jewish weddings for interfaith couples because people who are not Jewish are not subject to Jewish law, and under Jewish law a Jewish wedding involves a binding contract between two Jews.[7] Additionally, the Rabbinical Assembly, the Conservative movement's rabbis' association, does not allow its members to officiate or, until recently, even attend weddings of interfaith couples.[8]

Jewish law, however, has been reinterpreted in the past. For example, as traditionally understood, Jewish law prohibited homosexual relationships, but some rabbis who do not officiate for interfaith couples based on Jewish law do officiate at weddings for LGBTQ couples as long as both partners are Jewish. The Rabbinical Assembly allows its members to officiate at weddings of LGBTQ couples following a 2006 ruling of the Conservative movement's Committee on Law and Standards that changed previous interpretations of Jewish law and "normalize[d] the status of gay and lesbian Jews in the Jewish community."[9]

Reform Judaism seeks guidance from Jewish law but does not regard it as binding; the movement famously changed previous interpretations of Jewish law to recognize patrilineal descent. The Central Conference of American Rabbis (CCAR), the association of Reform rabbis, permits its members to make their own decisions about officiation. However, the CCAR still has an official resolution dating from 1973 that disapproves of officiation because intermarriage "should be discouraged," expressing the second main reason not to officiate: so as not to approve or encourage intermarriage because it leads to fewer Jews and less Judaism.[10] In InterfaithFamily's early years, I met with a Reform rabbi in Chicago who told me she didn't officiate for interfaith couples because of research showing that intermarried couples were not Jewishly engaged. She has since changed her position, along with many rabbis whose views on the impact of intermarriage and the impact of officiation have changed.

Reform rabbis who started to officiate for interfaith couples early on—I have been privileged to know Rabbi Mayer Selekman in Philadelphia; Rabbi Irwin Fishbein in Westfield, New Jersey; and Rabbi Michael Oppenheimer in Cleveland—told me they were excoriated by their colleagues. Critics of intermarriage suggested that rabbis who officiated for interfaith couples were only looking for money (*rent-a-rabbi* was the derogatory term) or were unscrupulous. When the Associated Press published a story about officiation in 2007, it included examples of rabbis whose status as rabbis was questionable, who did not respect Jewish tradition in the weddings they conducted, and who charged unreasonable fees for their services.[11] That was the year that InterfaithFamily launched its Jewish Clergy Officiation Referral Service, a free, high-quality referral system to over six hundred vetted rabbis, which in 2016 responded to almost twenty-three hundred requests.

Rabbis started to recognize the negative impact that their refusals to officiate had on future Jewish engagement. In InterfaithFamily surveys, 67 percent of respondents—all of whom were synagogue members raising children as Jews, and thus past the time when officiation would have been an issue for their own weddings—said they were attracted a lot or somewhat to synagogues if "the rabbi officiates at weddings of interfaith couples."[12] Similar comments on another survey I reviewed included: "It was painful for us when my childhood rabbi refused to perform our wedding ceremony, though I promised to raise my children exclusively in the Jewish faith and have done so"; and "Searching for a rabbi for our wedding was not a positive experience." In 2013, the Jewish Federation of Greater Washington convened a daylong program about welcoming interfaith families. After an interfaith couple told of their difficult experience, much of the concluding panel discussion concerned rabbinic officiation at weddings of interfaith couples.[13] To this day, if you ask interfaith couples about their experiences with the Jewish community, negative experiences with officiation come up frequently.

Refusal to officiate has negative impacts on the adult children of intermarriage as well. The Jewish Outreach Institute's *Listening to the Adult Children of Intermarriage* study contains this powerful statement:

> There are so many ways in which Jewish institutions can say implicitly that your family is second class such as the rabbi who won't do interfaith marriages. You are saying my parents' relationship is a problem, and you don't want to replicate couples who look like my parents. And I look at them and think "the world could use more people like my parents."[14]

In early 2008, the first academic study appeared that showed a correlation between having a rabbi officiate at interfaith couples' weddings and their later Jewish engagement. In *Intermarriage and Jewish Journeys*, Arnold Dashefsky described the negative experience many interfaith couples have seeking Jewish clergy to officiate at their weddings as a "huge turnoff."[15] Then in 2009, the Cohen Center at Brandeis, in one of its studies on the impact of Birthright Israel, acknowledged the following:

Marrying a Jewish person is not the only measure of Jewish commitment. Although such a commitment is difficult to assess, the
nature of the wedding ceremony is an additional indicator of Jewish commitment, particularly for intermarried couples. Although
not a perfect predictor of future choices, decisions about officiation and wedding rituals provide a window into the place of Jewishness in the lives of these individuals.

The study reports that trip participants who intermarried had a 31 percent chance of being married by a rabbi alone, which the authors describe
as "marrying Jewishly" and a marriage ceremony "where Jewish identity
is predominant."[16]

At about the same time, highly regarded Reform rabbis started
announcing that they were changing their positions and would officiate
for interfaith couples. In 2009, Daniel Zemel, a rabbi in Washington, DC,
explained that refusing to officiate was inconsistent with building an "open
and attractive" community:

> As we look to the future, a fully American Jewish community will
> have to be as open and attractive a community as it can possibly
> be, laden with wisdom, values and meaning so that our children,
> grandchildren and their spouses, Jewish or non-Jewish, will want
> to be nourished, educated and live their lives within its doors. I
> have come to understand that an interfaith marriage that begins
> with rejection by the rabbi may have difficulty building the kind
> of "open and attractive" community that we all hope for. And that
> is the phenomenon that I wish to end.[17]

Rabbi James Ponet, who co-officiated at the Clinton-Mezvinsky wedding, changed his position when he realized that instead of intermarriage
threatening Jewish survival, "What if our people is in fact evolving into
new forms of identity and observance? What if we are indeed generating
new models of Jewish commitment and engagement with the world?" He
continued:

I believe we are the ever-evolving people and that there will always be among us those who are rigorously attached to ancient forms. I believe it is critical that there will also always be among us those who vigorously dream and search for new vessels into which to decant the *sam chayyim*, the living elixir of Torah. If we only look backward as we move into the future, we will surely stumble. We need scouts, envoys, *chalutzim*, pioneers to blaze new ways into the ancient-newness of Judaism.[18]

In 2010, the CCAR released a report from a task force on intermarriage that had studied officiation for three years.[19] The report continued to insist that encouraging inmarriage was important because of the greater likelihood of continuity, and the CCAR left standing the 1973 resolution. Despite that, the report was interpreted as creating a more comfortable, accepting atmosphere for Reform rabbis who officiate at interfaith weddings. It said:

There is an underlying respect for the integrity of colleagues across a broad spectrum of ideology and practice so long as it is consistent with the CCAR Code of Ethics and policies against officiation on Shabbat and co-officiation with non-Jewish clergy.[20]

In 2012, John Rosove, a Los Angeles Reform rabbi, explained in a Rosh Hashanah sermon why he was changing his long-held position:

I've come to the conclusion that based upon the new reality in which we find ourselves and the fact that many intermarried families are seemingly successful in raising their children as Jews . . . I now believe that I can better serve the Jewish people by officiating at their weddings.[21]

Rabbi Laura Geller of Temple Emanuel of Beverly Hills emphasized the potential for positive impact that officiation creates:

I came to understand that my role as a rabbi is to facilitate the creation of Jewish families, not Jewish marriages. I have discovered since that decision that when a rabbi takes planning a wedding very seriously, spending a lot of time with a couple, it becomes an opportunity to open a door that really can deepen a commitment to create a Jewish home.[22]

The culmination of these developments was the game-changing *Under the Chuppah* study in 2016. Now rabbis who don't officiate at weddings of interfaith couples can't rely on the argument that those couples won't engage in Jewish life. Reform rabbis who don't officiate are refusing to take action—one they are permitted to take by their association—that is strongly associated with interfaith couples raising their children as Jews and joining synagogues. This is no longer a tenable position. It's time for the CCAR to change its official position.

We now know that many more rabbis are in fact officiating for interfaith couples. The Rabbinic Center for Research and Counseling, starting in the 1980s, conducted a series of surveys of members of the Reform and Reconstructionist rabbinical associations (CCAR and RRA respectively). Published results from their 1995 survey indicate that 47 percent of respondents would officiate for interfaith couples, and 13 percent would co-officiate.[23] InterfaithFamily's 2017 survey—it had 881 responses, including 23 percent of CCAR members and 44 percent of RRA members—found that 85 percent officiate at weddings of interfaith couples.[24] In the survey, many rabbis explained their decision to officiate by referring to their experience with numerous interfaith couples who were creating Jewish homes and raising Jewish children. One said:

> I believe that interfaith families are a strength in our Jewish community. Many non-Jewish spouses are very committed to raising Jewish children. This has been my own life experience and what I see in my community presently. Interfaith couples are not a threat to Judaism.[25]

Another comment was particularly powerful:

> My reason NOT to officiate had always been, "It is my job description to create and sanctify new Jewish households." And I believed

that only two Jews could produce such a thing. However, real-life showed me something different and, after nearly ten years of turning down interfaith weddings, I announced my change in policy and began officiating under certain circumstances. I delivered a major sermon on the High Holy Days about my change in practice, and it was the first time that I actually received a standing ovation![26]

As noted previously, some rabbis say they oppose intermarriage before it happens but support intermarriages after. In the InterfaithFamily survey, some respondents said they felt it was hypocritical to decline to officiate for interfaith couples but then tell them they are welcome after the wedding. One said, "I felt that it was disingenuous to welcome couples into the community after the wedding but not be part of the wedding. That is when I began to officiate."[27]

ISSUES ON THE FRONTIER OF OFFICIATION

Couples who want their weddings to take place before Shabbat has ended may have a hard time finding a rabbi to officiate. As noted above, the CCAR Task Force in 2010 indicated that officiation on Shabbat is disapproved. After Chelsea Clinton's wedding on a Saturday before sundown, Leon Morris wrote an op-ed, "A Call for A Moratorium on Shabbat Weddings," arguing that Reform rabbis should "model what it means to take time seriously, to honor a day, to live in symbolic ways that speak to the kind of Jewish world we would like to see and are committing ourselves to creating."[28] In response, Evan Moffic said the proposed moratorium would "alienate the vast majority of American Jews" and not "honor the spirit of Reform Judaism":

> A wedding ceremony is an opportunity to create a Jewish memory at a critical moment in a couple's life. It is a chance to welcome a couple into the Jewish people with open arms and open hearts. It is the last area where we should seek to impose an obstacle that does not violate the spirit of Shabbat. Many couples have a strong

commitment to Jewish life and have legitimate concerns that lead them to get married a few hours before sunset on a Saturday evening. Are we going to turn them away?[29]

In InterfaithFamily's 2017 survey, 59 percent of rabbis said they officiate before sundown on Shabbat.[30]

The liturgy rabbis use in weddings for interfaith couples also remains an issue. While some rabbis use the traditional phrase that consecrates a Jewish marriage, "under the laws of Moses and Israel," many others use different formulations, feeling that an interfaith wedding is not "under the laws of Moses and Israel." Rabbi Angela Buchdahl has said, however, that "if a non-Jewish partner is willing to live in a home 'under the laws of Moses and Israel,' to study Jewish laws and practice, and to raise any future children as Jews, then a rabbi can consecrate that commitment with integrity."[31]

A bigger frontier issue is the requirements and conditions that many rabbis impose on their officiation: only for members of their synagogue, or only for couples who are committed to raising Jewish children and creating a Jewish home, or only if the partner from a different faith tradition will take an Introduction to Judaism class.[32] In the 2017 survey, of the rabbis who do officiate, 59 percent require as a condition of doing so that the couple commit to establish a Jewish home and/or raise their children as Jews.[33] Couples who aren't at that point yet, who may be reluctant or unwilling to make that commitment, are likely to have a harder time finding a rabbi to officiate. To be as inclusive as we need to be and avoid having interfaith couples turn away from Jewish engagement, more rabbis need to be willing to respond to sincere requests from interfaith couples and officiate without requiring these kinds of commitments.

Co-officiation is the biggest frontier issue for rabbis who want to be inclusive. As noted above, the CCAR Task Force in 2010 disapproved of co-officiation. The RRA allows its members to officiate but not co-officiate.[34] However, there is a lot of ambiguity in what "co-officiation" means. It can mean sharing a service with clergy from another faith, or it can mean being the sole officiant but allowing other clergy to participate. The biggest variable is whether the other clergy can make theological references to their particular faith, which usually means referring to Jesus.

In August 2010, Julie Wiener reported that the fact that Chelsea Clinton's wedding was co-officiated was a particular bone of contention: "Even as the number of liberal rabbis willing to preside at weddings of Jews to gentiles appears to be growing, co-officiation with clergy of another faith, while hardly unheard of, remains taboo." At that time, as I reported to Wiener, 40 percent of the rabbis on InterfaithFamily's officiation referral service were willing to co-officiate, and 43 percent of the requests for wedding officiation received in 2009 were for co-officiation.[35] There clearly is a lot of what could be called "customer demand" for co-officiation. Still, some Reform rabbis said they would have nothing to do with Interfaith-Family because our referral service provided co-officiating rabbis to those couples who wanted them.

Wiener reported comments by three rabbis about what they thought a couple's desire for co-officiation signified. Rabbi Ellen Dreyfuss, then the president of the CCAR, said:

> The rabbi's presence and officiation at a wedding is reflective of a commitment on the part of the couple to have a Jewish home and a Jewish family, so co-officiation with clergy of another faith does not reflect that commit. It reflects, rather, indecision on the part of the couple. . . . Religiously it's problematic because [the bride and groom are] (sic) trying to create a both and there's no such thing as a both.[36]

Rabbi Richard Hirsh, then the executive director of the RRA, also said that "having a co-officiated ceremony points in the direction of a home that won't be primarily Jewish." But Rabbi Kerry Olitzky aptly pointed out that "the common assumption is that when a couple wishes a rabbi to co-officiate, the couple is going to bring up the future children in two faiths or the couple has not made a decision. . . . That's probably a premature conclusion to make."[37]

In the InterfaithFamily 2017 survey, rabbis' opposition to co-officiation seemed to be primarily based on assumptions they made regarding the reasons why the couple wants co-officiation. One said, "[I]f there is clergy from other faith co-officiating, my interpretation is that this couple has decided to create a family and build their home (as the chuppah represents) as one that is not a family that is committed to Judaism."[38] Another said:

> I don't wish to support a view that Judaism is an "option" in the couple's life among other "co-existing" or "competing" cultural expressions or life paths. While this approach might be the reality for a given couple, affirming that reality doesn't align with my sense of rabbinic purpose.[39]

Of course, it is also entirely possible that couples may want co-officiation simply to honor the traditions of both of their families and have not decided what they will ultimately do in terms of their home or family or children being Jewish.

The main reason for the shift toward more openness to officiation is that rabbis have come to believe, as research has shown, that rejection pushes interfaith couples away, while officiation influences many to create Jewish homes, families, and children. That logic equally applies to couples seeking co-officiation, who will be pushed away by rejection and drawn in by the rabbi's participation. I thought it was significant that at Chelsea Clinton's wedding, a highly regarded rabbi was willing to co-officiate before Shabbat was over. I saw that as having potential positive influence on other rabbis. Rabbi Lev Ba'esh, a Reform rabbi and CCAR member who oversaw InterfaithFamily's referral service, said he co-officiates because:

> "my view is that any Jew who wants Jewish ritual in their life should have it." Even if a couple hasn't yet decided whether or not to have a Jewish household, "the wedding is a great opportunity to show Judaism is something that has meaning and value for them." The hope is that if they have a good experience, then "down the road" these

couples will get more engaged in Jewish life. "I know that I'm not just hoping this, because I also do a lot of [their] baby namings."[40]

In InterfaithFamily's 2017 survey, 25 percent of respondents said they co-officiate with clergy from other faiths. Another 20 percent said that they do not co-officiate but do permit clergy from other faiths to offer prayers or readings that contain no theological references to religions other than Judaism. Furthermore, 47 percent said they would offer a prayer, reading, or blessing at a service performed by clergy from another faith. Given that a 1995 survey reported that 13 percent of rabbis would co-officiate, there is clearly an increasing openness to doing so.[41]

To be as inclusive as we need to be, more rabbis need to be willing to respond to the demand from interfaith couples for co-officiation. There has been a trend among young couples, evident from even a cursory reading of the *New York Times* wedding announcements, toward having friends officiate, often with online "ordinations." Steve Roberts feels that couples getting married who decide to "just get a judge" because they have difficulty finding clergy "in most cases do a disservice to themselves." He asks those couples to consider the traditions they come from and find ways to reflect them, in order to "not pretend they are neutral characters."[42] It's also a lost opportunity for rabbis, who by officiating have a chance to influence the couples' later Jewish engagement. But the current trend toward more officiation and more co-officiation reflects a very promising shift in attitudes.

THE CONSERVATIVE MOVEMENT AND OFFICIATION

The strict prohibition against Conservative rabbis officiating for interfaith couples is probably the biggest impediment to the movement's ability to attract interfaith families and retain their relatives as members.

On Yom Kippur in 2014, Rabbi Adina Lewittes, who had served as assistant dean of the Jewish Theological Seminary, delivered a sermon in which she revealed that she would officiate at intermarriages and had resigned from the Rabbinical Assembly. She explained how she had been asked to officiate by a couple and found herself "struggling to refuse":

I was their rabbi before they married and would continue to be their rabbi afterwards. Who was I supposed to be for the moment they came together? Was there no way for me to stand with them at their wedding, bless the love that brought them together, send the message that the Jewish community wants their continued presence and involvement, all while maintaining my integrity and that of Jewish tradition?

Ultimately, knowing the movement's rules forbidding officiating at intermarriage, Rabbi Lewittes "had no choice but to withdraw [her] membership, [although] having to leave my spiritual home in order to be true to myself was painful."[43]

In December 2014, Rabbi Wesley Gardenswartz of Temple Emanuel in Newton, Massachusetts, one of the largest Conservative synagogues in the country, proposed a policy that would enable him to officiate at interfaith weddings where the couple had committed to a "Covenant to Raise Jewish Children." Apparently, significant congregational reservations led to withdrawal of the policy, although Rabbi Gardenswartz said the congregation would "explore ways to be more welcoming to interfaith families both before and after the wedding." Rabbi Chuck Simon, then head of the Federation of Jewish Men's Clubs, the most liberal voice in the movement on intermarriage issues, described "the move by someone of Gardenswartz's stature to review policy on interfaith unions" as a potential "game changer for the movement" and "the beginning of a huge paradigm shift."[44]

However, in 2015, Rabbi Jeremy Kalmanofsky, explaining why he wouldn't accept intermarriage, wrote that "celebrating interfaith weddings . . . [would] diminish a sacred covenantal tradition, and risk making liberal Judaism into a jumble of traditional gestures that might please individuals but demand nothing from them."[45] Rabbi Seymour Rosenbloom, the emeritus rabbi at a Philadelphia synagogue, said in 2016 that it's time to allow Conservative rabbis to officiate at weddings of interfaith couples; because he began to do so, he was expelled from the Rabbinical Assembly in 2017.[46]

Also in 2017, Rabbi Elliot Cosgrove weighed in on the topic. Researchers from the Cohen Center had presented their new *Under the Chuppah* report at the Rabbinical Assembly convention, but Rabbi Cosgrove was not persuaded. Although Jewish law "can, and oftentimes should, change," Jewish law has the right to limit what it validates. He "unapologetically want[s] young Jews to marry other Jews." Officiation at intermarriages "send[s] the message that all choices are equal, a message that I do not think wise given the undisputed place inmarriage has as the single most important determinant in ensuring Jewish continuity."[47]

When rabbis acknowledge that Jewish law can and oftentimes should change, the officiation debate turns on the consequences of the positions taken, which circles back to couples turning their backs on Judaism when rabbis turn their backs on them. Rabbi Cosgrove articulately says what he wants the Conservative movement's message to be: We want you to marry Jews; when you don't, the path to conversion is warm, embracing, and doable; if that's not an option, we will help you build a Jewish family and future while respecting your spiritual integrity. This message has not resonated for many years and has led to declining membership. Rabbi Cosgrove laudably says that when an intermarriage occurs, "we must be . . . passionate in creating a culture of warm embrace for Jew and non-Jew alike."[48] Unfortunately, the inability to officiate undermines a culture of warm embrace.

Between June and August 2017, there was a flurry of activity. Rabbi Amichai Lau-Lavie announced that he would officiate at weddings between Jews and those who were the modern-day equivalents of the *gerim toshavim*, whom he described as "resident aliens" who in the past were not Jewish but lived among and interacted with Jews and had some status under Jewish law. As a result, he resigned from the Rabbinical Assembly. The rabbis at B'nai Jeshurun, an influential synagogue in New York with roots in but unaffiliated with the Conservative movement, announced they would officiate for interfaith couples who commit to creating Jewish homes and raising Jewish children. The Rabbinical Assembly and the Jewish Theological Seminary reiterated their opposition, as did several Conservative rabbis in their own essays.[49] More recently the Rabbinical Assembly lifted the prohibition on rabbis attending interfaith weddings, but not on officiating at them.[50] It is encouraging to see strong voices working to address the issue; I look forward to seeing how the movement's position evolves in the future.

16

STATUS—RECOGNITION AND RITUAL PARTICIPATION

Interfaith families who want to engage in Jewish life encounter boundaries in terms of who is considered Jewish and who can participate in Jewish rituals. Different positions on these boundary issues stem from different attitudes toward intermarriage and partners from different faith traditions, along with different views of who Judaism is for—just for Jews or for all who want to engage. There have been promising developments toward more inclusive attitudes and policies in these areas, but more progress is needed.

RECOGNITION

As discussed in chapter 2, under traditional Jewish law and what is known as matrilineal descent, the child of a Jewish mother is Jewish. The Reform and Reconstructionist movements have interpreted Jewish law to potentially recognize the children of Jewish fathers as Jews—what is commonly known as patrilineal descent—if they are raised as Jews. The fact that Orthodox and Conservative Judaism officially, as well as many lay Jews from all denominations, do not recognize the children of Jewish fathers, raised as Jews, as Jewish is a serious obstacle to the involvement of interfaith families in Jewish life.[1] Fortunately, there is a solution to this divide. Everyone in the Jewish community could regard the children of Jewish fathers as Jews for all purposes except where halachic status—that a person is Jewish under traditional Jewish law—matters, typically around issues of marriage, death, and ritual participation.

In 1994, when my daughter, Emily, was sixteen, she began dating a Conservative Jew. One night she was invited for Shabbat dinner. Emily knew about the Reform movement's policy on patrilineal descent. I didn't know how her date's family felt about that issue, but I wanted to try to protect her against possible hurt, so I reminded her that in the eyes of some other Jews, she would not be considered Jewish. Emily very defiantly stated, "No one is going to tell me that I'm not Jewish!" This was a bittersweet moment for me. I was happy and proud of how strongly she felt. But I was, and still am, pained to think that any Jew might want to reject or exclude from the Jewish people my caring, intelligent, beautiful, and Jewishly committed daughter.

Almost ten years later, one child of intermarried parents wrote for InterfaithFamily that "perhaps the most significant problem children from interfaith families have, particularly us patrilineal Jews, is acceptance from others if or when we decide on a particular religion. I have been told over and over again that I am not a real Jew." Another wrote, "I'm struggling a lot with my Jewish identity. There's no question that I feel Jewish, but *halacha* says that I am not a Jew." A Jewish father wrote, "So what does it matter that her mother isn't a Jew? Don't I matter, too? Aren't my genes relevant?"[2]

Ten years after that, the Jewish Outreach Institute's *Listening to the Adult Children of Intermarriage* study found that patrilineal Jews are less comfortable identifying themselves as children of intermarriage in the context of a Jewish communal institution and that "Jews with one Jewish parent often feel excluded by the Jewish community; this feeling is more pronounced among those whose mother is not Jewish."[3]

InterfaithFamily's surveys corroborate the view that nonacceptance of patrilineal Jews is "a real turn-off . . . even if the kids want to learn, they are told that they can never be Jewish."[4] Edgar Bronfman said, "From my son Adam I learned how insulting it is if your children, who have a non-Jewish mother, are considered not Jews by other Jews."[5]

Rabbi Andy Bachman, former rabbi of Congregation Beth Elohim in Brooklyn, has suggested that children raised as Jews who are not considered Jews outside of the Reform or Reconstructionist movements because their mothers are not Jewish should be taken to the mikveh (ritual bath) for conversion by the age of bar or bat mitzvah.[6] The problem with that approach is that some Jews who don't consider those children Jewish wouldn't recognize such a conversion if it were under Reform or Reconstructionist auspices. If those conversions were so recognized, I would be in favor of making this kind of process more known and available to intermarried parents so that they could consider it. Conversion could be incorporated into a bris or baby naming ceremony in the same way.

In a collection of essays about patrilineal descent published in 2013, a Conservative rabbi, Alana Suskin, says it is "staggeringly painful" for patrilineal Jews to be told they aren't Jewish, but it's "something which is easy to fix" through conversion.[7] An Orthodox rabbi, Ben Greenberg, said that a child of Jewish patrilineal lineage "must be respected greatly for their identification with the Jewish people . . . people of patrilineal descent [should] be referred to as Jews who need to rectify their status vis-a-vis Jewish law."[8] But widespread conversion efforts among patrilineal Jews would be alienating and counterproductive, and the question of who would recognize whose conversions remains.

In the same collection of essays, Reform rabbi Rachel Gurevitz got it exactly right when she wrote that the recognition issue becomes relevant when people "seek access to our institutions, and especially our synagogues." At that point, she says, "we rabbis become the gatekeepers . . . let us be mindful of how and when we act as gatekeepers and what our purpose in those moments is."[9] In other words, are rabbis—and all Jewish leaders, for that matter—going to insist on limiting the Judaism they offer to only those who meet their standards of who is Jewish, or are they going to open the Judaism they offer to all who want to engage in it?

Additionally, Rabbi Gurevitz aptly points out that "if someone is observing Jewish practice, celebrating in Jewish time, identifying with the Jewish people, or perhaps doing none of these things but, when asked, makes a claim to be Jewish or 'part Jewish' because of their ancestry, it is largely irrelevant to them whether [rabbis] agree or approve."[10] Rabbis who don't widely open the Judaism they offer risk being left out of shaping the Jewish experiences of many who will engage without their approval.

There continue to be voices in the Jewish world who say that the Reconstructionist and Reform decisions to adopt patrilineal descent were a mistake. Orthodox rabbi Ben Greenberg, for example, says that they were because of the impact the decisions had on recognition of people as Jews among the denominations.[11] That disregards the impact the decisions had on enabling thousands of patrilineal Jews to engage in Jewish life and community.

The issue of recognition is aggravated by the situation in Israel. In 2010, Alana Newhouse wrote that if proposed legislation to give the Orthodox rabbinate control of all conversions in Israel were enacted, the State of Israel would be choosing to tell 85 percent of the Jewish world outside of Israel that their rabbis aren't rabbis, their religious practices are a sham, "the conversions of their parents and spouses were invalid, their marriages weren't legal under Jewish law, and their progeny were a tribe of bastards unfit to marry other Jews."[12] Reform rabbi Heidi Hoover writes that "Israel doesn't want me" because her conversion under Reform auspices is not recognized by the Chief Rabbinate:

> One of the messages that American Jews receive relentlessly is that we need to support Israel. There is much hand wringing over the perceived lessening of American Jewish connection to Israel among teens and young adults, and even among rabbinical students. I believe this lessening of connection is in part due to a growing number of American Jews who cannot fully live as Jews in Israel because their status as Jews is not recognized by the Chief Rabbinate.[13]

Rabbi Hoover tells people in her congregation who are converts under liberal auspices and people who identify as Jewish whose mothers were not Jewish that "they are, in fact, Jewish." Nevertheless, she wants them to be prepared that there are those who will not recognize them as such.[14] That's important, especially for the many young adults raised as Jews in interfaith families whose Jewish status would be questioned by others. Rabbi Gurevitz communicates this same message, although she does so "apologetically because I don't find these explanations to make Judaism very appealing."[15]

Rabbi Hoover concludes:

> It is crucial that American Jews of all denominations join to support religious pluralism in Israel, and in the United States as well. We need to find ways to respect and recognize each other's conversions and life-cycle rituals. There are not so many of us that we can afford to be divided, and if Israel continues to disenfranchise American Jews, she cannot expect their support to continue indefinitely.[16]

In January 2011, US Representative Gabrielle Giffords was shot in Arizona. Giffords comes from an interfaith family—her father is Jewish, her mother is not—and she did not claim her Jewish identity until she was an adult. The *Jerusalem Post*, not exactly liberal on intermarriage issues, wrote an editorial that basically said that Giffords should be considered a Jew, even though she is not halachically Jewish:

> Is it conceivable to exclude Giffords, another "non-Jew," who is so unequivocally Jewish? With all our desire for a universally accepted definition of "Who is a Jew?" that would unify the Jewish people, we cannot ignore the complicated reality that many "non-Jews" are much more Jewish than their "Jewish" fellows. Congresswoman Giffords is one of them.[17]

It took a tragedy for leading conservative Jewish commentators to arrive at the conclusion that Gabrielle Giffords is Jewish. Not everyone agreed, however. The editors of the *Forward* weighed in:

> This warm embrace is notable because, according to traditional Jewish law, Giffords is no more Jewish than Chelsea Clinton. Both were born of non-Jewish mothers and have never formally converted. (Only through patrilineal descent is Giffords, whose father was Jewish, considered a Jew.) Still . . . synagogues around the country are offering prayers for healing in her name, "yet they would be violating their own religious policy if they ever called her to the Torah for an aliyah honor." This disconnect between

religious standards and actual behavior is deepening across a wide swath of American Jewry.[18]

The *Forward* editors said the embrace of Giffords was cause for cheer, because tolerance and inclusion are good. But they also said it was also cause for dismay, lamenting the divide on this issue between the Orthodox and everyone else.

The solution to this divide is for everyone in the Jewish community, Orthodox included, to regard patrilineal Jews such as Gabrielle Giffords as Jews for all purposes except where halachic status matters. Halachic status, when important, can be taken on through conversion. Without minimizing the seriousness of conversion in any way, here's what that means:

- When an Orthodox Jew, for whom a halachically Jewish marriage partner is important, becomes involved with someone who is not halachically Jewish, the prospective partner can convert according to the Jewish partner's Orthodox halachic standards.
- A patrilineal Jew or a partner from a different faith tradition who wants to participate in synagogue rituals—such as reciting the Torah blessings—in a community that restricts that participation to halachic Jews, can choose to convert under the auspices of that community (e.g., Orthodox, Conservative, or other).[19]
- If a patrilineal Jew or a partner from a different faith tradition wants to be buried in a Jewish cemetery in which only halachic Jews are permitted to be buried, they can convert according to the halachic standards recognized by the cemetery.

But halachic status does not matter in all situations. There should not be any prohibition against patrilineal Jews celebrating Shabbat and other Jewish holidays, participating in Jewish life-cycle events, or praying in Jewish settings. In addition, many would say that the Jewish community benefited from having a non-halachic Jew such as Gabrielle Giffords, who was a staunch Jewishly identified supporter of Israel, in the US Congress.[20]

The recognition issue is perhaps the purest expression of the different views of Judaism as a system just for Jews or a system for anyone who wants to engage. It would be a major advance if the idea took hold that Judaism is a system for a Jewish community broadly defined to consist of Jews who are halachic and who are not halachic, with issues of halachic status to be addressed if and when they arise. One thing should be very clear: it is incomparably preferable to have patrilineal Jews engaging and to deal with the recognition issue by addressing halachic status when it matters, than to not have patrilineal Jews engaging at all.[21]

RITUAL PARTICIPATION

I experienced radical inclusivity in 2015, at the b'nei mitzvah of the children of my Jewish cousin, Nancy Sharp. Nancy's first husband, Brett, a very wonderful young man, died of brain cancer when their twins were two years old. Nancy decided to move from Manhattan to Denver, where she had one friend. There, Nancy read a magazine article about eligible bachelors that featured Steve Saunders, a local TV journalist who was raised Catholic. Steve's wife had died of cancer and he was raising two teen boys. Nancy wrote to Steve. They met, married, and combined their families.[22]

The Saunders family was not unfamiliar with what happens at a bar or bat mitzvah—Steve's sons had many Jewish friends growing up. One of Steve's nephews even attended the preschool at Temple Micah, where Nancy and Steve are members and the b'nei mitzvah took place. What was remarkable was how Rabbi Adam Morris included Steve and his family in the service. The Torah was passed not only from Nancy's parents and Brett's mother but also from Steve's Catholic parents, then to Steve and Nancy, and finally to the twins. That wouldn't be allowed in many synagogues. And that's not all—Steve joined with Nancy in the parents' *aliyah*, reciting the blessings over reading from the Torah. That wouldn't be allowed in many synagogues either.

The decision by religious leaders to limit participation in ritual to Jews is another serious obstacle to engagement and another expression of the "who is in" versus "who is engaging" positions.[23] In the fall 1999 issue of *Reform Judaism* magazine, Rabbi Eric Yoffie, then president of the Reform movement, wrote, "We all understand that those who have not converted cannot participate in certain rituals."[24] Over the years, when I asked Reform rabbis whether they would allow a parent from a different faith background to have an *aliyah* at their child's bar or bat mitzvah, most rabbis were categorically opposed. How could people who were not Jewish recite a prayer that thanks God for choosing "us" (the Jewish people) among the nations and giving "us" (the Jewish people) the Torah? How could they be given the highest honor that a Jew can have?

The answer is that an intermarried partner who has participated in raising a child as a Jew to the point of that child becoming bar or bat mitzvah could say, with complete integrity and authenticity, that his or her family is included among the "us" who were chosen and to whom the Torah was given. Moreover, such a parent, who has given a child permission to have an identity different from theirs, deserves the highest honor that the Jewish community can bestow. Given the sacrifices involved, profound gratitude is exactly what these parents deserve.

There are some who argue—using the analogy of citizenship, where certain rights such as voting pertain to citizens only—that only those who are born Jewish or converts should have certain rights, such as having an *aliyah*. However, applying that approach in this context—telling people in interfaith relationships that only born Jews or converts can participate fully—discourages the partners from different faith traditions, as well as their Jewish partners, from engaging with Judaism at all. They may never get involved in the first place, or they may not stay long enough to get to the point where they would consider conversion, which is a deeply personal, often years-long process.

Telling a parent that he or she cannot have an *aliyah* because he or she isn't included in the "us" is destructive and counterproductive. Telling them that it's fine for them to say the prayers in the pews, just not up on the bimah receiving an honor reserved for Jews, isn't logical or convincing. They are left questioning whether they can authentically say any of the many Jewish prayers that refer to "us."[25]

Intermarried partners from different faith backgrounds want to be accepted as they are. They want to feel united with their Jewish spouse and children, not divided or unequal. At this critical life-cycle event, they don't want their child given the message that one of their parents isn't allowed to participate and be honored fully. Instead of encouraging such people to live Jewishly, maintaining the boundary that only a Jew can have an *aliyah* makes them feel excluded, as many told InterfaithFamily:

> We are here because we thought we could pray together as a family. To say that my silence is mandated—even at the single moment of the *aliyah*—strikes at the reason why we are here.

> I would feel put out if I was told, no matter how committed I was, that I couldn't participate fully. Do you mean to tell me that my Jewish brother-in-law, who is totally secular and whose only connection to Judaism is to have matzah ball soup at the Seder at my house, could have an *aliyah* at my son's bar mitzvah, and I couldn't?

> I feel I've made a huge commitment in raising our children as Jews. Differentiation would feel punitive and exclusive. People need to understand what it would be like for the non-Jewish parent to be excluded at this moment despite all of the sacrifices he or she had made.[26]

Rabbi Carl Perkins contends that partners from different faith backgrounds may have these feelings because they have chosen not to convert despite being welcomed to do so, not because of communal boundaries.[27] Feelings of difference arise for a host of reasons: Jewish liturgy's emphasis on Jewish peoplehood and chosenness, Jews' attitudes that distinguish between negative *them* and positive *us*, restrictions on ritual participation by partners from different faith traditions, and more. Addressing these reasons can significantly reduce feelings of difference and encourage intermarried partners to live more Jewishly. It's true that eliminating boundaries may not completely eliminate the discomfort that partners from different faith traditions experience; indeed, some people convert after years of living Jewishly because they are uncomfortable continuing to experience that dissonance and seek an inner harmony or unity instead.[28] But that's not a reason to maintain restrictions on ritual participation.

In InterfaithFamily's surveys on what attracts interfaith families to Jewish organizations, inclusive policies on participation by interfaith families was the second most important factor. Organization or synagogue policies about interfaith families participating in worship services and at life-cycle events attracted 64 percent of the respondents "a lot." One said, "My previous synagogue did not allow the non-Jewish members of my family to fully participate in my son's bar mitzvah. We have since left that congregation."[29]

The issue of who is included in the *us* is not limited to parents sharing in an *aliyah* at their child's bar or bat mitzvah.[30] Many Jewish blessings include the phrase *asher kid'shanu b'mitzvotav, v'tzivanu*, "who made us holy with commandments, and commanded us." At Friday night services in many synagogues, a member leads the congregation in the blessing over lighting Shabbat candles, presenting the issue of whether a member from a different faith tradition can refer to commanding "us." More symbolically, at many synagogues during a bar or bat mitzvah ceremony, the Torah is passed from grandparents to parents to the bar or bat mitzvah child, signifying the transmission of tradition through the generations. Even though there is no prohibition against people who are not Jewish from touching the Torah, at many synagogues the grandparents and parent from different faith traditions don't get to participate, on the theory that the Torah is not "theirs" to pass or that they couldn't have passed Judaism to the child.[31]

In 2014, a rabbi who leads one of the thriving urban groups that is attracting young Jews and interfaith couples to worship services, text study, and other Jewish experiences told InterfaithFamily that she imposes no restrictions whatsoever on participation. She doesn't ask whether a person is Jewish or not Jewish or some place in between. Whatever anyone wants to do Jewishly, she allows. That is the kind of radically inclusive policy that will most certainly maximize Jewish engagement. Another similar group describes their approach as "radical accessibility"—the idea that everyone is welcome to find meaning and community there.[32]

Perhaps if rabbis who don't permit parents from different faith traditions to join in an *aliyah* could be present at occasions such as my cousin's b'nei mitzvah, they might have a change of heart. Seeing the contribution that someone like Steve, not to mention his extended family, has made to passing Judaism on to Nancy's children might lead them to consider the family of a person like Steve to be the *us* to whom the Torah was given, making it fully authentic and appropriate for a person like Steve to thank God for giving the Torah to his family—to *us*.[33] I hope that Rabbi Morris's inclusive approach, which by choosing to privilege love and family facilitates the transmission of Jewish tradition, becomes increasingly adopted by his colleagues.

END OF LIFE

Fortunately, participation in Jewish mourning and burial rituals by partners from different faith traditions—whether they are saying Kaddish for their relatives who are not Jewish or having a rabbi officiate at their own funeral—has become pretty much a nonissue. Sticky questions do come up, including co-officiation, but for the most part they are dealt with sensitively.[34] Burial in Jewish cemeteries, however, is still an issue.

In a traditional Jewish cemetery, the ground is considered consecrated, and only Jews can be buried there. While this can be off-putting to interfaith couples, in the traditional view, burying someone not Jewish makes the ground no longer consecrated. There are many people who were buried in Jewish cemeteries with the understanding that they would be forever in a Jewish—that is, consecrated—cemetery. Burying someone not Jewish there would violate that understanding.

Jewish law deals with this issue, however, by permitting a divider to separate different sections of a cemetery, much like a *mechitzah* (partition in a traditional synagogue that separates men and women). This allows a cemetery to remain Jewish and consecrated, while also allowing interfaith couples to be buried together in their own section. In 2006, I heard a representative of a Jewish cemetery established in the 1950s—before there was much intermarriage—say that they recognized demographic trends and decided to create a section in which interfaith couples could be buried together. They subsequently added a second, then a third.

A representative of another cemetery, established in the 1990s with interfaith couples and families specifically in mind, said they have designated sections of their cemetery as Conservative, Reform, and "open." In the Conservative and Reform sections, they follow the respective rules for who is a Jew. In the open section, they'll bury interfaith couples. At that cemetery, the different sections—divided by paved walkways that serve as dividers—look the same. You can't tell by just looking which section is which. In a growing trend, another cemetery, owned by a Conservative synagogue in New Jersey, announced in 2017 that it would open a section for interfaith couples, as did another in Toronto in 2018.[35]

End-of-life issues will become more prominent as more and more interfaith couples age. Jewish cemeteries with dividers that establish sections where only Jews can be buried and sections where interfaith couples can be buried, where the sections look the same and the divider is subtle, are sensitively addressing halachic issues when they need to, in ways that work.

17

INTERMARRIED RABBIS

In 2002, an intermarried congregant of a Pittsburgh synagogue sought to be admitted as a rabbinical student at Hebrew Union College (HUC), the Reform seminary. The fact that an intermarried Jew would want to become a rabbi was a striking testament to the depth and strength of Jewish commitment that is possible in an intermarriage. But the Central Conference of American Rabbis' Responsa Committee reaffirmed HUC's ban on ordaining intermarried Jews as rabbis, reasoning that rabbis are role models and should teach, by personal example, the ideal of inmarriage.[1]

Having more intermarried people get more involved in Jewish life would serve the value of Jewish continuity more than anything else could. Why not encourage intermarried Jews to become rabbis and thus role models for extensive engagement in Jewish life by others like them? Indeed, what better role model for engaged interfaith families could there be?

The debate over intermarried rabbis is yet another example of the influence of underlying attitudes about intermarriage on policies that, in turn, influence engagement by interfaith families. Progress has been made—with the Reconstructionist movement again leading the way and accepting intermarried rabbinic students—but more is needed.

Over the years at InterfaithFamily I talked with a number of exceptional people who were frustrated that they couldn't be accepted by seminaries because they were intermarried. One was Edie Mueller, who in 2009 wrote "Why I'm Not a Rabbi," which describes her 1994 experience of this rejection.[2] Another was David Curiel, the lead subject of "The Coming of the Intermarried Rabbi," an article about men and women seeking to attend and be ordained by rabbinical schools that will not accept them because they are intermarried.[3] Yet another was Peter Bregman, who many years later, in 2017, was honored by Romemu, a prominent emerging Jewish Renewal spiritual community, along with his wife, Reverend Eleanor Harrison Bregman, who works at Romemu.[4]

In 2009, I reasoned that while it made sense for denominations that consider halachah binding to require rabbis to live in halachically recognized marriages, the seminaries training rabbis for other denominations were free to consider that their graduates will be serving constituencies with many interfaith couples and families. Rabbis presumably want to inspire their constituents to more Jewish engagement; intermarried rabbis would be particularly inspiring to the interfaith couples who they served—and there is no reason they could not be inspiring to inmarried couples as well.[5]

I further contended that when congregations hire rabbis, lay leaders are the ones who select them. Congregations that wanted to promote inmarriage wouldn't hire rabbis that they perceive to encourage interfaith marriage. Presumably those lay leaders would choose not to hire an intermarried rabbi. By the same token, congregations that wanted to promote conversion as the desired response to the issue of interfaith marriage also presumably would choose not to hire a rabbi whose partner had not chosen to convert. However, congregations that were focused on supporting the Jewish engagement of all community members might well welcome an intermarried rabbi. Congregations are diverse, and rabbis could be as well.

Later in 2009, *Tablet* published an article about Ed Stafman, a former attorney who intermarried, became active in a Reform synagogue, and eventually received ordination by the Aleph Rabbinic Program, affiliated with the Renewal movement, the only seminary at the time that did not reject intermarried students outright. Rabbi Stafman was becoming the rabbi at Beth Shalom, a heavily intermarried Reform synagogue in Bozeman, Montana, whose members' comments support the notion of an intermarried rabbi as a role model and inspiration for interfaith couples. One person in the hiring process said that Stafman's being intermarried "might be a great asset because we're so intermarried here that you might have a better understanding of the congregation." Another said, "I think it will be very beneficial to those interfaith families in the community, and that they will really feel they have a home at Beth Shalom."[6]

In 2013, Daniel Kirzane, a rabbinic student at Hebrew Union College and the child of intermarried parents, wrote in a debate in *Reform Judaism* magazine that HUC's seminary should admit students with partners from different faith traditions.[7] In his scathing response, "Rabbis Married to Gentiles?" Rabbi Mark Miller lamented what he called Reform Judaism's "embrace of assimilation."[8] An intermarried woman, Aliza Worthington, wrote an equally heated response to Rabbi Miller:

> You are taking people who have chosen Judaism—*chosen* it!—and shoving them away. Here is someone [Kirzane] who was born of an intermarriage of faiths, and he not only *chose* Judaism to follow, to study, but to live and to teach! And you belittle his parents' love because it somehow makes his Judaism less authentic to you? You deny him his learning and his future livelihood should he fall in love with someone who is not Jewish? You're worried that a rabbi who marries a gentile is threatening and disgraceful to the Jewish faith? Even though he cherishes Judaism?[9]

Worthington's essay also attracted scathing comments that spurred Adin Feder, a high school student at a Boston Jewish day school, to write:

> The problem is the absolutism and rigidity of those who write off and bash Jews who intermarry or subscribe to a different religious philosophy. Attacking and disowning a fellow Jew who decided to marry a Catholic isn't just wrong. It's also impractical.
>
> In a recent survey I took of my grade at my pluralistic Jewish high school, I found that over half of the grade, 51%, is "open to marrying someone who is not Jewish." A further 19% said that they "don't know" if they would be open to it. Only 30% of the grade said that they are not "open to marrying someone who is not Jewish." Keep in mind that these results are from students at a Jewish school!

Is the peanut gallery that claims to have been invested with the power to define "real Judaism" and therefore insult all other Jews who don't fit that definition, prepared to repudiate a huge portion of the next generation of American Jews? Perhaps their energy would be better spent appealing to rather than insulting Jews, in order to ensure the continuity of the Jewish people.[10]

Let's hope that Feder's survey, coming from a Jewish high school, is indicative of a serious shift in attitudes among younger Jews that will marginalize negative views about intermarriage.

Later in 2013, Rabbi Ellen Lippman, who has an unconverted partner from a different faith tradition, wrote an open letter to HUC, her alma mater:

We are like the thousands of Jews across America who commit to strongly Jewish lives with their non-Jewish spouses. Interfaith families tell me that having a rabbi who mirrors their relationships makes an enormous difference to being able to commit to Jewish life.[11]

Rabbi Lippman argued that an "inclusive vision of Jewish leadership" meant that "we should not push away those who want to become leaders of the Jewish community as rabbis just because they are intermarried." She argued that

a rabbi is a role model, and there are many kinds of role models. Intermarriage is a fact of American Jewish life. We can do a better job of connecting intermarried Jews to synagogues, rabbis and Jewish life. One way is to knowingly ordain intermarried rabbis.[12]

In 2015, the Reconstructionist movement once again led the way to a more inclusive Judaism by taking the bold step to accept and graduate rabbinic students who are intermarried or in committed relationships with partners who are not Jewish. Responding to the role model argument, the movement, led by Rabbi Deborah Waxman, reaffirmed that "all rabbinical candidates must model commitment to Judaism in their communal, personal, and family lives"—but explained their decision was in large part because "Jews with non-Jewish partners demonstrat[e] these commitments every day in many Jewish communities":

> Reconstructionism approaches Jews and Judaism not simply as representing a culture or a religion, but as a people and a civilization. Its borders and boundaries are porous and constantly evolving. The Jewish present and Jewish future depend on our shifting focus toward Jews "doing Jewish" in ways that are meaningful to them rather than on "being Jewish" because of bloodline or adherence to mandated behaviors. . . . The issue of Jews intermarrying is no longer something we want to police; we want to welcome Jews and the people who love us to join us in the very difficult project of bringing meaning, justice, and hope into our world.[13]

The Reconstructionist decision was very controversial. In a *Forward* editorial, Jane Eisner said we should expect a rabbi to raise his or her children in a Jewish home, to maintain that home as the most sacred place in the Jewish ecosystem.[14] Her assumption that intermarried rabbis would not do so is unfounded. When Eisner says we should expect a rabbi to partner with another Jew, that's the tribalism that the Reconstructionist decision says alienates many younger progressive Jews and current or would-be rabbinical students. If the goal is Jewish commitment to the home, synagogue, and beyond, and if interfaith couples can demonstrate that commitment—as more and more do—then why is it necessary for Jews to partner with other Jews, beyond the assertion that "Jews should marry Jews," or worse, that "Jews are better."

Eisner said that "it is a propitious time to offer bold ideas to make Judaism more accessible and welcoming, to strengthen commitment among those born Jews and encourage others to join."[15] The Reconstructionist decision is precisely such a bold idea.

18

WORKING WITH FAMILIES DOING BOTH

As many as 25 percent of interfaith couples say they are raising their children both—partly Jewish and partly something else. Although it's not completely clear what doing both means, as discussed in chapter 12, how Jewish leaders and organizations respond to these families is a frontier issue in the intermarriage field.

In InterfaithFamily's early years, the idea of doing both seemed inconsistent with its stated mission to encourage Jewish choices. When I wrote or spoke about interfaith families raising Jewish children with unambiguous Jewish identities, I was clearly adopting the framing of the critics of intermarriage.[1] Initially InterfaithFamily did not allow the Interfaith Community, an organization that supports families doing both, to be included on its directory of Jewish organizations that supported interfaith families making Jewish choices.

Over the years, my thinking has changed. I was persuaded initially by Sheila Gordon, founder of the Interfaith Community, that they did not support merging the religions, that the Jewish partners in the couples they served saw their Jewish identity strengthened, and that the children of these couples could and sometimes did decide to identify as Jewish because of the education they received. Accordingly, we listed the Interfaith Community on InterfaithFamily's website. I was further persuaded by Susan Katz Miller, author of *Being Both: Embracing Two Religions in One Interfaith Family*, that these couples were respecting the integrity of each religion and teaching about and celebrating both. She makes a compelling case that "American religious institutions must acknowledge, rather than ignore, the reality of dual-faith identity and the children who represent the flesh and blood bridges between religions."[2]

To the extent that Jewish leaders and organizations focus on doing Jewish as desirable, with being Jewish less important, it is easier to negotiate the doing-both boundary—because they should facilitate people doing Jewish even if they are doing both and identify partly but not exclusively as Jewish. However, even if they focus on being Jewish—in particular, wanting children of interfaith families to identify as Jews—including couples who say they are doing both opens the door to children going in that direction.

That doesn't mean that Jewish organizations need to recommend raising children in two religions. InterfaithFamily did not do that; our mission consistently was to encourage Jewish choices while respecting the traditions of both members of the family. If people inquired about that approach, we directed them to other organizations. We didn't presume to pass judgment or suggest parents doing both were making a mistake. It just was not the approach we recommended.

Welcoming and including those who are taking this approach may seem as if it is undermining Judaism, but doing so will maximize the numbers of interfaith families who will engage in Jewish traditions. As a logical extension of the co-officiation issue, Jewish clergy and mohels, for example, shouldn't refuse Jewish baby welcoming ceremonies to parents who are also having their child baptized. A baptism doesn't have conclusive effect on how a child will identify and act as a teen or an adult. That will depend on how the child is raised, their experiences, and many other factors.

At the Interfaith Opportunity Summit in October 2016, Susan Katz Miller argued that families doing both are already part of synagogues and Jewish communities and that these couples want to engage in Judaism while educating their children about both religious traditions in the family without merging them together. She argued that having interfaith communities that celebrate and teach about both religions is "good for the Jews" because this approach exposes people to Judaism who otherwise would not learn about it, and some couples will not choose just the Jewish route. She encouraged Jewish institutions to engage openly with these families without alienating them.

There also is no reason why Jewish education at appropriate levels should not teach about Jesus. Rabbi Evan Moffic says that Rabbi Maurice Eisendrath, a mid-twentieth-century leader of the Reform movement, believed Reform Jews could embrace Jesus as a Hebrew prophet; Moffic says he doesn't go that far, but says "Jesus is a Jewish teacher whom we can respect and learn about, even as we do not see him as divine or messianic."[3] As also discussed in chapter 12, Jesus's conduct, as opposed to his nature as divine, can be a role model for Jews and others.

In 1995, the Reform movement adopted a policy in a "clear but close vote" to encourage congregations to establish "a clearly articulated policy that offers enrollment in Reform religious schools and day schools only to children who are not receiving formal religious education in any other religion."[4] When I was a Reform synagogue president from 1997 to 2000, I thought that was the right policy. I remember hearing that the purpose of our synagogue's religious school was to teach children not about Judaism but to "be" Jewish. If that's the purpose, maybe the policy makes sense, especially if you don't think someone can "be" Jewish and something else.

Because today I put more value on doing Jewish than being Jewish exclusively, I believe this is the wrong policy. I view children learning about Jewish life in a Reform synagogue religious school as increasing the chances they will do Jewish in the future, even if they are learning about another religion's traditions elsewhere. As stated in chapter 12, I think it's best for interfaith couples to choose one religious identity for their children, but for parents interested in doing both, the current policy—telling them they can't get help from the Jewish side—will increase the chances of no Jewish engagement in the future. (I would not, however, open up Jewish organizations in any way to so-called Messianic Jews, whose theology is incompatible with Judaism.)

A post on the InterfaithFamily Facebook page elicited this comment:

> I'm the Christian spouse of a Jewish man. I'm not sure whether the idea—you can't be both—is true or not. But I am sure that if the main thrust of Judaism's engagement with interfaith families

is the promulgation of the idea that if your identity and practice are not exclusively Jewish, you aren't Jewish at all—Judaism will continue to appear unwelcoming to interfaith families.

If Judaism wants interfaith families to be involved, it should get us excited about being involved by welcoming us, meeting us where we are, teaching us about Judaism, and taking the time to learn about who we are, rather than telling us what we should do to be Jewish enough to participate.

If Jewish congregations and communities spent half the energy figuring out how to and trying to be actively welcoming interfaith families that they do coming up with standards and conditions for our participation, Judaism wouldn't have to worry about losing interfaith families.[5]

Susan Katz Miller also points out that more of the teenagers and young adults raised in interfaith communities "lean Jewish," in her words, than Christian. "Perhaps, having been given a love for Judaism and basic Hebrew literacy in childhood, they will choose at some point in their lives to practice Judaism exclusively."[6] She says it is a "Jewish choice" to give children access to both cultures instead of choosing nothing, only Christian, or a third religion.[7] Miller refers to Judaism's "streamlined theology":

> Judaism can seem like an "easier" religion than Christianity. It does not require belief in the Virgin Birth, the Trinity, God appearing in the form of a man, or resurrection. While supernatural events also abound in the Torah, one can live as a "good Jew" through ritual observance without believing in these events, or even . . . without believing in God at all. . . . The simpler Jewish theology may explain in part why many grown children raised with both religions end up leaning toward Judaism.[8]

I also believe that many children raised with both religions will "lean toward Judaism" when they experience the inherent beauty and value of a Judaism of meaning.

In hindsight, that is why InterfaithFamily started to present the Jewish side of things in the kinds of interfaith communities Miller describes. We became comfortable presenting—to people who gravitate to the doing-both approach—the Jewish perspective and the model of interfaith families choosing Jewish engagement and Jewish identity for their children while learning about and respecting the other religious tradition in the family.

Finally, the factors that influenced Susan Katz Miller and her husband to raise their children in two religions are worth considering. She was a patrilineal Jew who did not feel accepted: "Often, I felt marginalized as an interfaith child and had to fight to defend my claim to Judaism." She and her husband wanted their children not to be "tolerated or on the periphery in a single-faith context."[9] She said, "I didn't want to subject my quarter-Jew children to the experience I'd had of constantly having to defend my Jewish identity."[10] They did not want one spouse "to feel left out—to feel like an 'out-parent' or guest in a church or synagogue."[11] As she explained, "My mother went to Hebrew classes and virtually dropped her own religious practice. However, I was always conscious that she had not converted; and if I forgot, there was always someone from the Jewish community there to remind me."[12]

Interfaith families shouldn't have to worry about their children being marginalized, just tolerated, or feeling as if they are on the periphery. The Jewish partners shouldn't have to worry that the partner from a different faith tradition might feel left out. If Jews and Jewish organizations adopted radically inclusive attitudes and policies, they wouldn't have to.

A Serious Campaign to Engage Interfaith Families

The Jewish community is filled with talented, committed, and philanthropic funders and leaders of organizations. When there has been vision and collaboration, the response to issues and programs has been massive. It is hard to find a community, federation, or organization that is not actively supporting disability inclusion, teen engagement, day schools, PJ Library, summer camps, Hillel, or Birthright Israel. It's wonderful to see the attention given to all these important, deserving causes. Without detracting from any of them, however, the potential impact of engaging interfaith families Jewishly is vastly larger.[1]

The *Millennial Children of Intermarriage* study makes it clear that programmatic interventions work. It found that formal and informal Jewish educational experiences "launch children on a pathway to Jewish involvement in college and beyond."[2] In order to set our children on the pathway of this rich tradition, a massive, concerted programmatic response to engage interfaith families in Jewish life and community is needed. Chapter 19 describes programmatic efforts to date and why programs designed for and marketed to interfaith families are needed. Chapter 20 lays out a model of pathways to that engagement, and chapter 21 shows the positive impacts that can be achieved by these efforts.

19

Building a Future of Programmatic Efforts

In 2005, Michael Rukin, a senior lay Jewish communal leader, called for a "massive investment in creative programs of outreach" to interfaith families and their children. Rukin called for:

> a significant change in the language (both verbal and nonverbal) toward [them] . . . a broad base of institutions working together . . . a major commitment from the federation system to infuse their agencies with a thrust of creative outreach programs . . . a renewed commitment from the religious movements . . . [and] the continued prodding of inspired philanthropists . . . with a rollout plan to massive numbers . . . [and] budget, way beyond the minuscule amounts currently available.[1]

Promising steps have been taken, but much more needs to be done to implement such a serious campaign to engage interfaith families—and reap the positive results.

Building on Past Efforts

Designing and building interfaith family engagement programs does not have to start from scratch. The Boston Jewish community, led by Combined Jewish Philanthropies (CJP), has taken the most concrete efforts to welcome interfaith families of any American community since the late 1990s. When the 2005 Boston survey showed that 60 percent of interfaith families were raising their children as Jews, I attributed that result to those programmatic efforts in an op-ed in the *Forward* co-written with Kathy Kahn, then director of outreach for the Reform movement.[2] CJP had a dedicated line item in its budget expressly for "services to the intermarried" that funded enhanced outreach programming of the Reform and Conservative movements and other agencies, including InterfaithFamily. In 2006, CJP's $300,000 of funding for this area was the highest in the country, representing 1 percent of CJP's total annual allocations.

All told, Boston couples and families could find discussion groups, programs for families with young children, short-term educational programs such as "Taste of Judaism" (a free, widely advertised, three-session class for those who are curious, focused on ethics, spirituality, and community, developed by the Reform movement but also taught in Conservative and other settings), and longer Introduction to Judaism courses that could lead to conversion. Each of the funded programs devoted a significant portion of its funding to marketing, including advertising and generating stories in secular media and on the Internet.

InterfaithFamily had a bulletin board in its office and put a copy of the *Forward* op-ed on it under a sign that read, "Look what 1% can do!" One day Michael Rukin attached a large yellow sticky note to the sign on which he wrote, "THINK ABOUT WHAT 10% WOULD DO!" He was a rare, bold thinker who understood the importance of vastly increased attention to efforts to engage interfaith families Jewishly. We need more thinkers like him today.

In 2008 a consortium of major foundations put together a funding proposal for an interfaith initiative.[3] Citing a "critical moment in the history of modern-day Jewry," the consortium said the "vibrancy, size, and strength of the Jewish people" depended upon "a powerful new vision that empowers and enables the Jewish community to better serve" the "rapidly expanding population" of interfaith families with children. The proposal called for $7.5 million over three years to create a national entity, a "state-of-the-art" website, inclusivity training of Jewish professionals and lay leaders, and a comprehensive array of integrated programs and services, targeted to interfaith families with children, in three pilot communities. Because of the 2008–9 financial downturn and the Madoff scandal, this proposal unfortunately was never funded, but the structure it envisioned is still needed.

The three-pronged approach of publicizing what is available in the Jewish community, training for professional and lay leadership, and programs for interfaith families was also recommended in a historic December 2011 report of the UJA-Federation of New York's Task Force on Welcoming Interfaith Families. The task force, staffed by Dru Greenwood, former director of outreach for the Reform movement, recognized that the potential for Jewish engagement among interfaith families was not being fulfilled. The task force recommended "an approach that unapologetically announces its welcome, provides sustained, networked, professionally staffed, and well-advertised gateway educational programs targeted to interfaith couples and families, and provides ongoing training for professionals and lay leaders."[4] Some of the recommendations of the task force have been implemented in New York but on a much more limited scale than the task force envisioned.

In 2011, InterfaithFamily launched the InterfaithFamily/Your Community initiative with a pilot in Chicago, followed by projects in San Francisco and Philadelphia (through a merger with an existing organization, InterFaithways) in 2012, Boston in 2013, Los Angeles in 2014, and Atlanta and Washington DC in 2016. (Cleveland started an affiliate of InterfaithFamily, called jHUB, in 2014.) The InterfaithFamily/Your Community model placed two on-the-ground full-time staff—a rabbi and a project manager—to offer a range of programs and services in local communities. Their jobs were entirely devoted to engaging interfaith families and supporting those Jewish organizations that wanted to engage interfaith families.

The desired results of this initiative were that people in interfaith relationships would feel comfortable and confident in Jewish settings and when making Jewish choices, would maintain connections with other Jewishly engaged families and Jewish organizations, and would make Jewish choices using the skills and assets they had acquired—and Jewish institutions would be fully inclusive of them. Evaluations of the initiative described in chapter 21 indicated that the desired results were being realized. In 2018, InterfaithFamily began to transition the InterfaithFamily/Your Community initiative to a rabbinic fellowship model, in order to expand the number of rabbis who would be trained, available, and ready to do interfaith family engagement work. The fellowship was to launch with a pilot cohort in 2019.

Every community should have staff devoted to engaging interfaith families. Basing that staff in an organization focused on engaging interfaith families is one good approach. Housing staff devoted to engaging interfaith families in community agencies that address a number of populations (Jewish community centers, family service agencies, federations, and the like) runs the risk that engaging interfaith families will lose priority to other causes or be susceptible to turf issues that often arise in Jewish communities, which happened more than once between 1999 and 2015. However, housing dedicated staff in a broader community agency can work, as it has with the jHUB program supported by the Cleveland federation.[5]

Honeymoon Israel is a newer program that provides immersive nine-day trips to Israel for locally based cohorts of couples—70 percent of the participants are interfaith couples. Honeymoon Israel provides a safe, nonjudgmental space that facilitates discussion, negotiation, and compromise between partners, and deep relationship building both between couples, and between couples and staff (who are often rabbis).[6]

THE NEED FOR PROGRAMS SPECIFICALLY "FOR INTERFAITH FAMILIES"

Some people have the notion that interfaith families are not interested in interfaith-specific programming, that they don't want to be "segregated," and that they prefer to attend general programs for everyone. While that is true for some interfaith families, many others are, in fact, interested in programs designed specifically for them, or in attending programs where they will find others like them. Especially when couples first put a toe in the water of Jewish life and community, they are likely to be more comfortable with others like them, while later they may no longer feel that need.

InterfaithFamily's surveys on what attracts and repels interfaith families asked if they preferred "targeted" (interfaith-family specific) or general programs. The responses of nearly seven hundred intermarried parents raising their children as Jews confirmed our hypothesis: significant percentages of interfaith families are interested in programs designed and marketed as "for interfaith families" and are attracted to organizations that offer them. Forty-five percent were attracted "a lot" by the Jewish organization or synagogue offering programs "that are described as being 'for interfaith families.'" Thirty percent of respondents said they were attracted "a lot" by the organization or synagogue organizing "groups of interfaith couples (*havurah*, interfaith discussion group, etc.)." The absence of such programs and groups was identified as a barrier.[7]

Respondents explained the reasons behind their preferences: they want to be with and share stories with others like them; interfaith families have unique issues, and some topics are best addressed in interfaith-family-specific programs; programs for interfaith families are more comfortable for partners who are not Jewish. Some pointed out that when interfaith couples start out, they may be more interested in interfaith-family-specific programs than they would be later, after they feel more integrated. In addition, some pointed out that the fact that an organization offers programs for interfaith families is an important statement that interfaith families are welcome.[8]

Some people have taken the position that focusing on a group, such as interfaith families, problematizes or pathologizes that group.[9] While it's true that people won't go where they are considered to be problems or to have problems, programs for interfaith families don't have to convey that message. Every social intervention responds to a perceived need, often of a particular group.

Others contend that interfaith families are not different, and that interfaith families no longer have issues particular to their interfaith relationships, therefore programs to address those issues are no longer needed.[10] While the needs of interfaith couples overlap with those of inmarried couples, they are also qualitatively different in important ways. Two basic examples: many partners from different faith backgrounds are starting out with no knowledge about Jewish traditions and have experienced negative, unwelcoming comments and behaviors, whether from disapproving Jewish relatives or professionals.

At InterfaithFamily, we frequently heard from partners in interfaith relationships who were asking for help to resolve issues that arose because of their interfaith relationship or who said they were more comfortable becoming acquainted with Judaism by being with people on a similar journey. Hosting interfaith-specific or general programs is not an either/or equation. Ignoring or pretending that interfaith couples do not have at least two religious traditions in their backgrounds does not make any sense. Responding to the particular needs of interfaith families does not conflict with and in fact is an essential support for a strategy of opening up Judaism in ways that attract everyone and making it accessible and usable. The need for interfaith-specific programs at a wide range of Jewish organizations, especially at gateway portals such as Jewish community centers, is clear.

A SERIOUS CAMPAIGN SHOULD BEGIN NOW

There are no persuasive arguments against implementing a massive concerted effort to engage interfaith families now. Some funders cite limited resources, competing priorities, and programs not fitting with their strategies. However, anyone who wants to see more people more Jewishly engaged in any activity—learning, social justice, spirituality—must realize that getting interfaith couples and families involved is essential to reaching those goals.

Some organization leaders view interfaith-specific programs as competitive with their own efforts. Local synagogue rabbis at the outset viewed InterfaithFamily/Your Community rabbis as competitors with respect to prospective members. Over time, most realized that the Your Community rabbis not only were reaching many couples who were not yet ready to become synagogue members but also were frequently referring couples to synagogues.

Some think Birthright Israel, with fewer trip participants intermarrying than nonparticipants, is the cure for intermarriage. However, many people have already aged out of Birthright, and significant percentages of trip participants do intermarry.[11] A December 2017 study reported that the likelihood of average trip participants intermarrying was 38 percent.[12]

Some say we don't need to address the intermarriage issue explicitly, that if we build up preschools, camps, teen and college programs, and so forth, those will capture enough interfaith families. But the leaders of those programs (including PJ Library and Birthright Israel) understand that interfaith families and their children are their growth markets, and they aren't satisfied with the numbers they're reaching. One basic truth about efforts to engage interfaith families is that they should form a continuum that starts as early as when couples are dating and getting married. Services and programs designed for and marketed to those interfaith couples will result in many more of their families getting involved later.

Some measure success by attracting large numbers of participants, and they say that interfaith family engagement programs don't draw the numbers of participants that indicate program success. Yet another truth: engaging interfaith families depends largely on one-on-one or small-group work with trained staff, or volunteers trained by staff, that don't reach large numbers. Interfaith family engagement efforts help create one Jewish family at a time, or at best, small groups of them. Another truth: "interfaithness"—that is, being in an interfaith relationship—is a salient characteristic for interfaith couples especially during transitional, life-cycle times but not all the time. High-attendance events or programs are not an effective programmatic solution to engage interfaith families. Even at holiday times, interfaith couples may not want to be together with others like themselves the way that LGBTQ people and Jews of color might.

Programmatic efforts that depend on relationship building and relational processes take time and are expensive. To the extent that reaching greater numbers requires more staff, the cost increases. Other well-funded programmatic interventions are expensive, most notably Birthright Israel. Given the critical importance of engaging interfaith families and the vital importance of relationship building in that process (see chapter 20), incurring the expense will generate a well-earned return on the investment. There is no reason to believe that the cost-per-participant-per-benefit is higher for efforts to engage interfaith families than it is for other programs.

Some indicate a desire to support or take action to engage interfaith families but don't know what works.[13] This isn't rocket science. There has been remarkable consensus on the kinds of programmatic efforts, described in chapter 20, that are needed to engage interfaith families.

Some say that evaluation of interfaith family engagement programs is insufficient without random sample, control group research like there has been for Birthright Israel. Yet other areas of Jewish life haven't had to wait for such gold standard proof of program effectiveness. Where information was inadequate, significant research was funded, with a commitment to then fund the directions indicated by the research. Efforts to engage interfaith families shouldn't be held to higher standards. Evaluations to date of interfaith engagement programs, including those described in chapter 21, demonstrate their positive impacts. There is no reason to doubt that additional evaluations of outreach programs would show similar positive results. While waiting for more research, the existing evaluation results should be regarded as compelling evidence justifying significant investment in interfaith engagement programs.

20

Model Pathways to Engagement

Best practices for nonprofit organizations now include developing what is called a "theory of change"—essentially a plan that states their desired ultimate impact, underlying beliefs and assumptions, and the measurable short-term and long-term outcomes of their programmatic efforts. To thrive into the future, the liberal Jewish world needs a theory of change to achieve two ultimate impacts: people in interfaith relationships engaging in Jewish life and community; and Jews, Jewish leaders, and Jewish organizations being radically inclusive of them.[1]

A Theory of Change for Interfaith Family Engagement

The beliefs and assumptions underlying a theory of change for interfaith family engagement are:

- Jewish communities will thrive with the inclusion of people in interfaith relationships and families.
- Families will be enriched when they engage in Jewish life and with Jewish communities.
- There are many individuals in interfaith relationships who are potentially or somewhat interested in but not yet engaging in Jewish life and communities.
- If more Jews, Jewish leaders, and Jewish organizations were inclusive and made well-designed programmatic efforts, then an increasing number of individuals in interfaith relationships and families will engage Jewishly.

The desired short-term outcomes of a theory of change for interfaith family engagement reflect a path that starts with interest and proceeds to learning and experience. Engagement starts when people in interfaith relationships who are potentially or somewhat interested in Jewish life and community have that interest sparked and are moved to act. Engagement proceeds through couples learning how to talk with each other about having religious traditions in their lives together and learning how to engage in those traditions with other interfaith couples and families. Experiencing Jewish life in communities of Jewishly engaged people follows, where they find their interest and learning supported and encouraged by inclusive Jews, Jewish leaders, and Jewish organizations.

The desired long-term outcomes of a theory of change for interfaith family engagement are:

- Individuals in interfaith relationships hear messages that they can be included in Jewish life and communities that can provide meaning to them and have reinforcing learning and relationship- and community-building experiences.
- Children of interfaith parents grow up in homes where Judaism is a visible and meaningful part of their lives.
- Jews, Jewish leaders, and Jewish organizations know how to and do include people in interfaith relationships and support their Jewish engagement.

MAKING RESOURCES AVAILABLE

Interfaith families connect with Jewish life at varied times and in sometimes random ways. The variety of possible connections emphasizes the importance of always being ready to capitalize on an opportunity to welcome that may arise. People make decisions about Jewish life before weddings; when children are born or start school or reach bar/bat mitzvah age; or while they are in college. People get involved in random ways: they read articles and books (one found her husband's childhood book about Jewish holidays and customs and starting learning from it); they see advertisements for programs in Jewish newspapers or parenting magazines, in emails forwarded by friends, or in temple bulletins; they talk to someone who invites them to something at a synagogue; they are put in touch with someone intermarried who welcomes them.[2]

Those interfaith families who are looking, are looking for friendly, welcoming information that respects their perspective. One website visitor told InterfaithFamily, "It's so hard to find positive interfaith articles/books/information out there."[3] Accessible, nonjudgmental educational information about Jewish traditions is needed, and the Internet is an ideal introductory medium for providing these families with engaging information available at their convenience, whenever they choose to look. We often encountered intermarried parents struggling to make their relatives from different faith traditions feel comfortable at Jewish life-cycle ceremonies and feel honored at holiday times. They were relieved and grateful to find resources where others similarly situated shared their experiences. One wrote, "It gave me inspiration to know I'm not the only one trying to do this." Another said, "Just seeing that issues are addressed makes people feel welcomed, that the non-Jewish spouse can participate with the Jewish spouse in his or her faith."[4]

InterfaithFamily was a pioneer in providing accessible resources designed to stimulate and support interfaith families' exploration of Jewish life. Today, many additional wonderful resources are available. The nonprofit Bimbam, whose tagline is "watch something Jewish," provides animated videos for learners of all ages; my grandsons love their extremely well-done videos for young children explaining Jewish values and holidays. While not marketed as "for interfaith families," Bimbam's videos are designed with sensitivity for that audience. JewBelong, another nonprofit, offers edgy, contemporary resources for adults, with interfaith families definitely in mind. One of their main slogans is "we don't care which half of you is Jewish."

MARKETING

How to spark interest in Jewish life and community in those who aren't looking yet, but who are potentially or even somewhat interested, is what back in the day was called "the $64,000 question." In part, this is a marketing challenge. Once, while driving along one of the three highways into Boston, I noticed the most effective advertisement I've ever seen. On a dark billboard, large white letters spelled out "TRY GOD." Smaller letters below spelled out "Catholic Radio," with a station frequency.[5]

I would have loved to put up billboards in every major city with "TRY JEWISH" in large letters and "visit InterfaithFamily.com" below, inviting interfaith couples in a quick, catchy way to make initial contact with Jewish resources available to them. I'm sure there are many talented marketing experts who with adequate resources could design and implement a plan for how to effectively push resources for interfaith families to the attention of interfaith couples who are not looking but are interested or potentially interested.

One thing that all Jewish organizations can do is be sure that their programs are marketed in ways that are sensitive to interfaith families. In 2011, InterfaithFamily developed a class for families with young children. We consciously decided to call the class "Raising a Child with Judaism in Your Interfaith Family," instead of "Raising a Jewish Child in Your Interfaith Family." "Raising a Jewish child" sounds as if it means exclusively Jewish, while "raising a child with Judaism" does not. A class about raising Jewish children might discourage parents who weren't at the point of raising them exclusively Jewish.[6]

RELATIONSHIPS

As important as marketing messages are, they are not likely to move most interfaith couples to action; personal relationships and invitations are needed for that. The Internet can provide an initial experience of virtual community building in a nonthreatening environment, but that is only a first step, and it must lead to face-to-face participation in local communities if interfaith families are to engage meaningfully in Jewish life.

The importance of invitation cannot be underestimated. One InterfaithFamily writer said, "I guess that's what I was hoping would fall from the sky all those years—someone to say, 'You're welcome. You can be one of us.'"[7] The One8 Foundation research, described in chapter 5, confirmed that couples especially rely on personal recommendations of friends in making decisions about activities in which to participate.[8]

Interfaith couples who aren't looking but are interested or potentially interested are most susceptible to being reached at touchstone, nodal moments in their lives. This may include when they are planning their future lives with each other—and possibly looking for wedding officiation; or perhaps when they are thinking about the possible role of religion in the lives of their children—and possibly looking for a synagogue. Those are times when invitations are most likely to be effective—in particular, invitations from other interfaith couples and from warmly embracing rabbis.

One thing heard over and again at InterfaithFamily is that interfaith couples want to be with others like themselves. Fifty-three percent of respondents to InterfaithFamily's surveys on what attracts interfaith families to Jewish organizations said they were attracted "a lot" if "there are a lot of interfaith families who are members." One said, "The visibility of non-Jewish members encouraged us to join."[9] Writers for Interfaith-Family made similar comments. One said, "I discovered a dozen other mommies struggling with the same kinds of issues." Another said, "We did visit the temple, and I was very relieved to meet the McVeighs, the O'Flahertys and the Gianninotos." Another said, "I needed a support system. We met other couples like us and joined a *havurah* made up of interfaith couples." Participating in a program enabled one couple "to meet other couples, make friends with people who are facing the same issues we face, and feel comfortable branching out into other communities of Judaism in a synagogue."[10]

Another key learning is that people in interfaith relationships benefit greatly from establishing and maintaining trusted advisor relationships, in particular with rabbis. The One8 Foundation research suggested that programs and services need to be offered by exceptionally welcoming and embracing leaders with whom interfaith couples can establish warm and supportive relationships.[11] Rabbis who officiate at weddings for interfaith couples are the greatest potential source of trusted advisor relationships, especially to the extent they can stay in touch and be a continuing source of guidance and connection to programs, organizations, and communities. Rabbis who provide other educational or life-cycle services for interfaith couples are also very important. Helping interfaith couples find rabbis to officiate at their life-cycle ceremonies has huge potential to foster the "sparking experiences" to connect couples to each other in a Jewish context that the One8 Foundation research found to be particularly impactful.

Individual rabbis can only work with so many interfaith couples, and if the rabbis have jobs with other responsibilities, the time they can devote to that work is even more limited. That makes relationships with other kinds of knowledgeable and embracing mentors even more important. Pairing interfaith couples who are more experienced with Jewish life with couples just getting started is one way to foster those kinds of relationships.

GRANDPARENTS

Depending on the families and the personalities involved, the ideal ambassadors or mentors to help spark and guide interfaith couples' Jewish engagement can be grandparents. I've heard Ruth Nemzoff, author of a book about parenting adult children and an expert on adult–adult child relationships, call grandparents "boots on the ground" in those efforts.[12] The *Millennial Children of Intermarriage* study observed that for children of intermarriage, being very close to Jewish grandparents had a positive impact on many Jewish attitudes and behaviors in young adulthood. At the same time, they noted that children of intermarriage by definition can have only one set of Jewish grandparents and as a result were less likely than children of inmarriage to have had a close relationship with Jewish grandparents.[13]

Communication is very important in both directions. If the parents approve, Jewish grandparents can model Jewish behaviors and share them with their grandchildren. Adult children can talk clearly with their parents, the grandparents, about what they are doing about religious traditions with their grandchildren, so that the grandparents can act consistently with their decisions.

Grandparents and other relatives deal with life-cycle celebrations in many different ways. InterfaithFamily published many stories of relatives from different faith traditions participating in Jewish life-cycle events and being very happy about it, including gladly participating in a bris or a bat mitzvah. Of course, conflict with in-laws over religious issues happens. Especially in those cases, the best couples can do is be clear on what they have agreed with each other and in explaining their decision to their parents, and hope that disappointed parents will respect their decisions.

When my daughter, Emily, was born, I knew it was a Jewish tradition to name a child after a deceased relative, but we hadn't done that. I thought that my parents were disappointed when I told them that Emily's middle name was going to be her mother's very English-sounding maiden name. However, my parents, very wisely, didn't push the subject of her name or of a Hebrew name. When Adam was born, they didn't raise the issue of a bris. Although they very much wanted their grandchildren to be Jewish, they must have been aware, consciously or not, that it wasn't a good time to push. Instead, they made sure to invite and include us in their celebrations of Jewish holidays and Friday night Shabbat dinners.

The Jewish in-laws and grandparents have it within their power to be embracing and supportive, and that is the best way to preserve the opportunity to influence the Jewish engagement of their children and grandchildren. One couple was getting married and wasn't sure whether the Jewish grandmother would come to the wedding. Eventually she came and danced with her new grandson-in-law, saying, "You're my grandson now."[14] That is the kind of warmth that can influence the Jewish future of a family.

OPPORTUNITIES TO TALK ABOUT RELIGIOUS TRADITIONS

Participating in discussions facilitated under Jewish auspices has a powerful impact that influences couples toward making Jewish choices for their family and their children. For many years, the Reform movement offered workshops at synagogues called "Times and Seasons," or "Yours, Mine and Ours," which is still offered by Reform Jewish Outreach Boston.[15] In

1994, Dr. Marion Usher, a clinical social worker with a private practice and a pioneer in efforts to engage interfaith families, began to offer the "Love and Religion" workshop for interfaith couples, mostly interdating or newly married, at a Jewish community center in Washington, DC.[16] The "Love and Religion" workshop and meet-up groups that discuss similar issues have been a standard feature of InterfaithFamily's programmatic offerings.

Discussion groups are grounded in couple and family theory as it relates to interfaith couples. Esther Perel says that new couples need the confidence to talk openly about their differences but may find it hard to do so. They may fear that their differences will threaten their relationship, caught between remaining silent to ensure togetherness and greater self-revelation. Because religious education for many Jewish partners ended at bar or bat mitzvah age, they may lack a cognitive framework and vocabulary to understand and describe what is important to them.[17]

Perel says the key is for the partners to engage in "a guided exploration of each partner's identity," becoming "anthropologists of each other's cultures and archaeologists of their own history." When each becomes more secure in him- or herself, the other becomes less threatening. Then the partners can proceed to negotiate the cultural fabric of their family and the future identity of their children. In addition, Perel says that to clarify the meaning and importance of their ethnic and religious identity, partners need to achieve "ethnic individuation," becoming differentiated from their families.[18]

Structured exercises can enable couples to revisit their childhood memories, draw out their involvement in ethnicity and religion, uncover what they heard about their partner's group and religion, examine people and events that influenced their identity, and share their views of restrictions and supports of their traditions. This allows them to establish commonalities in values that can serve as the foundation for creating a new world for their family, allowing them to bridge their differences. Perel says, "It is this simultaneous process of deconstruction and conservation in dealing with the past that underlies the potential for change."[19]

Perel did this kind of work in therapy with individual couples. Most rabbis officiating at weddings do premarital counseling. Paula Brody, the former director of Reform Jewish Outreach Boston, created a wonderful resource, the CCAR *Premarital Counseling Guide for Clergy*, to help clergy address these issues with respect to interfaith families.[20] Discussions in groups of interfaith couples have the important added benefits of reaching many more couples and connecting them to others in similar situations.

Marion Usher explains, in a video about her workshop, that couples participate because religious traditions matter to them, and they want to have a religious life together. However, they are facing challenges because of their different backgrounds. Some have not decided or are conflicted about what they will do with future children; some think they will raise future children "both"; and some have decided to raise children Jewish but are concerned whether they'll be able to do so. In one workshop session, the partners do the kind of structured exercise Perel describes, talking about their religious upbringings, what they find meaningful in those religious practices, and what they would like to bring forward into their lives together. In another session, they talk about their families of origin and how they conceive of their own identity. One of the most impactful features of the discussions is that they can foster ongoing connections among interfaith couples who go on to become friends.[21]

As mentioned before, all interfaith partners who are interested in having religion in their lives need to address and resolve certain issues. They're not eternal, in the sense that they never get resolved, but the issues that came up forty years ago in my own life are still coming up today for others. If asked to rank the most important programs Jewish communities can offer to engage interfaith families, the top spot would go to facilitating discussions for groups of couples. These are particularly important because, as the One8 Foundation research found, couples who make decisions about faith collaboratively and early on are more likely to establish a stable identity for their children.[22]

OPPORTUNITIES TO LEARN ABOUT JEWISH TRADITIONS AND BUILD COMMUNITY

Opportunities to learn about and experience Jewish traditions with other interfaith couples are another important pathway toward interfaith family engagement. When interfaith couples get interested, they look for help learning how they can live Jewishly and, as the One8 Foundation research shows, how doing so can add value and meaning to their lives.[23] Often the partners from a different faith tradition are eager to learn Jewish traditions and the Jewish partners are not well equipped to teach them. A range of classes and social events can be designed to provide that help, similar to the Reform movement's "A Taste of Judaism" and Interfaith-Family's "Raising a Child with Judaism in Your Interfaith Family."

In all of these kinds of programs, couples learn how and why to integrate various aspects of Jewish life and community into their lives and develop skills to navigate the Jewish communal landscape. Equally important, they connect more with other Jewishly engaged interfaith couples. The design of these programs is consistent with the One8 Foundation research in several respects. Programs to foster spiritual parenting are a great example of teaching Jewish practices that relate to day-to-day living. They can lead to feeling knowledgeable and having a sense of comfort from having faith and believing in something bigger, connected to the very practical context of raising young children. Offering social experiences around Jewish activities can build community among interfaith couples, match them with people they feel comfortable with and keep them together, recognizing they want authentic exchanges in small settings. All of this provides a solid foundation for further Jewish engagement.

21

THE POSITIVE IMPACTS THAT CAN BE ACHIEVED

The 2016 Interfaith Opportunity Summit marked a watershed moment. An at-capacity crowd of three-hundred-plus major foundation, federation, and organization leaders gathered to address the topic of engaging interfaith families in Jewish life and community. Engaging interfaith families nationally and in local communities finally appeared to be at a high level in the mainstream Jewish community's agenda, with the Jewish Federations of North America and the Jewish Funders Network partnering with InterfaithFamily on the event.[1]

During the summit there was considerable consensus about the applicability to interfaith families of a new emphasis on doing, as opposed to being, Jewish. Participants shared stories of interfaith couples valuing Judaism's gratitude practice, home family practice, focus on others, focus on improving the world, spiritual life, and ongoing questioning. One session on peoplehood affirmed that intermarried, unconverted partners from different faith traditions can feel included in Jewish communities.[2]

A dominant theme was the importance of relationships and relational processes in engaging interfaith families. At one session, the point was made that even Jewish identity is relationally constructed. Identity formation is lifelong and dependent on experiences people have in relationship with others—whether in college activities, as couples, or with trusted advisors or other couples. In a session on entry points and pathways for interfaith couples, speakers who represented early childhood programs, couples' groups, and Jewish learning programs all emphasized the importance of developing relationships. One said, "When relationships of trust and security are evident, families can thrive." Participants at yet another session emphasized the importance of reaching people through their friends: the disengaged "free roamers" have friends who are engaged and friends who are seekers, and all of them are social and on social media. People go to things when someone they know says, "Do you want to go to this? I'm going."[3]

There was great interest in a presentation by Wendy Rosov on evaluations of interfaith engagement programs. Rosov Consulting's evaluations of InterfaithFamily/Your Community, Honeymoon Israel, and jHUB (which have continued after the summit) demonstrate the powerful, positive impacts that interfaith engagement programs can have—impacts that every community that makes the effort can achieve.[4]

1. Positive Connections Between Rabbis and Officiation Seekers. In one evaluation, Rosov found that nearly one-quarter of the participants in InterfaithFamily programs had initially contacted the program with the goal of finding a rabbi to officiate at their wedding. In another, Rosov found that "particularly . . . in finding wedding officiants, [many] voiced a palpable sense of relief that this aspect of their wedding plans could finally be resolved." One participant said that a bad experience in the Jewish community "made me feel like I would never want to participate. I connected with [the local InterfaithFamily rabbi], and it was a 180. It was an emotional experience; she created an environment where good conversations happened. We feel welcomed and safe and that was a change."

2. Improved Family Dynamics. Many program participants report that structured discussions with other interfaith couples guided by trusted advisors helped them talk with their partners about the role of religious traditions in their family's life and how to incorporate religious traditions and cultures represented in their family in ways that work best for them. Rosov found the impact of engagement programs on shifting couple dynamics was both "significant and noteworthy." A high percentage of couples indicated the programs helped them when it came to talking with their partners about the role Jewish traditions can play in their lives and enabled them to appreciate the similarities and differences in their respective cultural and religious traditions. One participant said the class "helped us to talk to our families in terms of how we would live our lives." Another said the program "helped cement for us that when we have a child, s/he will be raised Jewish. Even before we were engaged, we planned to have a Jewish household, but that desire was strengthened."

3. Increased Knowledge, Comfort, and Participation in Jewish Traditions. High percentages of respondents to Rosov evaluation surveys said the programs helped them

- expand their knowledge of Judaism and/or Jewish life
- better understand the meaning behind specific Jewish rituals or traditions
- modify, experiment, or make their own home-based Jewish traditions to incorporate both partners
- incorporate Jewish traditions in life-cycle events (birth ceremonies, bar/bat mitzvah, weddings, funerals)
- participate in Jewish rituals (such as lighting Shabbat candles, lighting a Hanukkah menorah, participating in a Passover Seder, or saying Hebrew blessings over food)

In addition, high percentages of survey respondents said the programs helped them feel more confident participating in Jewish rituals, celebrations, and events and more comfortable in institutional Jewish settings such as a synagogue. In one in-house survey, a participant in Interfaith-Family's "Raising a Child with Judaism" class said that as a result of taking the class, their practices had changed to include saying the bedtime *Sh'ma*.

4. Connections with Other Jewishly Engaged Interfaith Couples. Drawing on all their evaluations of interfaith engagement programs, Rosov has reported that

the desire to create personal connections and learn from other interfaith couples is a recurring theme. Interfaith couples and families look for communities, opportunities, and spaces where they can discuss some of their experiences and challenges with other couples who share similar experiences. They appreciate the opportunity to learn from each other and are reassured by seeing the great diversity of approaches to creating a Jewish (or interfaith) family that different couples have chosen.

In one evaluation for InterfaithFamily, two-thirds of participants expressed interest in having space to discuss interfaith issues with other interfaith couples. In another, Rosov found that participants noted "the opportunity to engage with and get support from other Jewishly engaged interfaith individuals [was] particularly critical to their ongoing participation and engagement in Jewish life."

One participant said, "[W]e realized that we're not the only ones asking questions and figuring this out. . . . It's just nice to have that support." Another said, "Going to the workshops and dinners it has been a relief [to know] families [who] are going through [the] same issues and challenges." Still another said, "[M]eeting other people like myself has given me the confidence to seek out a Jewish community. I am now a member of a synagogue . . . I am becoming part of a Jewish community, so I'm very happy about that." Beyond a class, meet-up, or life-cycle event, participants appreciate being able to tap into like-minded interfaith couples and families for support. High percentages of participants said their programs helped them to develop relationships with other Jewishly engaged interfaith couples.

5. Providing Communities of Interfaith Families. Going beyond the finding that interfaith couples and families were building relationships to others like themselves, Rosov found that nearly one-third of InterfaithFamily participants initially sought to find an actual community of interfaith couples and families, while almost three-quarters said they were interested in developing a community of interfaith couples and families:

> For some, these interfaith-specific communities may satisfy their need for Jewish connection; for others, they may not. . . . [T]hese interfaith-specific communities allow couples and families to gain comfort and confidence in their own Jewish practice. In some cases, this can be a helpful stepping stone into greater communal involvement.

Rosov noted that after couples become parents, they often seek greater involvement in Jewish life, which can be in an interfaith-specific community or in their local Jewish community.

6. Connections with Local Jewish Communities. Program participants did in fact learn about and connect with programs and organizations in their local Jewish communities. High percentages of survey respondents said the programs helped them learn about the organizations and professionals in the Jewish community and what they provide. This enabled them to connect with local and online Jewish community resources. As a result, their sense of connection to the Jewish community was enhanced. Rosov found that participants "noted a variety of activities and programs that they became aware of through their connection with IFF." One said, "There are programs for interfaith couples that are more visible to me now. I know I can access the IFF website and figure something out. I have a contact in an organization that I can reach out to if I have questions." Another said, "I would say, 100% I feel more connected to finding a Jewish community, and more engaged in the question of how to find it. Without IFF, I would not have done that at all."

7. Ongoing Connections with Trusted Advisors. Rosov found that participants developed trusting relationships with program staff, especially with rabbis in the area of wedding officiation. Rosov noted that participants "resoundingly noted that they had positive experiences" with program staff. One participant emphasized the importance of the positive, accepting approach she experienced: "They are not trying to say that people need to convert; they honor other faiths, and that is important. If I continue to have those positive feelings, then I will continue to be involved in the Jewish community."

8. More Welcoming Organizations. Finally, Rosov found that institutions were developing more inclusive policies as a result of InterfaithFamily programs. A synagogue education director said, "[W]e've begun to discuss various issues related to interfaith families here at our congregation in our weekly staff meetings. Thanks for helping get that very important conversation started." A rabbi said he was influenced in "the way I talk and write about interfaith Jews in our community and beyond."

It should be beyond question that feeling more comfortable, confident, and connected in Jewish settings is conducive to desired outcomes such as raising children with Judaism or sending children to Jewish preschool, summer camp, or Jewish education. It should also be beyond question that programs designed and marketed for interfaith families can be part of a network of interconnected programs and feed into general programs for everyone.[5] One of Rosov's key findings is that InterfaithFamily's impact "begins at home, and expands outward to support couples' and families' awareness and exploration of Jewish communal resources and organizations . . . setting participants on a path toward greater involvement."

EVERYTHING FOLLOWS
FROM ATTITUDES

In 2008, when Edgar and Adam Bronfman espoused a positive response to intermarriage at the federations' General Assembly, I expressed hope that those in attendance would take the message to heart and that positive attitudes and concrete actions would follow.[1] If more policy makers and funders in the Jewish community adopted positive attitudes toward intermarriage, we would see inclusive policies and a much greater communal effort to attract interfaith families to Jewish life. We need more Jewish leaders to pick up the mantle Edgar Bronfman left behind.

Some signs indicate that is happening. At the Reform movement's biennial in November 2013, Rabbi Rick Jacobs called for "audacious hospitality."[2] In later press reports he said he wanted to build "on-ramps to Jewish life" for the majority of the next generation who will be the children of intermarriages, that "finger-wagging" is a turnoff for intermarried Jews and their partners who might otherwise make Jewish choices,[3] and that "Jewish living, values, commitments . . . can be upheld in interfaith families" and are not the "exclusive province of Jewish-Jewish couples."[4] The commitment to audacious hospitality is extremely important. I look forward to seeing the Reform movement's programmatic follow-up.

Many speakers and participants at the 2016 Interfaith Opportunity Summit spoke of the need for a shift in the dominant narrative, referring to the remaining ambivalence about intermarriage. More than one said that organizations that think they are welcoming, really aren't. One said that if a couple has just one bad experience, they may not come back. Another said that "we all need to be educated that we are all ambassadors." A Protestant woman married to a Jewish man, raising their children

Jewish, told about how she was deeply moved when she held the Torah for the first time at Simchat Torah immediately before the Summit. She reported that she had reached that point because a rabbi said yes when asked to officiate at her wedding and because at her emerging spiritual community she experienced "radical hospitality, not just tolerance." There was no hint of "do more Jewish, be more Jewish, convert." It was a safe place to explore while feeling truly part of a community.[5]

Ultimately the reason there hasn't been a massive concerted effort to engage interfaith families is the same reason that more interfaith families don't engage Jewishly in the first place—negative to ambivalent attitudes about intermarriage that are still prevalent among Jews and Jewish leaders. The dominant narrative about intermarriage must change—and it can. There has been much progress since the "continuity crises" began. But much more progress needs to be made.

As far back as 1994, a federation task force recognized that "some significant changes may need to occur in both staff attitudes and approaches at every level in federation and community agencies and organizations."[6] Recognizing that "some" changes "may" be needed was an understatement. I would say huge changes must occur before attitudes are as radically inclusive as they need to be. But when the liberal Jewish world adopts radically inclusive attitudes toward intermarriage and partners from different faith traditions, policies and programs that facilitate and encourage their engagement will follow, and more and more interfaith families will be attracted to Jewish life and experience the meaning it can add to their lives.

Some people think that negative attitudes among Jews about intermarriage will lessen over time because today's young adults don't share those attitudes, so we don't need to do anything. I don't think we should or can wait that long—and I'm not sure how fast it will happen, given the studies that continue to report young adults questioning the Jewishness of other young adults.[7]

In the Hornstein Program, I learned from Ron Heifitz's *Leadership Without Easy Answers* that leaders move people to adapt their attitudes.

The prime example was Lyndon Johnson, who ironically, given the positions he had previously taken as a senator from Texas, led Americans to give up their opposition to civil rights.[8] Given the fractured nature of the Jewish community, I can't foresee a single leader—someone like Lyndon Johnson—being able to move Jews to be inclusive of interfaith couples. However, a coalition of key leaders who jointly have the capability to lead an adaptation of attitudes in the community—and to fund and take action to engage interfaith families—is possible and very much needed.

In 2014, after Steven M. Cohen and Jack Wertheimer issued another critical analysis of intermarriage,[9] Chip Edelsberg, then the executive director of the Jim Joseph Foundation, cowrote "The Ever-Renewing People," with a subheading that aptly summarizes the essay: "Jewish life in America is actually flourishing, thanks in part to the energy of children of intermarriage." Cohen and Wertheimer had cited sociologist Milton Himmelfarb, who decades ago, when asked what the grandchildren of intermarried Jews should be called, responded "Christian." Edelsberg dismisses that notion as neither apt nor helpful, noting that thousands of young Jews—up to half of whom would be dismissed by Cohen and Wertheimer as "Christian"—attend Jewish summer camps, Jewish teen programs, Hillel, and Moishe Houses.[10] He responded to Cohen and Wertheimer in no uncertain terms:

> In the end, Wertheimer and Cohen's depiction of [American Jewish] life as in need of being pulled back "from the brink" is another caricature of Jews as (in the phrase of the late Simon Rawidowicz) an "ever-dying people." This belies our extraordinary history as a people and an ever-renewing faith tradition that, time and again, have demonstrated an ability to evolve and adapt, thereby avoiding the cliff that Wertheimer and Cohen have artificially constructed.[11]

This optimistic view of the future, on the part of one of the Jewish community's most important philanthropists, supports increased efforts to engage even more interfaith families and children of interfaith families in

Jewish life and community—to ensure, in Edelsberg's words, that diverse Jews "will continue to invigorate contemporary Judaism and invent new ways to experience American Jewish life."[12]

Movie actor Michael Douglas was told his whole life that he wasn't Jewish because his mother wasn't Jewish. When told that he was being given the Genesis Prize in 2015 as an outstanding Jew, he said, "This is a mistake, I'm not Jewish."[13] However, his son had gotten the family interested in Judaism, and become bar mitzvah. They traveled to Israel. The head of the Genesis Prize Foundation said their goal in choosing Douglas was to highlight "a growing reality, which must be addressed" and to emphasize "inclusiveness of Jews of intermarriage" in Jewish life.[14] Another Genesis Prize leader said:

> In the strictest sense, our laureate this year is not a "perfect" Jew. His mother is not Jewish. I even suspect that he does not spend every Friday evening in a synagogue and does not follow kashrut. Yet, he is someone who put his energy and determination into being Jewish, who exercised his free will and showed commitment to follow the path of his ancestors in search for a foundation. Should we deny his Jewishness on the basis of his mother's birth or should we celebrate it on the basis of his commitment to embrace Judaism and pass his Jewish heritage to his children? Are not free will and determination the essential qualities of the Jews? We can respond to freedom by building barriers and closing up, or we can respond to it by being inclusive and supportive of those who chose a path of Judaism. I choose the latter. . . . [W]e should support and encourage those who have made a decision to embrace their Jewish identity and pass their Jewish heritage to their children, like Michael Douglas is doing. We should welcome them with open arms—not turn away from them.[15]

When Douglas received the award in June 2015, he announced that he would donate the prize to support efforts to reach out to other Jews from intermarried families seeking a connection to the Jewish community.[16]

The Genesis Prize Fund and the Jewish Funders Network simultaneously announced a $1.65 million matching grant fund for organizations and projects that support and enhance avenues to Jewish engagement for intermarried couples and their families. The goals of the matching grant were:

> To encourage the creation of a culture of welcoming and acceptance within the Jewish community of intermarried couples, their families, and individuals who come from these families.

> To energize and strengthen organizations working in this field and to encourage the creation of new programs in that area.

> To use the leverage of matching funds to foster the field and bring both new funders and new funding into the field. These new funders offer a prospect of long-term sustainability to the field.

> To encourage funders to engage with nonprofits and other organizations on particular projects and take an active role in developing the field.[17]

With this extremely welcome development, we were finally seeing more philanthropic resources devoted to the most pressing opportunity the Jewish community has to grow and be enriched. There is a strong foundation for the massive concerted effort that's needed, and there is growing interest and awareness of the importance of the issue. But we have a long way to go to achieve an inclusive culture and strengthened programs working in this field. It is my urgent hope that organization leaders and the funding community will resolve to follow through. This is the time for action!

EPILOGUE

Changing attitudes is hard work—not only for Jews who might embrace interfaith couples but also for interfaith couples who might accept our invitations to embrace Jewish life and community. Interfaith couples may be uncertain about whether they want to participate in any religious traditions, or Jewish ones in particular. They may feel they don't know what's involved and embarrassed or unsure how to find out. They may be worried, from experience or anticipation, what kind of reception they will find. How these feelings get resolved plays out against strong couple and sometimes strong family dynamics.

Many thousands of interfaith couples have found meaning and value in Jewish traditions. It happened with Wendy and me, and with our children as well. While writing this book, I asked them why they were Jewishly involved, providing their children with a Jewish education while many other young adult Jews and children of intermarriage were not. Their brief answers were telling. Adam said he saw how much being Jewishly involved had added to our family's lives growing up and he wanted his children to have that. Emily's husband, Brett, said he welcomes Jewish education for his sons because central tenets of Judaism are compatible with his own beliefs that "we are all connected to one another, our planet and the universe; that we should treat each other with respect and dignity; and that we all deserve to be free." Adam's wife, Alicia, who grew up a Quaker, feels that "we can find within the Jewish community the important cultural, community, and social justice pieces of religion that I valued growing up and that we both value for our kids."

Emily, on the other hand, explained her involvement by the attitudes she experienced in her Jewish community: she said she was able to raise her children with Judaism because "we are fortunate enough to have access to a temple and Jewish organizations that are inclusive. In these settings, rituals and traditions are explained and all are invited to participate as they are comfortable. There really seems to be no differentiation between the parents—no one is checking your Jewish credentials." Brett added, "I always feel like a welcome participant without putting my own background or beliefs behind those of Emily or the boys. I feel confident that the boys will learn about their Jewish heritage without making me feel like an outsider."

In a nutshell, there you have the two arenas where attitudes need to adapt. As happened with my children, interfaith couples can come to see the meaning that Jewish life can provide, and when Jews and Jewish organizations are truly inclusive, interfaith couples may come to stay.

Jewish attitudes toward intermarriage and the *other* are very deep-seated. It will be challenging to adapt them into the radically inclusive attitudes from which inclusive policies and a serious engagement campaign will flow. But I know it's possible because I've seen fundamental attitudes change in very personal ways.

The rabbi who spoke so callously to Wendy when we got engaged experienced intermarriage in his own family, and he became involved in efforts to welcome interfaith families. It took about thirty years before we spoke again, but when we finally met, he was supportive of the work I was doing at InterfaithFamily.

When my mother died at ninety-five, I said in my eulogy that my parents had a choice to make. They chose their love for me and their devotion to their family above anything else, even when it wasn't clear whether or not Jewish traditions would continue to be part of my life. If you look at our wedding album (we were married by a judge), my father looks very grim—but he was there, and Wendy feels he and my mother came to embrace her as their own daughter.

A cousin visited with my father while my mother's funeral was taking place (my father was unable to travel). At about the same time as I was giving my eulogy, my father started telling her exactly the same thing: "Bea and I talked about it. We decided that we didn't want to turn our backs and lose our son. And look at the wonderful family that we got."

At the *shiva*, my mother's childhood next-door neighbor, Elaine, told Wendy that my mother lived a "charmed" life. Wendy said, "Probably the worst thing that happened to her is that Ed married me." Elaine said, "That's right." Wendy said, "If I'm the worst thing that happened to her, I guess she did have a pretty charmed life," and Elaine readily agreed.

I would like to think that my mother and my father could see into the future the whole small universe of our loving family that would result from their choosing love. But that choice made something more than a loving family possible. They opened doors that set the possibility of an ongoing Jewish future in motion.

So it's not only interfaith couples who I hope will choose both to love each other and to engage with Jewish tradition. I hope that Jews, Jewish leaders, and the Jewish organizations they lead will maximize the chances of Jewish traditions continuing into the future by choosing to love interfaith couples and partners from different faith traditions.

To follow and join in advocacy for a radically inclusive Judaism that engages interfaith families, please visit the website of the Center for Radically Inclusive Judaism, www.CFRIJ.com, or email info@CFRIJ.com.

ACKNOWLEDGMENTS

At the outset I thought I was a pretty good writer and would not benefit from editing. How foolish! Judy Bolton-Fasman introduced me to Jamie Bernard, whose developmental edit improved my draft dramatically. Dena Neusner helped to shape the manuscript. I am especially indebted to my friend and colleague Kathy Bloomfield, whose line editing refined the manuscript into the book you have before you, and to Stuart Matlins, who guided me throughout the publication process. Thank you also to Emily Wichland and Tim Holtz for the expert editing and design they contributed, and to Debra Corman for her above-and beyond proofreading. I am solely responsible for the content and positions taken in the book.

I'm grateful to so many people who helped me in my work to engage interfaith families Jewishly, and I apologize to anyone whom I fail to mention here. First, to the people who helped me get involved—initially Paula Brody, and then Judy Krell, who staffed CJP's intermarriage task force. The outstanding Hornstein Program faculty—especially Bernie Reisman z"l, Susan Shevitz, Sherry Israel, Joe Reimer, Larry Sternberg, and Liza Stern—supported my independent studies of intermarriage, and I learned much more at my fieldwork placements at Jewish Family & Children's Service, with Ira Schor, Debbie Whitehill, and Elana Kling Perkins, and at CJP. Through this work I started to get to know many of the pioneering professionals in the field, including Rosanne Levitt, Dawn Kepler, Lynne Wolfe, Phyllis Adler, Marion Usher, Arlene Chernow, and Debbie Antonoff, and later Karen Kushner, Rayzel Raphael, and Elana MacGilpin, as well as Kathy Kahn, Catherine Fischer, Joyce Schwartz, and all of the other outstanding Reform movement outreach professionals.

I'm especially indebted to Yossi Abramowitz, who started the web magazine www.interfaithfamily.com with Ronnie Friedland as editor, and later supported my founding InterfaithFamily as an independent nonprofit with Ronnie as the first employee. I'm equally indebted to Esta

Epstein, Ginny Wise, Mamie Kanfer Stewart, and Lynda Schwartz, who served as chairs of InterfaithFamily's board while I was CEO, and to the founding InterfaithFamily board members, Arthur Obermayer z"l, and my dear friend Gary Furst. I had long and close relationships with Ken Grandberg, Steve Kris, Jim Ball, Eve Coulson, Jonathan Wornick, Carol Targum, Lydia Kukoff, David Rokoff, Rebecca Hoelting Short, Bill Schwartz, Nancy Gennet, Paul Cohen, Ruth Nemzoff, Mindy Fortin, and Laurie Toll Franz, and I thank them and every other InterfaithFamily board member.

Heather Martin, InterfaithFamily's chief operating officer, truly made it all work. Thank you to Jodi Bromberg for taking over as CEO. We had a terrific staff, including Micah Sachs, Ruth Abrams, Benjamin Maron, and Lindsey Silken as editors; Susan Edni, who made the office run; and others too many to name. I learned a great deal from the staff of the Your Community initiative, especially its director, Stacie Garnett-Cook, and several of the rabbis who served as local Your Community directors with whom I worked the longest: Robyn Frisch, Mychal Copeland, and Jillian Cameron.

Over the years I was fortunate to have steady encouragement from Jon Woocher z"l and Ron Wolfson. Generous institutional funders made InterfaithFamily's work possible, and I benefited greatly from their guidance, including, in roughly chronological order: Debbie Findling, Stephanie Rapp, Amy Lyons, and the Goldman and Haas families in San Francisco; Brenda Zlatin and the Blaustein family; Edgar M. Bronfman Jr. z"l, Adam Bronfman, and Dana Raucher; Sandy Cardin and the Schusterman family; Terry Rubenstein and the Meyerhoff family; Barbara Picower; Lesley Said Matsa and the Crown family; Alicia Oberman, Suzanne Knoll, and the Jack and Goldie Wolfe Miller family; Kimberly Miller Rubenfeld; Felicia Hermann and Jackie Fishman; Jay Kaiman, Daniel Sperling, Elisa Levy, and the Marcus family; Joe Kanfer, Marcella Kanfer Rolnick, Dara Weinerman Steinberg, and the Lippman Kanfer family; Mike Leven; Batya Olsen; Prudence L. Steiner; Michael Frieze; Dvora Joseph Davey; Sheila Lambert; Jey Auritt and Andy Cable; Michael Rukin z"l and Morreen Rukin Bayles; Ben Binswanger and the Joyce and Irving Goldman family; Sandra Fisher and Jodi Jarvis of CJP; Jeff Zlot and Phil Strause, lay leaders of the San Francisco federation; Karyn Cohen and the Jacobson family; Newt Becker z"l, and David and Ann Peckenpaugh Becker; Ari Ritvo-Slifka and Sarah Silver; Edward M. Ackerman z"l; Harold Grinspoon and Winnie Sandler Grinspoon; Jim Adler; Uri Herscher; Steve Grossman; Charles Steiner; Dorothy and Leonard z"l Wasserman; and Faye Kimerling. I'm grateful to every funder of InterfaithFamily, and to Joseph Hyman for his introductions to funders and his role with the 2008 funders consortium.

Over the years I learned from many rabbis who were leaders in engaging interfaith families, including Rachel Cowan z"l, Jerry Davidson, Brian Field, Laura Geller, David Kudan, Evan Moffic, Stephen Pearce, Steven Carr Reuben, Sam Gordon, Peter Rubinstein, and Alvin Sugarman, among others. As detailed in the book, my views were significantly shaped in dialogue with Carl Perkins. Rim Meirowitz served on InterfaithFamily's board and was a wonderful rabbinic advisor.

I was fortunate to have known and worked for too short a time with Egon Mayer z"l. He was an exceptionally warm and visionary leader who deserves credit along with Rabbi Alex Schindler z"l for the first significant efforts to change the Jewish world's attitudes toward intermarriage. I hope that I have contributed to some degree in furthering their agenda.

I like to say that Dru Greenwood, who inherited Rabbi Schindler's and Lydia Kukoff's outreach leadership, knows more about engaging interfaith families than anyone in the world. I am grateful for her friendship and trusted advice for over thirty years, including commenting on more than one version of this book.

I am grateful to Barry Shrage, the most enlightened federation leader of our times, for his ongoing friendship and support. At our first meeting over twenty years ago, I asked Barry how he would feel if his Orthodox son got involved with my not halachically Jewish daughter. Barry said he hoped his son would live a halachic life and to do that with my daughter would require her to convert, but he wouldn't reject them if that didn't happen. Barry's amazing inclusivity extended from that personal level to his communal leadership advocating for and funding interfaith engagement efforts. I hope that this book will inspire more federation professional and lay leaders to follow in Barry's footsteps.

There are three rabbis to whom I am grateful above all. Lev Ba'esh, the model of inclusivity, who worked at InterfaithFamily for a time, officiated at the weddings of both my children and at the bris of my oldest grandson (we call him the "Grand Rabbi of the Case Family"). Ari Moffic was the first director of the first Your Community project in Chicago. Her passion for engaging interfaith families Jewishly is unmatched, and she always pushed me toward the most liberal positions. And Mayer Selekman, a pioneer in interfaith engagement efforts who was excoriated for being so far ahead of his time, has become my closest rabbinic advisor.

Finally, this book and my work with interfaith families happened, like most of what I've done with my life, because of Wendy. She was the cause of the first great leap I took—to love and marry her—and she supported without hesitation every leap I took thereafter. There are no words to express how grateful I am.

NOTES

Over the past twenty years I talked with or heard many people in inter-faith relationships as well as Jewish professionals and lay leaders whose statements are quoted in this book. I also read many such statements in private, unpublished documents, including in emails, in-house evaluations at InterfaithFamily, and other surveys. Original sources for these statements, whenever I could find them, are cited in the notes. In cases where there are no or not easily accessible original sources (and sometimes even when there are), I cite essays and blog posts I wrote contemporaneously in which I quoted them. I know I am asking readers to put a good deal of faith in my reliability as an accurate reporter.

1 Choosing Love—the Rise of Intermarriage in America

1. Sidney Goldstein, "Profile of American Jewry: Insights from the 1990 National Jewish Population Survey," in *American Jewish Year Book 1992* (New York: American Jewish Committee, 1992), 125, http://www.jewishdatabank.org/Studies/downloadFile .cfm?FileID=3004. Traditional Jews say Jewish law forbids intermarriage. They cite the Talmud and a provision in the Torah, Deuteronomy 7:3–4, that literally prohibits intermarriage with only seven specified Canaanite tribes that no longer exist and states the rationale that the Canaanite partners would "turn aside your son from (following) after me and they would serve other gods." However, as W. Gunther Plaut explains in *The Torah: A Modern Commentary*, rev. ed. (New York: URJ Press, 2005), intermarriages "did take place throughout the early centuries of Israel's existence; thus, Moses [and] Solomon . . . took foreign wives, as did the tribal forefathers Simeon and Joseph"; Plaut describes this as "the tension of contrasting tendencies in Jewish history: its expanding and contracting heartbeats, the broadening and narrowing of peoplehood" (1214). The dominant tendency in Jewish history until recently has been contraction and a narrow concept of peoplehood, with Jews living in host societies that disapproved of or forbade intermarriages or discriminated against Jews.
2. Goldstein, "Profile of American Jewry," 125.
3. Goldstein, 125.
4. Goldstein, 125; United Jewish Communities, *National Jewish Population Survey 2000–2001* (New York: United Jewish Communities, 2003), 16, http://www.jewishdatabank .org/Studies/downloadFile.cfm?FileID=1490.

2 Choosing Tradition—the Jewish Community's Response

1. Harry Bliss, *Boston Globe*, October 31, 2006, used with permission of Pippin Properties, Inc.

2. Sidney Goldstein, "Profile of American Jewry: Insights from the 1990 National Jewish Population Survey," in *American Jewish Year Book 1992* (New York: American Jewish Committee, 1992), 124, http://www.jewishdatabank.org/Studies/downloadFile.cfm?FileID=3004.

3. Marianne R. Sanua, "AJC and Intermarriage: The Complexities of Jewish Continuity, 1960–2006," in *American Jewish Yearbook 2007* (New York: American Jewish Committee, 2007), 12–20, http://www.ajcarchives.org/AJC_DATA/Files/AJYB703.CV.pdf.

4. Jacob Staub, "A Reconstructionist View of Patrilineal Descent," in *Judaism* 34, no. 1 (Winter 1985): 97–98, http://archive.jewishrecon.org/resource-files/files/Reconstructionist%20view%20on%20patrlineal%20descent.pdf.

5. Alexander M. Schindler, *Rabbi Schindler 1978 Speech Establishing Outreach* (speech, Board of Trustees of the Union of American Hebrew Congregations, Houston, TX, December 2, 1978), https://urj.org/rabbi-schindler-1978-speech-establishing-outreach; Committee on Patrilineal Descent, *The Status of Children of Mixed Marriages* (New York: Central Conference of American Rabbis, 1983), http://www.jewishvirtuallibrary.org/reform-movement-s-resolution-on-patrilineal-descent-march-1983. The Conservative movement's position at the time could be summarized as opposing intermarriage, promoting conversion in the event of intermarriage, and being as welcoming as was consistent with Conservative standards. The incidence of intermarriage among Orthodox Jews is low; how Orthodox Judaism does or might respond to intermarriage is beyond the scope of this book.

6. Egon Mayer, *Love and Tradition: Marriage Between Jews and Christians* (New York: Plenum Press, 1985).

7. Ari L. Goldman, "Long Island Interview: Egon Mayer; Intermarriage: Public Issue, Private Fear," *New York Times*, May 21, 1989, https://www.nytimes.com/1989/05/21/nyregion/long-island-interview-egon-mayer-intermarriage-public-issue-private-fear.html.

8. Sanua, "AJC and Intermarriage," 23–26.

9. Goldstein, "Profile of American Jewry," 127.

10. Sanua, "AJC and Intermarriage," 26–27. More recent statements include Jack Wertheimer, "New Outreach to Intermarrieds Makes Wrong Assumptions," *New York Jewish Week*, December 13, 2011, http://jewishweek.timesofisrael.com/new-outreach-to-intermarrieds-makes-wrong-assumptions; Jack Wertheimer and Steven M. Cohen, "The Pew Survey Reanalyzed: More Bad News, but a Glimmer of Hope," *Mosaic Magazine*, November 2, 2014, https://mosaicmagazine.com/essay/2014/11/the-pew-survey-reanalyzed; and Sylvia Barack Fishman, Steven M. Cohen, and Jack Wertheimer, "Michael Chabon's Views on Intermarriage Are Increasingly Mainstream. They Are Also Morally Abhorrent," Jewish Telegraphic Agency, June 8, 2018, https://www.jta.org/2018/06/08/news-opinion/michael-chabons-views-intermarriage-increasingly-mainstream-also-morally-abhorrent.

11. Sanua, "AJC and Intermarriage," 30.

12. Sylvia Barack Fishman, *Jewish and Something Else: A Study of Mixed-Married Families* (American Jewish Committee, 2001), 6, research.policyarchive.org/9961.pdf; Steven Bayme, foreword to *Jewish and Something Else*, v.

13. In 2018, there was publicity that Steven M. Cohen had repeatedly sexually harassed numerous women in his field (Hannah Dreyfus, "Harassment Allegations Mount Against Leading Jewish Sociologist," *Jewish Week*, July 19, 2018, https://jewishweek .timesofisrael.com/harassment-allegations-mount-against-leading-jewish-sociologist). Some argued that his work should be reevaluated or discounted as a result (see Gary Rosenblatt, "Cohen's Fall Tests Border of Demography and Sexism," *Jewish Week*, August 1, 2018, https://jewishweek.timesofisrael.com/cohens-fall-tests-border-of -demography-and-sexism). Cohen is perhaps the most prominent critic of intermarriage; I strongly disagree with his views. I believe that Cohen demonstrated a subjective bias against intermarriage and agree with Jane Eisner that Cohen "and a few other select sociologists evolved from being dispassionate researchers and analysts to advocates for policy solutions" ("My Personal and Professional Reckoning with Steven Cohen's #MeToo Moment," *Forward*, July 26, 2018, https://forward.com /opinion/406679/my-personal-and-professional-reckoning-with-steven-cohens-me too-moment). However, Cohen's arguments about intermarriage need to be challenged on their merits, not because of his bad conduct.

14. Steven M. Cohen, *A Tale of Two Jewries: The "Inconvenient Truth" for American Jews* (New York: Jewish Life Network/Steinhardt Foundation, 2007), 11, http://www .bjpa.org/search-results/publication/2908. In a 2004 paper, Benjamin Phillips and Fern Chertok of the Cohen Center for Modern Jewish Studies at Brandeis wrote that a child's Jewish identity is determined not simply by the fact that the parents are intermarried, but rather largely by the environment the family creates, and in particular by their decision to raise the children as Jews. They concluded that "tarring all intermarriages with the same brush" makes the loss of Jewish identity "a self-fulfilling prophecy" (Benjamin Phillips and Fern Chertok, "Jewish Identity among the Adult Children of Intermarriage: Event Horizon or Navigable Horizon?" [paper presented at the 36th Annual Conference of the Association for Jewish Studies, Chicago, IL, December 21, 2004], 11, http://www.bjpa.org/search-results/publication/3468).

15. Council of Jewish Federations, *Jewish Community Services to the Intermarried: Report of the Task Force on the Intermarried and Jewish Affiliation* (New York: Council of Jewish Federations, 1994).

16. Combined Jewish Philanthropies, "Report of the Strategic Planning Committee: A Culture of Learning, a Vision of Justice, a Community of Caring," January 1998, 14–15.

17. United Jewish Communities, *National Jewish Population Survey 2000–2001* (New York: United Jewish Communities, 2003), 16, http://www.jewishdatabank.org/Studies /downloadFile.cfm?FileID=1490.

18. Pew Research Center, *A Portrait of Jewish Americans* (Washington, DC: Pew Research Center's Religions and Public Life Project, 2013), 35–37, http://www.jewishdatabank .org/studies/downloadFile.cfm?FileID=3088.

19. Many published articles on the Pew report refer to the intermarriage rate among non-Orthodox Jews as 71 percent, but Alan Cooperman, primary author of the Pew report, says the correct figure is 72 percent. Alan Cooperman, email to me, January 27, 2017. There are different ways to describe the frequency and extent of intermarriage. The finding that 44 percent of all Jews who were married as of 2013 were intermarried describes the percentage of intermarried Jews at a point in time, not a rate of intermarriage. If one in two Jews intermarry in a period, the *individual* rate of intermarriage is 50 percent; that is, 50 percent of Jews who married in that period of time intermarried. In that case, the *couples* rate of intermarriage is 67 percent because if there are 100 Jews, and 50 percent of them marry other Jews, 25 couples (each with two Jews) are formed, while if 50 percent of them intermarry, 50 couples (each with one Jew) are formed, so out of 75 couples total, 50, or 67 percent, are intermarried. The couples rate of intermarriage will always be higher than the individual rate.

20. By 2021, "2/5 of the largest communities in Canada are projected to have intermarriage rates above 50% and over 1/3 of all individuals residing in couples or families will be living in interfaith arrangements" (Alan Simons, "The Changing Face of Jewish Canada," *JewishInfoNews.com*, July 29, 2009, https://jewishinfonews.wordpress.com /2009/07/29/the-changing-face-of-jewish-canada-%E2%80%9Ca-potentially -critical-situation-%E2%80%9D).

21. The intermarriage rate in the United Kingdom was 26 percent for those marrying after 2010, "reflective of an upward trend" (David Graham, *Jews in Couples: Marriage, Intermarriage, Cohabitation and Divorce in Britain* [London: Institute for Jewish Policy Research, 2016], 2, http://archive.jpr.org.uk/object-uk401).

3 How Many Jews Will There Be?

1. W. Gunther Plaut, ed., *The Torah: A Modern Commentary*, rev. ed. (New York: URJ Press, 2005), 899.

2. Surveys include:

1990 national: Barry Kosmin et al., *Highlights of the CJF 1990 National Population Survey* (New York: Council of Jewish Federations, 1991), http://www.bjpa.org /Publications/details.cfm?PublicationID=13841.

2000–2001 national: United Jewish Communities, *National Jewish Population Survey 2000–2001* (New York: United Jewish Communities, 2003), http://www .jewishdatabank.org/Studies/downloadFile.cfm?FileID=1490.

2013 national ("Pew report"): Pew Research Center, *A Portrait of Jewish Americans* (Washington, DC: Pew Research Center's Religions and Public Life Project, 2013), http://www.jewishdatabank.org/studies/downloadFile.cfm?FileID=3088.

2011 New York ("2011 New York study"): Steven M. Cohen, Jacob B. Ukeles, and Ron Miller, *Jewish Community Study of New York: 2011* (New York: UJA-Federation of New York, 2012), http://www.jewishdatabank.org/studies/downloadFile.cfm ?FileID=2852.

2015 Boston ("2015 Boston study"): Leonard Saxe et al., *2015 Greater Boston Jewish Community Study* (Waltham: Brandeis University, Cohen Center for Modern

Jewish Studies, 2016), http://www.jewishboston.com/2015-greater-boston-jewish
-community-study-cjp-overview-cohen-center-report.

2018 Washington, DC: Janet Krasner Aronson et al., *2017 Greater Washington Jewish Community Demographic Study* (Washington, DC: Jewish Federation of Greater Washington, DC, 2018), https://www.shalomdc.org/wp-content/uploads/2018/03/DCJewishCommunityStudy.pdf.

2018 San Francisco: Steven M. Cohen and Jacob B. Ukeles, *A Portrait of Bay Area Jewish Life and Communities, Community Study Highlights* (San Francisco: Jewish Community Federation of San Francisco, the Peninsula, Marin and Sonoma Counties, 2018), http://jewishdatabank.org/Studies/downloadFile.cfm?FileID=3721.

2018 Pittsburgh: Matthew Boxer et al., *The 2017 Greater Pittsburgh Jewish Community Study*, pittsburghjewishcommstudy021918.2.pdf, available at http://www.jfedpgh.org/history.

3. For example, the *Jewish Community Study of New York* frequently attributes cause and effect to intermarriage but not other factors. Thus intermarriage—not other factors such as what the partners bring to the marriage—"strongly influences" whether children are raised as Jews, the Jewish engagement level of the home, and the Jewish educational choices for their children. In contrast, on the question whether having fewer Jewish acquaintances causes less engagement: "Of course, the chicken and egg here are difficult to discern. Do people with many Jewish intimates acquire and sustain Jewish engagement, or do Jewishly engaged people form and sustain Jewish friendships and family relationships?" (Cohen et al., *Jewish Community Study of New York*, 162, 191).

4. Theodore Sasson, "New Analysis of Pew Data: Children of Intermarriage Increasingly Identify as Jews," *Tablet*, November 11, 2013, 8, https://www.bjpa.org/search-results/publication/18694.

5. Cohen et al., *Jewish Community Study of New York*, 180–81. (Figures total more than 100 percent due to rounding.)

6. Saxe et al., *2015 Greater Boston Jewish Community Study*, 34. In two studies released in 2018, in Washington, DC, 75 percent of intermarried parents said they were raising their children exclusively (61 percent) or partly (14 percent) as Jews; in Pittsburgh the corresponding figures were 44 percent, 33 percent, and 11 percent. Aronson et al., *2017 Greater Washington Jewish Community Demographic Study*, 44; Boxer et al., *2017 Greater Pittsburgh Jewish Community Study*, 32.

7. Pew Research Center, *Portrait of Jewish Americans*, 8. (Total is less than 100 percent due to rounding.)

8. Sasson, "New Analysis of Pew Data," 1, 4, 6, 8–9. A 2016 study of millennial children of intermarriage (those born between 1981 and 1995) asked what their parents told them about their religious identity: 41 percent said they were told they were Jewish only; 17 percent were told they were both; 18 percent were told it was their choice; 18 percent were not raised in any religion; 5 percent were raised in the other religion (Theodore Sasson et al., *Millennial Children of Intermarriage: Touchpoints and Trajectories of Jewish Engagement* [Waltham: Brandeis University, Cohen Center for

Modern Jewish Studies, 2016], 14, http://www.brandeis.edu/cmjs/pdfs/intermarriage
/MillennialChildrenIntermarriage1.pdf).

9. Steven M. Cohen, "Which of Our Grandchildren Will Be Jewish in This Age of Intermarriage?" *Forward*, October 24, 2016, http://forward.com/opinion/352405 /which-of-our-grandchildren-will-be-jewish-in-this-age-of-intermarriage.

10. Steven M. Cohen, email to me, October 25, 2016.

11. Pew Research Center, *Portrait of Jewish Americans*, 37.

12. Sasson et al., *Millennial Children of Intermarriage*, 43–44.

4 What Will Jewish Life Look Like?

1. "The index consists of 12 items that cover a variety of conceptual domains . . . touch[ing] on communal affiliation, ritual observance, salience of Jewish life, and social interaction. . . . The items are attending a program or event at a . . . Jewish community center; belonging to a synagogue; belonging to a Jewish organization; usually or always attending a Passover seder; usually or always lighting Sabbath candles; usually or always lighting Chanukah candles; feeling it's very important to be part of a Jewish community; regularly talking about Jewish-related topics with Jewish friends; feeling a lot a part of a Jewish community; volunteering for Jewish organizations or causes; having closest friends who are mostly or all Jewish; and contributing to any Jewish charity" (Steven M. Cohen, Jacob B. Ukeles, and Ron Miller, *Jewish Community Study of New York: 2011* [New York: UJA-Federation of New York, 2012], 118, http://www.jewishdatabank.org/studies/downloadFile.cfm?FileID=2852). The 2015 Boston study also created an index of Jewish engagement based on fourteen Jewish behaviors (Leonard Saxe et al., *2015 Greater Boston Jewish Community Study* [Waltham: Brandeis University, Cohen Center for Modern Jewish Studies, 2016], 21–23, http://www.jewishboston.com/2015-greater-boston-jewish-community -study-cjp-overview-cohen-center-report).

2. Steven M. Cohen, "The Great Divorce," *Foreign Policy*, May 21, 2010, http://foreign-policy.com/2010/05/21/the-special-relationship-2, quoted in Edmund Case, "Young American Jews, Israel, and Intermarriage," *EdmundCase.com* (blog), June 4, 2010, http://www.edmundcase.com/israel/young-american-jews-israel-and-intermarriage, originally published at InterfaithFamily.com.

3. David Graham, *Jews in Couples: Marriage, Intermarriage, Cohabitation and Divorce in Britain* (London: Institute for Jewish Policy Research, 2016), 2, http://www.jpr.org .uk/documents/JPR_2016.Jews_in_couples.Marriage_intermarriage_cohabitation _and_divroce_in_Britain.July_2016.pdf.

4. Steven M. Cohen and Arnold M. Eisen, *The Jew Within: Self, Family and Community in America* (Bloomington: Indiana University Press, 2000), 189, 198–99. See also Jack Wertheimer, *The New American Judaism: How Jews Practice Their Religion Today* (Princeton, NJ: Princeton University Press, 2018), 20; Mary C. Waters, *Ethnic Options: Choosing Identities in America* (Berkeley: University of California Press, 1990), 4–5.

5. Cohen et al., *Jewish Community Study of New York*, 111–12. See also Irwin Kula, "From the Cathedral to the Bazaar: What Chelsea Clinton's Wedding Says about Religious Syncretism," *Huffington Post*, last modified May 25, 2011, http://www .huffingtonpost.com/rabbi-irwin-kula/from-the-cathedral-to-the_b_659871.html.

6. Pew Research Center, *A Portrait of Jewish Americans* (Washington, DC: Pew Research Center's Religions and Public Life Project, 2013), 14, http://www.jewishdatabank .org/studies/downloadFile.cfm?FileID=3088.

7. Saxe et al., *2015 Greater Boston Jewish Community Study*, 3, 21–31.

8. Ben Sales, "The Fall of a Top Sociologist Could Change the Field of Counting Jews," *Jewish Telegraphic Agency*, August 3, 2018, https://www.jta.org/2018/08/03/news -opinion/united-states/the-fall-of-a-top-sociologist-could-change-the-field-of -counting-jews.

9. For example, in the 2015 Boston study, 37 percent of the intermarried with children are synagogue members (compared to 64 percent of the inmarried with children); 83 percent of the intermarried with children attended services in the past year (compared to 93 percent), 100 percent lit Hanukkah candles (compared to 100 percent), 93 percent attended a seder (compared to 99 percent), 59 percent lit Shabbat candles sometimes (compared to 81 percent), 22 percent follow some kosher practice (compared to 45 percent); 60 percent of the intermarried donate to Jewish causes (compared to 80 percent); 86 percent are concerned with worldwide anti-Semitism (compared to 95 percent); 72 percent feel very much, somewhat, or a little emotionally connected to Israel (compared to 93 percent) (Saxe et al., *2015 Greater Boston Jewish Community Study*, 41–43, 49, 55, 59). For further analysis of the 2015 Boston study, see Edmund Case, "A Review of the 2015 Greater Boston Jewish Community Study," *EdmundCase.com* (blog), December 2, 2016, http://www.edmundcase.com /wp-content/uploads/2016/12/A-Review-of-the-2015-Greater-Boston-Jewish -Community-Study.pdf.

10. An important 2008 paper supports this position. See Fern Chertok, Benjamin Phillips, and Leonard Saxe, *It's Not Just Who Stands Under the Chuppah: Intermarriage and Engagement* (Waltham: Brandeis University, Cohen Center for Modern Jewish Studies, 2008), 1–2, https://www.bjpa.org/search-results/publication/3417. The authors are critical of "most attempts to capture the impact of intermarriage" by comparing Jewish engagement measures between those who come from intermarried and inmarried households. While there are differences in how the adult children of intermarried and inmarried households were raised, those who were exposed to similar levels of Jewish experiences look very much alike. In other words, the Jewish behaviors and attitudes of children of intermarried families are not determined simply by the fact that the parents are intermarried but rather by what those parents chose to do Jewishly. The "fundamentally flawed narratives of intermarriage that have dominated discussion need to be replaced by" a new framework that should "focus on understanding the factors that motivate individuals and families . . . to participate actively in Jewish life." These findings were confirmed in later research. See Theodore Sasson et al., *Millennial Children of Intermarriage: Touchpoints and Trajectories of Jewish Engagement* (Waltham: Brandeis University, Cohen Center

for Modern Jewish Studies, 2016), http://www.brandeis.edu/cmjs/pdfs/intermarriage/MillennialChildrenIntermarriage1.pdf.

11. Cohen et al., *Jewish Community Study of New York*, 142. The Pew report similarly treats intermarrieds who are engaged Jewishly and those who are not, together, and reports that as a group they have lower rates of engagement. The Pew report does not make comparisons between Jewishly engaged intermarrieds and inmarrieds (Pew Research Center, *Portrait of Jewish Americans*, 60, 62, 76–77).

12. Cohen et al., *Jewish Community Study of New York*, 187–88.

13. The 2011 New York study's index of Jewish engagement does not include five indicators of Jewish behaviors and attitudes that can be undertaken individually or with friends and family: going to a Jewish cultural event or museum; having been to Israel; fasting on Yom Kippur; studying on their own (or informally with a friend or teacher); and accessing Jewish websites (Cohen et al., *Jewish Community Study of New York*, 119). The authors of a 2016 United Kingdom study similarly reported that the gap between intermarried and inmarried Jews is smaller on ethical and cultural variables, and wider on "socially exclusivist" and religiously observant variables (Graham, *Jews in Couples*, 21).

14. Pew Research Center, *Portrait of Jewish Americans*, 51–52.

15. Steven M. Cohen, email to me, February 7, 2017.

16. Pew Research Center, *Portrait of Jewish Americans*, 60.

17. The Pew report also says that one half of Reform-affiliated Jews who are married are intermarried (Pew Research Center, *Portrait of Jewish Americans*, 37). Steven M. Cohen has stated that the Pew report data indicate that there were approximately 756,000 members of Reform synagogues in 2013 (Steven M. Cohen, "As Reform Jews Gather, Some Good News in the Numbers," *Forward*, November 5, 2015, http://forward.com/news/national/324227/as-reform-jews-gather-some-good-news-in-the-numbers). Assuming for purposes of example that all members were married would mean 378,000 couples, and if half are intermarried, that would mean 189,000 intermarried couples who were members of Reform synagogues.

18. David Gregory, *How's Your Faith? An Unlikely Spiritual Journey* (New York: Simon & Schuster, 2015).

19. Lauren Ashburn, "David Gregory Interview on Judaism," *Daily Beast*, September 28, 2011, http://www.thedailybeast.com/articles/2011/09/28/david-gergory-interview-on-judaism.

20. Ashburn, "David Gregory Interview on Judaism."

21. Ashley Parker, "All the Obama 20-Somethings," *New York Times Sunday Magazine*, April 29, 2010, http://www.nytimes.com/2010/05/02/magazine/02obamastaff-t.html. Lesser wrote for InterfaithFamily about his experiences on a Birthright Israel trip. See Eric Lesser, "Integrating My Identity in Israel," InterfaithFamily.com, accessed October 1, 2018, http://www.interfaithfamily.com/news_and_opinion/israel/Integrating_My_Identity_in_Israel.shtml. Later he wrote one of the very best articles InterfaithFamily published; the title conveys the substance: Eric Lesser, "How My Italian-American Catholic Mother Strengthened My Jewish Identity," InterfaithFamily.com, accessed October 1, 2018, http://www.interfaithfamily.com

/relationships/growing_up_in_an_interfaith_family/How_My_ItalianAmerican_Catholic
_Mother_Strengthened_My_Jewish_Identity_Lessons_in_Intermarriage.shtml.

22. Arnold Eisen, "A Reply to Ed Case's Review of *The Jew Within*," *EdmundCase.com*
(blog), January 2001, http://www.edmundcase.com/media/essays/an-intermarried
-perspective-on-the-jew-within-by-steven-m-cohen-and-arnold-m-eisen, originally
published at InterfaithFamily.com.

5 Choosing Love *and* Tradition—Couple and Family Dynamics

1. Esther Perel, "Ethnocultural Factors in Marital Communications Among Intermarried Couples," *Journal of Jewish Communal Service* 66, no. 3 (January 1990): 244,
https://www.bjpa.org/search-results/publication/4.

2. Perel, "Ethnocultural Factors in Marital Communications," 244, 246, 248.

3. Perel, "Ethnocultural Factors in Marital Communications," 246, 248. There is some
evidence that interfaith couples divorce more often because of their interfaith backgrounds. See Naomi Schaefer Riley, *'Til Faith Do Us Part: How Interfaith Marriage
Is Transforming America* (New York: Oxford University Press, 2013); Graham, *Jews
in Couples*, 31. However, a 2009 study found "absolutely no difference in marital satisfaction between" inmarried and intermarried people (Janice Aron, "Interfaith Marriage Satisfaction Study Yields Answers and More Questions," InterfaithFamily.com,
August 28, 2009, quoted in Edmund Case, "Are Interfaith Marriages Really Failing
Fast?" *EdmundCase.com* [blog], June 6, 2010, www.edmundcase.com/divorce/are
-interfaith-marriages-really-failing-fast, originally published at InterfaithFamily.com).

4. Perel, "Ethnocultural Factors in Marital Communications," 249.

5. Perel, "Ethnocultural Factors in Marital Communications," 252.

6. The Jacobson Family Foundation, now the One8 Foundation, funded the research,
which was conducted by the firm Continuum. The results are contained in an unpublished presentation, *Interfaith Insights & Workbook*.

7. One8 Foundation, *Interfaith Insights & Workbook*.

8. One8 Foundation, *Interfaith Insights & Workbook*.

9. One8 Foundation, *Interfaith Insights & Workbook*.

10. See Edmund Case, "What We Can Learn from the InterfaithFamily.com Network
Essay Contest," *EdmundCase.com* (blog), September 2003, http://www.edmundcase
.com/media/essays/what-we-can-learn-from-the-interfaithfamily-com-network
-essay-contest, originally published at InterfaithFamily.com.

11. Quoted in Case, "What We Can Learn."

12. Steven M. Cohen and Arnold M. Eisen, *The Jew Within: Self, Family and Community in America* (Bloomington: Indiana University Press, 2000), 62, 116.

6 Jewish Traditions for a Life of Meaning

1. Lee Moore and Jonathan Woocher, "What Are Jewish Sensibilities?" *Sh'ma Now*,
accessed October 1, 2018, http://forward.com/shma-now/jewish-sensibilities.

2. Irwin Kula, "From the Cathedral to the Bazaar: What Chelsea Clinton's Wedding
Says about Religious Syncretism," *Huffington Post*, last modified May 25, 2011, http://

www.huffingtonpost.com/rabbi-irwin-kula/from-the-cathedral-to-the_b_659871.html.

3. Barry Shrage, "Story Tellers: A New Story of Jewish Identity," *Sh'ma: A Journal of Jewish Ideas* 40, no. 668 (March 1, 2010): 1–2, https://www.bjpa.org/search-results/publication/6836.

4. Faustine Sigal, "Moishe House: (How) Is Our Jewish Learning Different from All the Other Jewish Learnings?" *eJewishPhilanthropy*, August 8, 2018, https://ejewishphilanthropy.com/moishe-house-how-is-our-jewish-learning-different-from-all-the-other-jewish-learnings.

5. Emily Bazelon, "So the Torah Is a Parenting Guide?" *New York Times Sunday Magazine*, October 1, 2006, http://www.nytimes.com/2006/10/01/magazine/01parenting.html. The Parenting with a Jewish Lens class offered by Hebrew College, http://www.hebrewcollege.edu/parenting, addresses child-raising issues with wisdom from Jewish texts.

6. Nicki Greninger, "Why Bother? A Religious School Manifesto," *eJewishPhilanthropy*, August 1, 2017, http://ejewishphilanthropy.com/why-bother-a-religious-school-manifesto.

7. In *The Jew Within*, Steven M. Cohen and Arnold Eisen reported that instead of involvement in the public sphere of Jewish organizations, institutions, and causes such as the Holocaust, Israel, or Jewish philanthropy, the dominant sources of Jewish meaning for moderately affiliated Jews had become participation in family Jewish holiday observance. Their main recommendation for fostering Jewish involvement was to maintain "the positive influence of families," with communal funding to provide "the spaces and resources outside the home that make possible the activities in the home"—primarily the holiday observances "which American Jews find so meaningful" (Steven M. Cohen and Arnold M. Eisen, *The Jew Within: Self, Family and Community in America* [Bloomington: Indiana University Press, 2000], 205).

8. Jewish life-cycle events—baby welcoming and coming of age ceremonies, weddings, and death and mourning rituals—also express values and continue to be adapted to meet contemporary needs. Resources to help interfaith couples design inclusive life-cycle ceremonies can be found at https://www.interfaithfamily.com/life_cycle.

9. Paula Yablonsky, "How I Used My Christmas Tree Decorations to Light Up My Sukkah," InterfaithFamily.com, accessed October 1, 2018, https://interfaithfamily.com/holidays/shabbat_and_other_holidays/how_i_used_my_christmas_tree_decorations_to_light_up_my_sukkah.

10. Quoted in Edmund Case, "What We Can Learn from the InterfaithFamily.com Network Essay Contest," *EdmundCase.com* (blog), September 2003, http://www.edmundcase.com/media/essays/what-we-can-learn-from-the-interfaithfamily-com-network-essay-contest, originally published at InterfaithFamily.com.

11. Cindy Sher, "The Power of Caring, the Power of Chelsea," *Jewish United Fund of Metropolitan Chicago*, May 9, 2013, quoted in "What Chelsea Clinton Loves about Judaism," *EdmundCase.com* (blog), May 10, 2013, http://www.edmundcase.com/celebrities/what-chelsea-clinton-loves-about-judaism, originally published at InterfaithFamily.com.

12. HIAS, *Haggaddah Supplement 2018–5778*, 2, https://www.hias.org/sites/default/files/hias_haggadah_2018_color.pdf.

13. Steven Carr Reuben, "Why Hanukkah?" InterfaithFamily.com, accessed October 1, 2018, http://www.interfaithfamily.com/holidays/hanukkah_and_christmas/Why_Hanukkah.shtml.

14. Carr Reuben, "Why Hanukkah?"

7 What about Christmas?

1. Quoted in Daniela Martin, "Negotiation and Accommodation in Mixed Marriages," *Aufbau* 67, no. 25 (December 6, 2001), http://www.archive.org/stream/aufbau666720002001germ#page/n601/.

2. Local community studies started asking questions about Christmas celebrations only recently. The 2011 New York study found that in nine of ten intermarried households, synagogue affiliated or not, Christmas was celebrated by a household member. The study states that "in about half, it is celebrated as a religious holiday," but does not explain what that means (Steven M. Cohen, Jacob B. Ukeles, and Ron Miller, *Jewish Community Study of New York: 2011* [New York: UJA-Federation of New York, 2012], 144, http://www.jewishdatabank.org/studies/downloadFile.cfm?FileID=2852).

3. Sylvia Barack Fishman, *Jewish and Something Else: A Study of Mixed-Married Families* (New York: American Jewish Committee, 2001). In an op-ed for the *New York Jewish Week*, I described the results of the survey as "biased" and "part of an orchestrated campaign against intermarriage" (Edmund Case, "Discouraging Intermarriage Is Not the Way to Preserve Jewish Identity," *New York Jewish Week*, May 18, 2001, reprinted at http://www.edmundcase.com/media/essays/discouraging-intermarriage-is-not-the-way-to-preserve-jewish-identity).

4. Edmund Case, "What We Can Learn from the InterfaithFamily.com Network Essay Contest," *EdmundCase.com* (blog), September 2003, http://www.edmundcase.com/media/essays/what-we-can-learn-from-the-interfaithfamily-com-network-essay-contest, originally published at InterfaithFamily.com.

5. Quoted in Case, "What We Can Learn."

6. Quoted in Case, "What We Can Learn."

7. Sylvia Barack Fishman, *Double or Nothing: Jewish Families and Mixed Marriage* (Lebanon, NH: University Press of New England, 2004), 13, 62–63, 68, 95–96. For a detailed criticism of *Double or Nothing*, see Edmund Case, "Social Science and the Intermarriage Debate," *EdmundCase.com* (blog), accessed October 1, 2018, http://www.edmundcase.com/media/essays/social-science-and-the-intermarriage-debate, originally published at InterfaithFamily.com.

8. Fishman, *Double or Nothing*, 97, 159. Similarly, I attended a program about intermarriage in Boston where Barry Shrage and Steven Bayme were the speakers; Bayme said that a Jew attending an Easter dinner was affirming the divinity of Jesus. In 2013, Bayme said in an article that featured a family that belonged to a synagogue and sent the children to Jewish religious school—but also had a Christmas tree—that a Christmas tree is "suggestive of the very thin nature of the Jewish identity of the home"

(D. Michaels, "A Merry Little Chanukah?" *Jewish Exponent*, March 8, 2013, http://
jewishexponent.com/2013/03/08/a-merry-little-chanukah).

9. Fishman, *Double or Nothing*, 142. *Double or Nothing* still gets cited in papers critical
of intermarriage. See, for example, Sylvia Barack Fishman and Steven M. Cohen,
Family, Engagement, and Jewish Continuity among American Jews (Jerusalem: Jewish
People Policy Planning Institute, 2017), 37, http://jppi.org.il/new/wp-content/uploads
/2017/06/Raising-Jewish-Children-Research-and-Indicators-for-Intervention.pdf.

10. To view all of InterfaithFamily's surveys, see "Surveys and Resources,"
InterfaithFamily.com, http://www.interfaithfamily.com/about_us_advocacy/advocacy
/Surveys.shtml.

11. Edmund Case, "What We Learned from the December Dilemma Survey,"
InterfaithFamily.com, accessed October 1, 2018, 1, 3–4, 5, http://www.interfaithfamily
.com/files/pdf/surveyreport.pdf. InterfaithFamily also conducted ten years'
of Passover/Easter surveys, with similar results. See Edmund Case, "What
We Learned from the 2013 Passover/Easter Survey," InterfaithFamily.com,
accessed October 1, 2018, 4–5, http://www.interfaithfamily.com/files/pdf
/WhatWeLearnedfromthe2013PassoverEasterSurvey.pdf.

12. Jodi Bromberg, "What We Learned from the Tenth Annual December Holidays
Survey," InterfaithFamily.com, accessed October 1, 2018, 3, 4, 10, http://www
.interfaithfamily.com/files/pdf/WhatWeLearned2013DecemberHolidaysSurvey.pdf.

13. Theodore Sasson et al., *Millennial Children of Intermarriage: Touchpoints and
Trajectories of Jewish Engagement* (Waltham: Brandeis University, Cohen Center for Modern Jewish Studies, 2016), 18–20, http://www.brandeis.edu/cmjs/pdfs
/intermarriage/MillennialChildrenIntermarriage1.pdf.

14. The surveys consistently showed a higher percentage of respondents treated Hanukkah as a religious holiday; in 2010, for example, 55 percent said they would tell the
Hanukkah story, and when asked to rate the religious or secular nature of their holiday participation, 23 percent said their Hanukkah celebrations were religious and
28 percent said they were secular (49 percent said half and half), compared to 2
percent who said their Christmas celebrations were religious and 89 percent who
said they were secular (only 9 percent said half and half) (Edmund Case, "What
We Learned from the Seventh Annual December Holidays Survey," InterfaithFamily
.com, accessed October 1, 2018, 4–5, 12, http://www.interfaithfamily.com/files/pdf
/WhatWeLearnedfromthe2010DecemberHolidaysSurvey.pdf).

15. Jordana Horn, "Actually, You Can't Celebrate Hanukkah and Christmas," *Kvel-
ler*, December 14, 2011, http://www.kveller.com/actually-you-cant-celebrate
-hanukkah-and-christmas; Jordana Horn, "The Grinch Stole Chrismukkah," *Forward*, December 22, 2011, http://forward.com/opinion/148344/the-grinch-stole
-chrismukkah; Debra Nussbaum Cohen, "Interfaith Mom Is Wrong about Chrismukkah," *Forward*, December 19, 2011, http://forward.com/sisterhood/148176
/interfaith-mom-is-wrong-about-chrismukkah.

16. Kate Bigam, "In Response to an Anti-Interfaith Voice," InterfaithFamily.com,
December 20, 2011, http://www.interfaithfamily.com/blog/iff/december-holidays/in
-response-to-an-anti-interfaith-voice. For a convert's perspective, see Sue Fishkoff,

"My Family Tree Is Loaded with Tinsel," *j. The Jewish News of Northern California*, December 16, 2011, http://www.jweekly.com/2011/12/16/my-family-tree-is-loaded -with-tinsel.

17. While Jewish traditions are adaptable to meet the needs of interfaith families, some adaptations go too far, such as "Chrismukkah," which mushes Hanukkah and Christ-mas together (Ron Gompertz and Edmund Case, "Imagine . . . It's Chrismukkah Time Again!" *EdmundCase.com* [blog], December 2005, http://www.edmundcase .com/media/essays/imagine-its-chrismukkah-time-again, originally published on InterfaithFamily.com). In InterfaithFamily's 2004 holiday survey, more than two-thirds of the respondents said they kept their Hanukkah and Christmas celebrations separate (Case, "What We Learned from the December Dilemma Survey," 5). In 2005, 78 percent said they thought Chrismukkah was a bad idea:

> We try to honor both traditions in our family, while raising our children Jewish. To blend the two makes it impossible to truly understand and appreciate what the holidays mean.

> The fact that we are in interfaith relationships does not mean that we have an interfaith religion. Our religions are still two separate, individual traditions that should be honored as such. Celebrating both Christmas and Hanukkah is one thing, but pretending they are the same holiday is another.

> It confuses children. I think they need to be given one clear and consistent mes-sage about which holiday is which, and why each is important in its own right. Mixing the two diminishes the meaning for both.

(Edmund Case, "What We Learned from the Second Annual December Dilemma Sur-vey," InterfaithFamily.com, accessed October 1, 2018, 3–4, http://www.interfaithfamily .com/about_us_advocacy/advocacy/Surveys.shtml).

18. Edmund Case, "Memo to Elena Kagan: Not All Jews Spend Christmas at Chinese Restaurants," *EdmundCase.com* (blog), June 30, 2010, http://www.edmundcase.com /christmas/memo-to-elena-kagan-not-all-jews-spend-christmas-at-chinese -restaurants, originally published at InterfaithFamily.com.

19. Quoted in Case, "What We Can Learn."

8 Expressing Spirituality in Jewish Settings

1. Barry Shrage, "Story Tellers: A New Story of Jewish Identity," *Sh'ma: A Journal of Jewish Ideas* 40, no. 668 (March 1, 2010): 1–2, https://www.bjpa.org/search-results /publication/6836.

2. Steven M. Cohen and Arnold M. Eisen, *The Jew Within: Self, Family and Commu-nity in America* (Bloomington: Indiana University Press, 2000), 8, 196.

3. The seven communities in the Jewish Emergent Network (http://www .jewishemergentnetwork.org) share "a commitment to approaches both traditionally rooted and creative, and a demonstrated success in attracting unaffiliated and disengaged Jews to a rich and meaningful Jewish practice" and are "rethinking

basic assumptions about ritual and spiritual practice." The website of the Mussar Institute is https://mussarinstitute.org/.

4. Edmund Case, "We Need a Religious Movement That Is Totally Inclusive of Interfaith Families," *EdmundCase.com* (blog), March 2000, http://www.edmundcase.com/media/essays/we-need-a-religious-movement-that-is-totally-inclusive-of-intermarried-jewish-families, originally published on InterfaithFamily.com.

5. Quoted in Case, "We Need a Religious Movement."

6. Quoted in Edmund Case, "What We Can Learn from the InterfaithFamily.com Network Essay Contest," *EdmundCase.com* (blog), September 2003, http://www.edmundcase.com/media/essays/what-we-can-learn-from-the-interfaithfamily-com-network-essay-contest, originally published at InterfaithFamily.com.

7. Cohen and Eisen, *Jew Within*, 189.

8. Jews are less spiritually inclined, less likely to have spiritual mentors, less involved with God, and less attached to religion and prayer. Although 71 percent say they believe in God, as compared to 81 percent of other white Americans, only 35 percent have a "certain" belief in God, as compared to 58 percent of others (Steven M. Cohen and Lawrence A. Hoffman, "How Spiritual Are America's Jews? Narrowing the Spirituality Gap Between Jews and Other Americans," *S3KReport*, no. 4 [March 2009]: 6, http://www.hollishillsjc.org/wp-content/uploads/2014/02/S3K-How-Spiritual-Are-American-Jews.pdf).

9. Cohen and Hoffman, "How Spiritual Are America's Jews?" 13.

10. Julia Duin, "Study Finds US Jews Drifting Away from Faith," *Washington Times*, August 5, 2009, https://www.pressreader.com/usa/the-washington-times-daily/20090805/282668978365667.

11. Duin, "Study Finds US Jews Drifting Away from Faith."

12. Pew Research Center, *A Portrait of Jewish Americans* (Washington, DC: Pew Research Center's Religions and Public Life Project, 2013), 60, 72, 74–75, http://www.jewishdatabank.org/studies/downloadFile.cfm?FileID=3088.

13. Theodore Sasson, "New Analysis of Pew Data: Children of Intermarriage Increasingly Identify as Jews," *Tablet*, November 11, 2013, 8, https://www.bjpa.org/search-results/publication/18694.

14. Pew Research Center, *Portrait of Jewish Americans*, 9. Interfaith couples may come to say that their religion is not Jewish because of the reception they experience in Jewish communities, as discussed in chapter 13.

15. Sasson, "New Analysis of Pew Data," 4.

16. Arthur Green, "From Pew Will Come Forth Torah," *eJewishPhilanthropy*, October 23, 2013, http://ejewishphilanthropy.com/from-pew-will-come-forth-torah.

17. Erika B. Seamon, *Interfaith Marriage in America: The Transformation of Religion and Christianity* (New York: Palgrave Macmillan, 2012).

18. Cohen and Eisen, *Jew Within*, 162.

19. Cohen and Eisen, 162.

20. Chaim Stern, ed., *Gates of Repentance: The New Union Prayerbook for the Days of Awe* (New York: Central Conference of American Rabbis, 1978), 119; Edwin C.

Goldberg et al., eds., *Mishkan Hanefesh: Machzor for the Days of Awe, Rosh Hasha-nah* (New York: CCAR Press, 2015), 220.

21. Stern, *Gates of Repentance*, 86.
22. Phillip Birnbaum, *Daily Prayer Book* (New York: Hebrew Publishing Company, 1949), 15–16. One of the same morning blessings thanks God "for not making me a woman"; past Conservative and Reform prayer book editors eliminated that blessing, or changed it to one that thanks God for being made in the divine image.
23. Morris Silverman, ed., *Sabbath and Festival Prayer Book* (New York: Rabbinical Assembly, 1946), 45.
24. Jules Harlow, ed., *Siddur Sim Shalom* (New York: Rabbinical Assembly, 1985), 11.
25. David Teutsch, ed., *Kol Haneshamah* (Wyncote, PA: Reconstructionist Press, 1994), 160.
26. Private conversation with David Teutsch, quoted in Edmund Case, "Let's Make the Language of Jewish Prayer Inclusive," *EdmundCase.com* (blog), November 2000, http://www.edmundcase.com/media/essays/lets-make-the-language-of-jewish -prayer-inclusive, originally published at InterfaithFamily.com.
27. Elyse Frishman, email message to me, November 27, 2000.
28. Elyse D. Frishman, ed., *Mishkan T'filah: A Reform Siddur* (New York: CCAR Press, 2007), 202; Edwin C. Goldberg et al., eds., *Mishkan Hanefesh: Machzor for the Days of Awe, Yom Kippur* (New York: CCAR Press, 2015), 162.
29. The Society for Classical Reform Judaism argues that Jewish worship services would be more comfortable and appealing to liberal Jews, and especially interfaith families, if they were conducted more in English than in Hebrew (Cynthia L. Conley, Nadia Sir-itsky, and Devon A. Lerner, "The Effect of Hebrew on Worship Satisfaction and Con-gregational Membership," Society for Classical Reform Judaism, accessed October 1, 2018, http://renewreform.org/impact-hebrew-worship-satisfaction-congregational -membership). This worthwhile option should be available for those to whom it is appealing, but Hebrew is also a distinctive Jewish tradition that is and can be appeal-ing to many interfaith families.

Invitation Two Find Belonging in Jewish Community

1. Barry Shrage, "Story Tellers: A New Story of Jewish Identity," *Sh'ma: A Journal of Jewish Ideas* 40, no. 668 (March 1, 2010): 1–2, https://www.bjpa.org/search-results /publication/6836.

9 *Being* Jewish—Conversion

1. Neil Gilman, *Sacred Fragments: Recovering Theology for the Modern Jew* (Philadel-phia: Jewish Publication Society, 1990), xvii.
2. Rabbi Carl Perkins is the author of the revised edition of the Conservative move-ment's text for prospective converts. Simcha Kling and Carl Perkins, *Embracing Judaism* (New York: Rabbinical Assembly, 1999).

3. Noa Kushner, "Judaism for Gen X: Get Your Jewish On," SFGate, September 6, 2010, http://www.sfgate.com/entertainment/article/Judaism-for-Gen-X-Get-your-Jewish -on-3175716.php.

4. David Ellenson, "Courage to Create a Judaism of Meaning," *Sh'ma: A Journal of Jewish Ideas* 38, no. 645 (November 1, 2007): 1–2, shma.com/2007/11/courage-to-create -a-judaism-of-meaning. There is yet another perspective, espoused by Irwin Kula, that views Judaism as a wisdom system that helps people live better lives and is available to anyone—Jewish or not. See Irwin Kula, *Yearnings: Embracing the Sacred Messiness of Life* (New York: Hyperion, 2006). But because feelings of belonging motivate people to engage in Jewish traditions, and because it is rewarding doing so in community, it is critically important for interfaith couples, and in particular partners from different faith traditions, to feel that they belong.

5. For example, parents in conversionary marriages raise their children as Jews at a rate even higher than inmarried couples (Steven M. Cohen, "Which of Our Grandchildren Will Be Jewish in this Age of Intermarriage?" *Forward*, October 24, 2016, https://forward.com/opinion/352405/which-of-our-grandchildren-will-be-jewish -in-this-age-of-intermarriage).

6. Quoted in Edmund Case, "We Need a Religious Movement That Is Totally Inclusive of Interfaith Families," *EdmundCase.com* (blog), March 2000, http://www.edmundcase .com/media/essays/we-need-a-religious-movement-that-is-totally-inclusive-of -intermarried-jewish-families, originally published at InterfaithFamily.com.

7. Quoted in Case, "We Need a Religious Movement."

8. At the time, I said "total" instead of "radical" (Edmund Case, "Redefine Jewish Peoplehood," *Reform Judaism*, Spring 2000, http://www.reformjudaismmag.net/rjmag-90s /300ec.html).

9. The Conservative movement's advocacy for conversion is perceived as a roadblock to attracting interfaith families. At its biennial convention in December 2005, the Conservative movement announced a new initiative to bring intermarried families into congregational life, "encouraging the couple to raise Jewish children and encouraging the non-Jewish spouse to convert" (Sue Fishkoff, "Conservatives Reach Out to Intermarried," Jewish Telegraphic Agency, December 7, 2005, http://www.jta.org/2005/12/07 /life-religion/features/conservatives-reach-out-to-intermarried). In 2009, Rabbi Chuck Simon, leader of the Federation of Jewish Men's Clubs, said, "[Although] there is nothing wrong with saying conversion is important to us, . . . [t]here is not a realistic expectation in today's life to set a goal of conversion. Couples set their own goals; that is not where I would start the game" (Stewart Ain, "Conservatives End Push to Convert Intermarrieds," *New York Jewish Week*, July 8, 2009, http://jewishweek .timesofisrael.com/conservatives-end-push-to-convert-intermarrieds-2). In 2013, Rabbi Elliot Cosgrove proposed a "fast-track" conversion, in which a person would convert first, and then study later, in order to enable Conservative rabbis to officiate at that person's wedding (Benjamin Maron, "A New Conservative Approach to Conversion and Intermarriage," InterfaithFamily.com, February 28, 2013, http://www .interfaithfamily.com/blog/iff/conversion/a-new-conservative-approach-to -conversion-and-intermarriage). But promoting conversion appeared to get renewed

emphasis in a 2014 op-ed by Arnold Eisen, chancellor of the Jewish Theological Seminary (Arnold Eisen, "Wanted: Converts to Judaism," *Wall Street Journal*, July 24, 2014, https://www.wsj.com/articles/arnold-m-eisen-wanted-converts-to-judaism -1406244075).

10. Quoted in Edmund Case, "The Next Big Thing Is Now: Outreach to the Intermarried," *EdmundCase.com* (blog), March 2006, http://www.edmundcase.com/media /essays/the-next-big-thing-is-now-outreach-to-the-intermarried, originally published at InterfaithFamily.com.

11. Eric Yoffie, "Encourage Conversion; Judaism's Teachings on Teen Sexuality" (sermon, 68th Biennial Convention of the Union for Reform Judaism, Houston, TX, November 8, 2005). See also "At Reform Conference, Movement Calls for a Push Toward Conversion," Jewish Telegraphic Agency, November 22, 2005, http://www.jta.org/2005/11/22 /archive/at-reform-conference-movement-calls-for-a-push-toward-conversion.

12. Michael Luo, "Reform Jews Hope to Unmix Mixed Marriages," *New York Times*, February 12, 2006, http://www.nytimes.com/2006/02/12/nyregion/reform-jews-hope -to-unmix-mixed-marriages.html. A 2006 Associated Press article also overstated Jewish leaders' advocacy for conversion (Rachel Zoll, "Interfaith Couples Deal with Whether to Convert Spouse," *East Bay Times*, September 21, 2006, http://www .eastbaytimes.com/2006/09/21/interfaith-couples-deal-with-whether-to-convert -spouse; Edmund Case, "Conversion to Judaism," *Washington Times*, September 25, 2006, http://www.washingtontimes.com/news/2006/sep/25/20060925-092532-1895r/).

13. Quoted in Edmund Case, "Letter to the Editor of the Jewish Week: Mean-Spirited Approach," *EdmundCase.com* (blog), February 2006, http://www.edmundcase.com /media/essays/letter-to-the-editor-of-the-jewish-week-mean-spirited-approach, originally published on InterfaithFamily.com.

14. Steven Bayme and Jack Wertheimer, "Revisiting and Promoting Conversion," *Jewish Week*, January 13, 2006. See also Edmund Case, "Mean-Spirited Approach," *New York Jewish Week*, February 10, 2006, quoted in Case, "Letter to the Editor of the Jewish Week." Steven M. Cohen objected when I attributed Bayme and Wertheimer's views to him, resulting in dueling letters to the editor of the *New Jersey Jewish News* (Case, "The Next Big Thing Is Now," *EdmundCase.com* [blog], March 2006, http:// www.edmundcase.com/media/essays/the-next-big-thing-is-now-outreach-to-the-in-termarried, originally published on InterfaithFamily.com).

15. Case, "Mean-Spirited Approach," quoted in Case, "Letter to the Editor of the Jewish Week."

16. Sylvia Barack Fishman, *Choosing Jewish: Conversations About Conversion* (New York: American Jewish Committee, 2006), 83, 111, https://www.bjpa.org/content /upload/bjpa/choo/CHOOSING_JEWISH.pdf.

17. InterfaithFamily, "What Attracts Interfaith Families to Jewish Organizations?" InterfaithFamily.com, September 5, 2012, http://www.interfaithfamily.com/about _us_advocacy/What_Attracts_Interfaith_Families_to_Jewish_Organizations .shtml?rd=2.

18. A good example is Rabbi Lisa Rubin's Exploring Judaism program at Central Synagogue in New York, described at http://www.centralsynagogue.org/engage/adult_engagement/exploring_judaism.

10 *Doing* Jewish—Radical Inclusion

1. Edmund Case, "Redefine Jewish Peoplehood," *Reform Judaism*, Spring 2000, http://www.reformjudaismmag.net/rjmag-90s/300ec.html; Edmund Case, "We Need a Religious Movement That Is Totally Inclusive of Interfaith Families," *EdmundCase.com* [blog], March 2000, http://www.edmundcase.com/media/essays/we-need-a-religious-movement-that-is-totally-inclusive-of-intermarried-jewish-families, originally published at InterfaithFamily.com.
2. Case, "We Need a Religious Movement."
3. Case, "We Need a Religious Movement."
4. Case, "We Need a Religious Movement"; Everett Fox, *The Five Books of Moses* (New York: Schocken, 1983), 605.
5. Steven M. Cohen and Arnold M. Eisen, *The Jew Within: Self, Family and Community in America* (Bloomington: Indiana University Press, 2000), 130. See also Irwin Kula, "From the Cathedral to the Bazaar: What Chelsea Clinton's Wedding Says about Religious Syncretism," *Huffington Post*, last modified May 25, 2011, http://www.huffingtonpost.com/rabbi-irwin-kula/from-the-cathedral-to-the_b_659871.html.
6. Cohen and Eisen, *Jew Within*, 103–105.
7. Cohen and Eisen, 162.
8. InterfaithFamily felt strongly that Israel is threatened by negative opinion and vilification around the world, and that it was important to express support for Israel and for efforts to peacefully resolve conflict there, but we did not take positions on the Israeli-Palestinian conflict.
9. Brittany Ritell, "Seeing Israel Through My Interfaith Family's Eyes," InterfaithFamily.com, March 20, 2014, http://www.interfaithfamily.com/relationships/growing_up_in_an_interfaith_family/Seeing_Israel_through_My_Interfaith_Familys_Eyes.shtml. Birthright Israel is the largest Jewish educational intervention in the world, having sent more than four hundred thousand Jewish young adults from North America to Israel for a ten-day, immersive educational experience (Leonard Saxe et al., *Beyond 10 Days: Parents, Gender, Marriage, and the Long-Term Impact of Birthright Israel* [Waltham: Brandeis University, Cohen Center for Modern Jewish Studies, 2017], https://www.brandeis.edu/cmjs/pdfs/jewish%20futures/Beyond10Days.pdf).
10. Dan Brosgol, "Far Away and Still at Home: Israel and Our Interfaith Family," InterfaithFamily.com, May 9, 2014, http://www.interfaithfamily.com/relationships/parenting/Israel_and_Our_Interfaith_Family.shtml.
11. Edwin C. Goldberg et al., eds., *Mishkan Hanefesh: Machzor for the Days of Awe, Yom Kippur* (New York: CCAR Press, 2015), 266.
12. Fox, *Five Books of Moses*, 601.

13. Steven M. Cohen and Joy Levitt, "If You Marry a Jew, You're One of Us," Jewish Telegraphic Agency, April 2, 2015, http://www.jta.org/2015/04/02/news-opinion /opinion/op-ed-if-you-marry-a-jew-youre-one-of-us.

14. Yossi Beilin, a member of Israel's Knesset, proposed in 1999 to establish a process of secular conversion (Yossi Beilin, "Thoughts on Secular Conversion," InterfaithFamily .com, October 1999, http://www.interfaithfamily.com/spirituality/conversion/Thoughts _on_Secular_Conversion_An_Important_Alternative_to_Religious_Conversion. shtml). In 2006 he proposed legislation that someone would be considered Jewish who "has joined the Jewish people in a non-religious process and has linked his or her fate with the Jewish people, and is not a member of another religion." Beilin was quoted as saying, "If people see themselves as Jewish . . . why should the state define them as not Jewish?" The idea was that individuals would join the Jewish people by means of activities in the Jewish community and maintaining a Jewish lifestyle. The central consideration would be a family tie to Jews (Shahar Ilan, "Bill Would Recognize Judaism Through Father," Ha'aretz, December 3, 2006, https://www.haaretz.com /bill-would-recognize-judaism-through-father-1.206013).

15. Cohen and Eisen, Jew Within, 23, 184–85.

16. Quoted in Edmund Case, "What We Can Learn from the InterfaithFamily.com Network Essay Contest," EdmundCase.com (blog), September 2003, http://www .edmundcase.com/media/essays/what-we-can-learn-from-the-interfaithfamily -com-network-essay-contest, originally published at InterfaithFamily.com.

17. The article is no longer available online.

18. Susan Fendrick, "Beyond 'Yes or No' Jewishness," Forward, February 16, 2011, http://forward.com/opinion/135474/beyond-yes-or-no-jewishness.

19. Alina Adams, "What My Black-Jewish Son Teaches Me About Rachel Dolezal," Forward, June 15, 2015, http://forward.com/opinion/310094/what-my-black-jewish-son -teaches-me-about-rachel-dolezal/#ixzz3dFw5m1tb.

20. Adams, "What My Black-Jewish Son."

21. Adams, "What My Black-Jewish Son."

22. Ron Brown, "Letter to the Editor," New York Times, June 21, 2015, quoted in Edmund Case, "TransJewish?" EdmundCase.com (blog), June 17, 2015, http://www .edmundcase.com/identity/transjewish, originally published at InterfaithFamily.com.

23. Adams, "What My Black-Jewish Son."

24. Gary Tobin, Opening the Gates: How Proactive Conversion Can Revitalize the Jewish Community (New York: Jossey-Bass, 1999). At the time, I said we would be better off promoting proactive inclusion than proactive conversion—including partners from different faith traditions and encouraging them to make Jewish choices, with conversion one possible outcome among others. The benefits Tobin saw in more converts— that converts add a richness to Jewish life and inspire born Jews to participate, that having more racially and ethnically diverse Jews helps Jews bridge gaps with other groups—could equally be had with more interfaith families engaged.

25. Esther Perel, "Ethnocultural Factors in Marital Communications Among Intermarried Couples," Journal of Jewish Communal Service 60, no. 3 (January 1990): 248, https://www.bjpa.org/search-results/publication/4.

11 Welcoming a Baby

1. Jessica Firger, "Circumcision Rates Declining in US, Study Says," *CBS News*, April 2, 2014, https://www.cbsnews.com/news/circumcision-rates-declining-health -risks-rising-study-says.

2. InterfaithFamily offers booklets and a guide with helpful suggestions, available at https://interfaithfamily.com/life_cycle/pregnancy_and_birth_ceremonies.

3. See, for example, Lisa Braver Moss, "Circumcision: A Jewish Inquiry," InterfaithFamily.com, accessed October 1, 2018, https://www.interfaithfamily.com /life_cycle/pregnancy_and_birth_ceremonies/circumcision_a_jewish_inquiry.

4. Walter Cuenin, "Is Heaven Denied to an Unbaptized Child?" InterfaithFamily .com, April 2001, http://www.interfaithfamily.com/life_cycle/pregnancy_and_birth _ceremonies/Is_Heaven_Denied_to_an_Unbaptized_Child_Advice_and_Perspective _for_Catholic_Parents_Who_Are_Raising_Their_Children_within_Judaism.shtml.

12 Raising Children—Jewish or *Both*?

1. Esther Perel, "Ethnocultural Factors in Marital Communications Among Intermarried Couples," *Journal of Jewish Communal Service* 60, no. 3 (January 1990): 251, https://www.bjpa.org/search-results/publication/4.

2. Quoted in Edmund Case, "What We Can Learn from the InterfaithFamily.com Network Essay Contest," *EdmundCase.com* (blog), September 2003, http://www .edmundcase.com/media/essays/what-we-can-learn-from-the-interfaithfamily -com-network-essay-contest, originally published at InterfaithFamily.com.

3. Quoted in Case, "What We Can Learn."

4. Quoted in Case, "What We Can Learn."

5. Fern Chertok, Benjamin Phillips, and Leonard Saxe, *It's Not Just Who Stands Under the Chuppah: Intermarriage and Engagement* (Waltham: Brandeis University, Cohen Center for Modern Jewish Studies, 2008), 1–2, https://www.bjpa.org/search-results /publication/3417; Theodore Sasson et al., *Millennial Children of Intermarriage: Touchpoints and Trajectories of Jewish Engagement* (Waltham: Brandeis University, Cohen Center for Modern Jewish Studies, 2016), 47, 50, http://www.brandeis.edu /cmjs/pdfs/intermarriage/MillennialChildrenIntermarriage1.pdf.

6. The 2011 New York study found that 35 percent of children of intermarried households are sent to supplemental Jewish religious school (Steven M. Cohen, Jacob B. Ukeles, and Ron Miller, *Jewish Community Study of New York: 2011* [New York: UJA-Federation of New York, 2012], 188, http://www.jewishdatabank.org/studies /downloadFile.cfm?FileID=2852). The Pew report says about 22 percent of interfaith families enroll their children in formal Jewish programs, including day school (5 percent), religious school education (13 percent), or Jewish day or sleepaway camp (14 percent) (Pew Research Center, *A Portrait of Jewish Americans* [Washington, DC: Pew Research Center's Religions and Public Life Project, 2013], 68, http://www .jewishdatabank.org/studies/downloadFile.cfm?FileID=3088). The 2015 Boston study reports that 21 percent of children of the intermarried are getting part-time (19 percent) or day school (2 percent) Jewish education (Leonard Saxe et al., *2015*

Greater Boston Jewish Community Study [Waltham: Brandeis University, Cohen Center for Modern Jewish Studies, 2016], 36, http://www.jewishboston.com/2015-greater-boston-jewish-community-study-cjp-overview-cohen-center-report. The *Millennial Children* study found that 44 percent of children of intermarriage had formal Jewish education (Sasson et al., *Millennial Children of Intermarriage*, 15).

7. Pew Research Center, *A Portrait of Jewish Americans*, 8. Bruce Phillips stated the 140,000 figure in an email to me and Alan Cooperman dated November 14, 2017.

8. Susan Katz Miller, "Being 'Partly Jewish,'" *New York Times*, October 31, 2013, http://www.nytimes.com/2013/11/01/opinion/being-partly-jewish.html; Susan Katz Miller, *Being Both: Embracing Two Religions in One Interfaith Family* (Boston: Beacon Press, 2013). The Interfaith Community website says they provide "balanced education" and "nurture the distinctiveness of Judaism and Christianity" ("What Is IFC," InterfaithCommunity.org, accessed October 1, 2018, http://www.interfaithcommunity.org/what-is-ifc).

9. MJL staff, "What Do Jews Believe About Jesus?" MyJewishLearning.com, accessed October 1, 2018, http://www.myjewishlearning.com/article/what-do-jews-believe-about-jesus.

10. Kate Fridkis, "Interfaith Families: Can You Be Jewish and Christian at the Same Time?" *Huffington Post*, June 21, 2010, http://www.huffingtonpost.com/kate-fridkis/can-you-be-jewish-and-chr_b_618731.html.

11. Jane Larkin, "You Can't Be Both (Jewish and Not)," *Forward*, November 10, 2013, http://forward.com/opinion/187286/you-cant-be-both-jewish-and-not.

12. Miller, "Being 'Partly Jewish.'"

13. Miller, "Being 'Partly Jewish.'"

14. Miller, "Being 'Partly Jewish.'"

15. Miller, "Being 'Partly Jewish.'"

16. James Carroll, "Jesus and the Promise of Christmas," *Boston Globe*, December 22, 2008, http://archive.boston.com/bostonglobe/editorial_opinion/oped/articles/2008/12/22/jesus_and_the_promise_of_christmas.

17. Larkin, "You Can't Be Both."

18. Elettra Fiumi and Lea Khayata, "Mixed Messages," *Tablet*, August 3, 2011, http://www.tabletmag.com/jewish-life-and-religion/73818/mixed-messages.

19. Miller, "Being 'Partly Jewish.'"

20. Edmund Case, "My Interview with Cokie and Steve Roberts," *EdmundCase.com* (blog), April 10, 2011, http://www.edmundcase.com/children-of-intermarriage/my-interview-with-steve-and-cokie-roberts, originally published at InterfaithFamily.com.

21. Sue Fishkoff, "'Half-Jews' Fight for Acceptance," *Jewish Journal*, July 13, 2007, http://jewishjournal.com/news/world/15121.

22. Miller, "Being 'Partly Jewish.'"

Road Map One   Attitudes

1. Ron Heifitz, *Leadership Without Easy Answers* (Cambridge, MA: Harvard University Press, 1994).

2. Steven M. Cohen and Joy Levitt, "If You Marry a Jew, You're One of Us," *Jewish Telegraphic Agency*, April 2, 2015, http://www.jta.org/2015/04/02/news-opinion /opinion/op-ed-if-you-marry-a-jew-youre-one-of-us.

13 The Discouraging Attitudes That Need to Change

1. Marc Gellman, "God Squad," *Edmond Sun*, April 2, 2009, http://www.edmondsun.com /news/lifestyles/god-squad/article_ad060d14-904b-5f08-86f3-321051f5a476.html.

2. We don't make inmarried families pass an observance test before we include them without reservation in Jewish communities (Edmund Case, "How Should American Jewry Respond to the National Jewish Population Survey?" *EdmundCase .com* [blog], accessed October 1, 2018, http://www.edmundcase.com/media/essays /how-should-american-jewry-respond-to-the-national-jewish-population -survey-reach-out-to-intermarrieds, originally published in the *Forward* and reprinted at InterfaithFamily.com).

3. Ruth Abrams, "Chelsea Clinton to Marry," InterfaithFamily.com, November 30, 2009, http://www.interfaithfamily.com/blog/iff/intermarriage/chelsea-clinton-to-marry; Edmund Case, "Chelsea Clinton May Not Need Help Finding a Rabbi for Her Wedding, But . . . ," *EdmundCase.com* (blog), December 1, 2009, http://www.edmundcase .com/wedding-officiation/chelsea-clinton-may-not-need-help-finding-a-rabbi -for-her-wedding-but, originally published at InterfaithFamily.com.

4. Philip Weiss, "Hillary Clinton Says We Need More Intermarriage," *Mondoweiss*, July 19, 2010, http://mondoweiss.net/2010/07/hillary-clinton-says-we-need-more -intermarriage. I wrote a feature for the *Huffington Post* to explain to people who might not be familiar with Jewish wedding ceremony customs what they might be seeing if the couple decided to have a Jewish wedding. See Edmund Case, "Interfaith Weddings: What Chelsea Clinton's Wedding Might Look Like," *Huffington Post*, July 23, 2010, http://www.huffingtonpost.com/edmund-c-case/interfaith -weddings-what_b_654596.html.

5. See Marion L. Usher, "Chelsea Clinton and Marc Mezvinsky: Religion and Interfaith Marriage," On Faith, *Washington Post*, accessed October 1, 2018, https:// www.onfaith.co/onfaith/2010/07/25/chelsea-clinton-and-marc-mezvinsky-religion -and-interfaith-marriage/3040; Marion L. Usher, "Part II: Where Does an Interfaith Couple Go to Find Help?" On Faith, *Washington Post*, accessed October 1, 2018, https://www.onfaith.co/onfaith/2010/07/27/part-2-where-does-an-interfaith-couple -go-to-find-help/7898; Marion L. Usher, "Part III: Chelsea Clinton and Marc Mezvinsky: How to Raise the Children?" On Faith, *Washington Post*, accessed October 1, 2018, https://www.onfaith.co/onfaith/2010/07/28/part-iiil-chelsea-clinton-and -marc-mezvinsky-how-to-raise-the-children/2780; Marion L. Usher, "Part IV: Develop a Solid Relationship Foundation," On Faith, *Washington Post*, accessed October 1, 2018, https://www.onfaith.co/onfaith/2010/07/29/part-iv-develop-a-solid-relationship -foundation/3316; Edmund Case, "Part V: Mazel Tov! A Viewer's Guide to the Clinton/Mezvinsky Wedding," On Faith, *Washington Post*, accessed October 1, 2018, https://www.onfaith.co/onfaith/2010/07/29/part-v-mazel-tov-a-viewers-guide-to -the-clintonmezvinsky-wedding/6189.

6. Jack Moline, "Oppose Intermarriage, But Support the Intermarried," On Faith, *Washington Post*, accessed October 1, 2018, https://www.onfaith.co/onfaith/2010/07/26/its-the-wrong-question/6228; quoted in Edmund Case, "Mazel Tov in Advance to Chelsea and Marc," *EdmundCase.com* (blog), July 30, 2010, http://www.edmundcase.com/wedding-officiation/mazel-tov-in-advance-to-chelsea-and-marc, originally published at InterfaithFamily.com.

7. Jacob Berkman, "Clinton-Mezvinsky Wedding Raises Questions About Intermarriage," Jewish Telegraphic Agency, August 3, 2010, http://www.jta.org/2010/08/03/life-religion/clinton-mezvinsky-wedding-raises-questions-about-intermarriage.

8. Allison Gaudet Yarrow, "Wedding Blues: Rabbis at Odds with Their Rules," *Forward*, August 4, 2010, http://forward.com/news/129834/wedding-blues-rabbis-at-odds-with-their-rules.

9. Edmund Case, "The Missing 'Mazel Tov,'" *Forward*, August 11, 2010, http://forward.com/opinion/129999/the-missing-mazel-tov. The *Forward* recognized the impact of their celebrity later in the year when it named Clinton and Mezvinsky to the 2010 "Forward 50," saying they had "telegraphed to the world that Judaism has nothing to hide," captivated the American imagination, and energized the conversation around Jewish identity (Jane Eisner, "Forward 50, 2010," *Forward*, October 26, 2010, https://forward.com/articles/132454/forward-50-2010/#top5).

10. In 2009, there was publicity about the case of the Feinbergs, who wrote into their will that any descendant who intermarried would be disinherited (four of their five grandchildren did anyway). See Marcy Oster, "Court: Will Disinheriting Grandchildren Legal," Jewish Telegraphic Agency, September 24, 2009, http://www.jta.org/2009/09/24/news-opinion/united-states/court-will-disinheriting-intermarried-granchildren-legal. Alan Dershowitz was quoted in 2010 as saying that "we're going through a very challenging period right now with intermarriage" and "I'm not suggesting it's a good thing. I don't support it" (Edmund Case, "What I Would Like to Be Thankful For," *EdmundCase.com* [blog], November 25, 2010, http://www.edmundcase.com/inclusion-and-welcoming/what-i-would-like-to-be-thankful-for, originally published at InterfaithFamily.com). In October 2011, a Jewish woman going to a mikveh for a ritual immersion in advance of her interfaith wedding wrote in the *Huffington Post* that she was rebuffed by a mikveh lady who told her that her marriage would not be recognized in the eyes of God (Jessica Langer-Sousa, "Why I Got Naked and Jumped Into the Ocean Before My Wedding," *Huffington Post*, October 3, 2011, http://www.huffingtonpost.com/jessica-langersousa/why-i-jumped-ocean-wedding_b_984334.html).

11. Danielle Berrin, "Mark Zuckerberg Created Facebook to Get Non-Jewish Girls," *Huffington Post*, September 28, 2010, http://www.huffingtonpost.com/danielle-berrin/the-social-network-mark-z_b_741914.html.

12. Elad Benari, "Expert Concerned Over Zuckerberg's Intermarriage," *Arutz Sheva*, May 21, 2012, http://www.israelnationalnews.com/News/News.aspx/156017#.T7mpdL9yNiY.

13. Ben Sales, "How Mark Zuckerberg Is Embracing His Judaism," Jewish Telegraphic Agency, October 2, 2017, https://www.jta.org/2017/10/02/life-religion

/how-mark-zuckerberg-embraced-his-judaism. At the High Holidays in 2018, Zuckerberg posted a video of himself blowing a shofar (News Brief, "Mark Zuckerberg Posts Video of Himself Blowing Shofar," *Jewish Telegraphic Agency*, September 12, 2018, https://www.jta.org/2018/09/12/news-opinion/mark-zuckerberg-posts-video-blowing-shofar). In another celebrity example, an Israeli story commented on the appointment of two Jews to the Obama administration, Rahm Emanuel as chief of staff and Ron Klain as Vice President Joe Biden's chief of staff. The author knew that Klain and his wife raised their children as Jews—he cited a *New York Times* article that said so—but instead of taking pride in his appointment, he wrote that "while Emanuel is an observant Jew, Klain intermarried more than twenty years ago and his family observes Christmas" (Tzvi Ben Gedalyahu, "Another Jew from Clinton Gov't to Join Obama-Biden Team," *Arutz Sheva*, November 8, 2014, http://www.israelnationalnews.com/News/News.aspx/128387, citing Julie Scelfo, "A Holiday Medley, Off-Key," *New York Times*, December 6, 2007, http://www.nytimes.com/2007/12/06/garden/06Fight.html?partner=permalink&exprod=permalink).

14. Jane Eisner, "For 2013, a Marriage Agenda," *Forward*, January 7, 2013, http://forward.com/opinion/editorial/168529/for-2013-a-marriage-agenda.

15. J. J. Goldberg, "How Many American Jews Are There?" *Forward*, February 18, 2013, http://forward.com/opinion/171204/how-many-american-jews-are-there.

16. "Intermarriage Rorschach Test," editorial, *Forward*, January 16, 2014, http://forward.com/opinion/editorial/191024/intermarriage-rorschach-test.

17. Cnaan Liphshiz, "New Campaign Targets Jews 'Lost' to Assimilation," *Ha'aretz*, September 3, 2009, https://www.haaretz.com/1.5470096. This campaign featured a video clip with a top Israeli TV reporter stating that more than 50 percent of young Jews assimilate. It likened Jews who intermarried to missing persons, with fake notices and pictures that were plastered on walls around Israel. Officials from the Jewish Agency for Israel described intermarriage as a "strategic national threat." The advertisements asked anyone who "knows a young Jew living abroad" to call MASA and concluded, "Together, we will strengthen his or her bond to Israel, so that we don't lose them." I responded, "This has got to be the most stupid, ill-conceived effort coming out of Israel in many years" (Edmund Case, "A Stupid, Ill-Conceived Approach from Israel," *EdmundCase.com* [blog], September 3, 2009, http://www.edmundcase.com/israel/a-stupid-ill-conceived-approach-from-israel, originally published at InterfaithFamily.com.)

18. Jane Eisner, "New Jewish Agency Chief Learns Quickly about Intermarriage. It's Sensitive," *Forward*, June 28, 2018, https://forward.com/opinion/404272/new-jewish-agency-chief-learns-quick-lesson-about-intermarriage-its; Raoul Wootlif, "Lapid Slams Harsh Rap of TV Stars' Interfaith Marriage, But Says He Opposes It," *Times of Israel*, October 14, 2018, https://www.timesofisrael.com/lapid-slams-harsh-rap-of-tv-stars-interfaith-marriage-but-says-he-opposes-it.

19. In 2010, Prime Minister Benjamin Netanyahu said "the loss of identity through assimilation or through intermarriage or through both is the greatest toll-taker of Jewish numbers in the last half-century" ("Bibi on the Loss of Identity," *eJewishPhilanthropy*, February 22, 2010, http://ejewishphilanthropy.com/bibi-on-the-loss

-of-identity). In 2014, there was an uproar in Israel because a son of Netanyahu was dating a Norwegian woman who was not Jewish. Knesset members voiced dismay at the "big problem" of the son possibly intermarrying (Edmund Case, "It Happens in The Best of Families," *EdmundCase.com* [blog], January 2, 2014, http://www.edmundcase.com/news/it-happens-in-the-best-of-families, originally published at InterfaithFamily.com).

20. In an op-ed in the *Jerusalem Post*, I wrote that intermarriage does not necessarily lead to loss of Jewish identity and affiliation; that many interfaith couples and families are engaging in Jewish life; and that intermarriage has the potential to increase support for Israel in America. See Edmund Case, "What Israelis Need to Know about Intermarriage in North America," *Jerusalem Post*, October 3, 2009, http://www.jpost.com/Opinion/What-Israelis-need-to-know-about-intermarriage-in-North-America.

21. Paul Golin, "Intermarriage, Assimilation Are Not Interchangeable," *New York Jewish Week*, April 13, 2010, http://jewishweek.timesofisrael.com/intermarriage-assimilation-are-not-interchangeable. In October 2011, a *Jerusalem Post* editorial suggested that Israel should fight intermarriage by enacting legislation to encourage inmarriage, while acknowledging that "preventing Jews from marrying non-Jews through legislation or a lack thereof will not stop intermarriage. Love will overcome any obstacle" ("Debating Civil Marriage," editorial, *Jerusalem Post*, October 9, 2011, http://www.jpost.com/Opinion/Editorials/Debating-civil-marriage).

22. Gal Beckerman, "New Study Finds That It's Not a Lack of Welcome That's Keeping the Intermarrieds Away," *Forward*, July 7, 2010, http://forward.com/news/129228/new-study-finds-that-it-s-not-a-lack-of-welcome. A 2017 Jewish Telegraphic Agency article about interfaith couples forming community outside of synagogues reported people saying that "even a welcoming synagogue can be an intimidating space," noting that "couples may not know the prayers or rituals, may feel uncomfortable with the expectation of becoming members, or may just feel like they're in the minority"; Steven M. Cohen appeared to acknowledge that interfaith couples don't feel welcome when he reportedly said that "the people that fit the demographic of the active group are the people who feel most welcome" (Ben Sales, "Outside the Synagogue, Intermarried Are Forming Community with Each Other," Jewish Telegraphic Agency, February 10, 2017, http://www.jta.org/2017/02/10/news-opinion/united-states/outside-the-synagogue-intermarried-are-forming-community-with-each-other).

23. Quoted in Edmund Case, "Question: Can Jews Encourage In-Marriage AND Welcome Interfaith Families?" *EdmundCase.com* (blog), September 13, 2010, http://www.edmundcase.com/engaging-interfaith-families-jewishly/question-can-jews-encourage-in-marriage-and-welcome-interfaith-families, originally published at InterfaithFamily.com.

24. Quoted in Edmund Case, "Can the Jewish Community Encourage Inmarriage AND Welcome Interfaith Families?" (speech, General Assembly of the Jewish Federations of North America, New Orleans, LA, November 5, 2010), http://www.edmundcase.com/wp-content/uploads/2016/05/nov-2010-speech.pdf.

25. Quoted in Case, "Can the Jewish Community Encourage Inmarriage?"

26. Arnold Eisen, "A Reply to Ed Case's Review of *The Jew Within*," *EdmundCase.com* (blog), January 2001, http://www.edmundcase.com/media/essays/an-intermarried-perspective-on-the-jew-within-by-steven-m-cohen-and-arnold-m-eisen, originally published at InterfaithFamily.com.

27. InterfaithFamily, "What Attracts Interfaith Families to Jewish Organizations?" InterfaithFamily.com, September 5, 2012, http://www.interfaithfamily.com/about_us_advocacy/What_Attracts_Interfaith_Families_to_Jewish_Organizations.shtml?rd=2. We reported on nearly seven hundred survey responses, all from people in interfaith relationships who are raising Jewish children and are members of Jewish organizations. See also Edmund Case, "What Draws Interfaith Families to Jewish Life," *New York Jewish Week*, September 27, 2012, https://jewishweek.timesofisrael.com/what-draws-interfaith-families-to-jewish-life; Edmund Case, "A New Year to Engage Interfaith Families in Jewish Life," *Huffington Post*, September 12, 2002, http://www.huffingtonpost.com/edmund-c-case/new-year-engage-interfaith-families-in-jewish-life_b_1861603.html.

28. Quoted in Edmund Case, "Why Intermarrieds Stay Away," *EdmundCase.com* (blog), July 9, 2010, http://www.edmundcase.com/inclusion-and-welcoming/why-intermarrieds-stay-away, originally published at InterfaithFamily.com.

29. Janet Krasner Aronson et al., *2017 Greater Washington Jewish Community Demographic Study* (Washington, DC: Jewish Federation of Greater Washington, DC, 2018), 93, https://www.shalomdc.org/wp-content/uploads/2018/03/DCJewishCommunityStudy.pdf. InterfaithFamily received the following comments in 2006: "It's hard to love a Jew and feel such anger and resentment as a result of it." "I am considering raising my children Jewish . . . [but] I am afraid of how people will treat them because of my religion. This fear is based on my treatment by some Jews." "I want to participate in the synagogue with my children, and for them to see that I am comfortable and accepted there. How could they really feel wholly Jewish unless the community I've chosen for them accepts me, and therefore them?" (See Edmund Case, "Let's Encourage the Jewish Journeys of Interfaith Families," *EdmundCase.com* [blog], July 13, 2006, http://www.edmundcase.com/media/essays/lets-encourage-the-jewish-journeys-of-interfaith-families, originally published at InterfaithFamily.com.)

30. Steven M. Cohen, Jacob B. Ukeles, and Ron Miller, *Jewish Community Study of New York: 2011* (New York: UJA-Federation of New York, 2012), 145, 149, http://www.jewishdatabank.org/studies/downloadFile.cfm?FileID=2852.

31. Jack Wertheimer, "New Outreach to Intermarrieds Makes Wrong Assumptions," *New York Jewish Week*, December 13, 2011, http://jewishweek.timesofisrael.com/new-outreach-to-intermarrieds-makes-wrong-assumptions.

32. Pew Research Center, *A Portrait of Jewish Americans* (Washington, DC: Pew Research Center's Religions and Public Life Project, 2013), 51–52, http://www.jewishdatabank.org/studies/downloadFile.cfm?FileID=3088.

33. Kerry Olitzky, Paul Golin, and Zohar Rotem, *Listening to the Adult Children of Intermarriage: What Jews with One Parent Need and Want from the Jewish*

Community (New York: Jewish Outreach Institute, 2013), 3, 6, https://www.bjpa.org/search-results/publication/18778.

34. J. Correspondent, "Noted Philanthropist Goes to Bat for Intermarriage," *j. The Jewish News of Northern California*, June 11, 2010, http://www.jweekly.com/2010/06/11/noted-philanthropist-goes-to-bat-for-intermarriage. Bronfman understood the importance of genuine welcome; at his memorial service in 2014, Hillary Clinton expressed gratitude for the friendship and support he provided to Chelsea Clinton when she was getting married (Edmund Case, "Debate Reignited," *EdmundCase.com* [blog], January 29, 2014, http://www.edmundcase.com/inclusion-and-welcoming/debate-reignited, originally published at InterfaithFamily.com).

35. Edgar Bronfman, with Beth Zasloff, *Hope Not Fear: A Path to Jewish Renaissance* (New York: St. Martin's Griffin, 2008), 27.

14 Radically Inclusive Attitudes

1. Edgar Bronfman, with Beth Zasloff, *Hope Not Fear: A Path to Jewish Renaissance* (New York: St. Martin's Griffin, 2008), 27–28.

2. Bronfman, *Hope Not Fear*, 29. In 2013 a Jewish Telegraphic Agency story reported that Jewish institutions and religious denominations were not "fighting against intermarriage" so much any longer but rather reacting by engaging with the intermarried in an effort to have them embrace Judaism. The denominations differed in how far to go in that embrace, and how strongly to push for conversion, but intermarriage was viewed as "a potential gain, in the form of the non-Jewish spouse or children who may convert" (Uriel Heilman, "The War Against Intermarriage Has Been Lost. Now What?" Jewish Telegraphic Agency, August 6, 2013, http://www.jta.org/2013/08/06/news-opinion/united-states/the-war-over-intermarriage-has-been-lost-now-what). Engaging the intermarried with conversion as the focus is not the kind of attitudinal shift that is needed.

3. Adam Bronfman (speech, General Assembly of the Jewish Federations of North America, Jerusalem, November 2008), quoted in Edmund Case, "Breaking New Ground with Jewish Leaders," *EdmundCase.com* (blog), November 23, 2008, http://www.edmundcase.com/inclusion-and-welcoming/breaking-new-ground-with-jewish-leaders, originally published at InterfaithFamily.com. Excerpts of the speech are available in a video, "Adam Bronfman on Welcoming the Intermarried," Jewish Telegraphic Agency, November 21, 2008, https://www.youtube.com/watch?v=oPTvPAn9oh4.

4. Quoted in Edmund Case, "A Jewish Leader Who 'Gets It,'" *EdmundCase.com* (blog), June 18, 2010, http://www.edmundcase.com/inclusion-and-welcoming/a-jewish-leader-who-gets-it, originally published at InterfaithFamily.com. Shrage repeated the message in "Story Tellers: A New Story of Jewish Identity," *Sh'ma: A Journal of Jewish Ideas*, 40, no. 668 (March 1, 2010): 1–2, https://www.bjpa.org/search-results/publication/6836.

5. J. J. Goldberg, "Generation to Generation, Our Changing Judaism," *Forward*, March 31, 2010, www.forward.com/articles/126979.

6. Goldberg, "Generation to Generation."

7. A year later, Judy Bolton-Fasman, a columnist for the Boston *Jewish Advocate*, described the bar mitzvah of the son of friend. "[The bar mitzvah boy] talked about how his beautiful mother and his generous father supported his Jewish learning. His non-Jewish grandparents read the Schechehiyanu. . . . I took [his Lutheran-raised father] aside . . . and thanked him for being a beloved companion of the Jewish people" (Edmund Case, "Another Step Towards a Changing Judaism," *EdmundCase.com* [blog], June 4, 2011, http://www.edmundcase.com/inclusion-and-welcoming/another -step-towards-a-changing-judaism, originally published at InterfaithFamily.com.)

8. Naamah Kelman and Elan Ezrachi, "Expanding the Tribe in the Home of the Brave," *Ha'aretz*, February 8, 2011, http://www.haaretz.com/print-edition/features/expanding -the-tribe-in-the-home-of-the-brave-1.341934. In another positive comment, Israeli-American journalist Liel Leibovitz said Israelis should say "welcome and so nice to have you here" to the woman then dating one of Prime Minister Netanyahu's sons (Edmund Case, "It Happens in the Best of Families," *EdmundCase.com* [blog], January 2, 2014, http://www.edmundcase.com/news/it-happens-in-the-best-of-families, originally published at InterfaithFamily.com).

9. Gary Rosenblatt, "Jewish Renaissance in Europe Presents a Surprising Challenge," *New York Jewish Week*, January 18, 2011, http://jewishweek.timesofisrael.com /jewish-renaissance-in-europe-presents-a-surprising-challenge.

10. Rosenblatt, "Jewish Renaissance in Europe."

11. Julie Wiener, "A Secret Love No More," *New York Jewish Week*, December 7, 2010, http://jewishweek.timesofisrael.com/a-secret-love-no-more.

12. Abigail Pogrebin, *Stars of David: Prominent Jews Talk About Being Jewish* (New York: Broadway Books, 2005), 66. Portman later married Benjamin Millipied, who is not Jewish.

13. Edmund Case, "The Next Celebrity Interfaith Couple?" *EdmundCase.com* (blog), July 28, 2011, http://www.edmundcase.com/celebrities/the-next-celebrity-interfaith -couple, originally published at InterfaithFamily.com; Elizabeth Kwiatkowski, "Ashley Hebert and J. P. Rosenbaum Discuss 'The Bachelorette,'" *Reality TV World*, August 2, 2011, http://www.realitytvworld.com/news/ashley-hebert-and-jp-rosenbaum-open-up -about-the-bachelorette-12535.php#SJ2a2JFPErO3xYQa.99.

14. Quoted in Edmund Case, "What We Can Learn from the InterfaithFamily.com Network Essay Contest," *EdmundCase.com* (blog), September 2003, http://www .edmundcase.com/media/essays/what-we-can-learn-from-the-interfaithfamily -com-network-essay-contest, originally published at InterfaithFamily.com.

15. Case, "What We Can Learn."

16. InterfaithFamily, "What Attracts Interfaith Families to Jewish Organizations?" InterfaithFamily.com, September 5, 2012, http://www.interfaithfamily.com/about _us_advocacy/What_Attracts_Interfaith_Families_to_Jewish_Organizations .shtml?rd=2. Interfaith families may give more weight to differences in openness to them than to other important considerations. As one said: "Our synagogue doesn't offer childcare during services, and we have begun attending a different synagogue that offers a wonderful children's program that our kids adore. The problem is that

that synagogue is not as open to interfaith families, so while we enjoy attending services there, we are unlikely to become members there."

17. Edmund Case, "A Stupid, Ill-Conceived Approach from Israel," *EdmundCase.com* (blog), September 3, 2009, http://www.edmundcase.com/israel/a-stupid-ill-conceived -approach-from-israel/, originally published at InterfaithFamily.com.

18. Leonard Saxe et al., *Beyond 10 Days: Parents, Gender, Marriage, and the Long-Term Impact of Birthright Israel* (Waltham: Brandeis University, Cohen Center for Modern Jewish Studies, 2017), 4, https://www.brandeis.edu/cmjs/pdfs/jewish%20futures /Beyond10Days.pdf.

19. Combined Jewish Philanthropies, "Report of the Strategic Planning Committee: A Culture of Learning, a Vision of Justice, a Community of Caring," January 1998, 14–15.

20. See, for example, "From Strength to Strength," Invitation to Combined Jewish Philanthropies October 3, 2018, event.

21. Allison Berry, "The View from Mt. Sinai—Building Our Inclusive Community," September 25, 2017, https://www.templeshalom.org/blogs?post_id=205891.

22. Berry, "The View from Mt. Sinai."

23. Arnold Eisen, "A Reply to Ed Case's Review of *The Jew Within*," *EdmundCase.com* (blog), January 2001, http://www.edmundcase.com/media/essays/an-intermarried -perspective-on-the-jew-within-by-steven-m-cohen-and-arnold-m-eisen, originally published at Interfaithfamily.com.

24. Edmund Case, "Let's Not Promote Inmarriage Without Promoting Outreach to the Intermarried," *EdmundCase.com* (blog), March 2001, http://www.edmundcase.com /media/essays/lets-not-promote-in-marriage-without-promoting-outreach-to-the -intermarried, originally published at InterfaithFamily.com. I made similar comments when I spoke at the General Assembly in 2002 ("Interfaith Families Raising Jewish Children" [speech, General Assembly of the United Jewish Communities, Philadelphia, PA, November 20, 2002], http://www.edmundcase.com /media/in-the-news/interfaith-families-raising-jewish-children, originally published at InterfaithFamily.com), and in a 2006 newspaper interview (Daniela Martin, "Negotiation and Accommodation in Mixed Marriages," *Aufbau* 67, no. 25 [December 6, 2001], http://www.archive.org/stream/aufbau666720002001germ#page/n601/).

25. Paul Golin, "God's Covenant, Judaism and Interfaith Marriage," *Huffington Post*, September 3, 2010, http://www.huffingtonpost.com/paul-golin/jews-can-welcome -inmarrie_b_699621.html. This reminded me of a friend who complained to me about people who said, about his adult child who was in a same-sex relationship, "It's wonderful that she has a partner, but wouldn't you prefer that she be straight?"

26. Edmund Case, "Can the Jewish Community Encourage Inmarriage AND Welcome Interfaith Families?" (speech, General Assembly of the Jewish Federations of North America, New Orleans, LA, November 5, 2010), http://www.edmundcase.com /wp-content/uploads/2016/05/nov-2010-speech.pdf.

27. Leonard Saxe et al., *2015 Greater Boston Jewish Community Study* (Waltham: Brandeis University, Cohen Center for Modern Jewish Studies, 2016), 31, http://

www.jewishboston.com/2015-greater-boston-jewish-community-study-cjp
-overview-cohen-center-report.

Road Map Two   Policies

1. Rabbi David Wolpe, "A Blessing and a Threat," On Faith, *Washington Post*, accessed October 1, 2018, https://www.onfaith.co/onfaith/2010/07/26/a-blessing-and-a-threat /6185.
2. Mamie Kanfer Stewart, "No Conversion Required," *Sh'ma: A Journal of Jewish Ideas*, April 3, 2013, http://shma.com/2013/04/no-conversion-required.
3. Edgar Bronfman, with Beth Zasloff, *Hope Not Fear: A Path to Jewish Renaissance* (New York: St. Martin's Griffin, 2008), 39.

15 Radical Inclusion Starts at the Wedding

1. Leonard Saxe et al., *Under the Chuppah: Rabbinic Officiation and Intermarriage* (Waltham: Brandeis University, Cohen Center for Modern Jewish Studies, 2016), http:// www.brandeis.edu/cmjs/pdfs/jewish%20futures/RabbinicOfficiation102616.pdf.
2. Saxe et al., *Under the Chuppah*, 9, 11.
3. Saxe et al., 18.
4. Sara Holtz, "Why I Am a Unitarian," InterfaithFamily.com, August 2002, http://www .interfaithfamily.com/news_and_opinion/synagogues_and_the_jewish_community /Why_I_Am_a_Unitarian.shtml.
5. Quoted in Edmund Case, "Birthright Israel, Jewish Wedding Ceremonies, and Jewish Commitment," *EdmundCase.com* (blog), October 27, 2009, http://www.edmundcase .com/wedding-officiation/birthright-israel-jewish-wedding-ceremonies-and-jewish -commitment, originally published at InterfaithFamily.com.
6. InterfaithFamily, *Report on InterfaithFamily's 2017 Survey on Rabbinic Officiation for Interfaith Couples*, August 2018, 1, https://www.interfaithfamily.com/wp-content /uploads/2018/08/Rabbi-Officiation-Report-Final.pdf.
7. "Rabbi David Wolpe, Los Angeles' Sinai Temple, Explains Why He Won't Perform Interfaith Wedding Ceremonies" *Huffington Post*, August 20, 2013, http://www .huffingtonpost.com/2013/08/20/interfaith-couples-weddings_n_3787445.html.
8. Ben Sales, "Conservative Rabbis Can Now Attend Intermarriages," Jewish Telegraphic Agency, October 22, 2018, https://www.jta.org/2018/10/22/news -opinion/conservative-rabbis-can-now-attend-intermarriages?utm_source =JTA%20Maropost&utm_campaign=JTA&utm_medium=email&mpweb=1161 -6485-193083.
9. Ben Sales, "Conservative Rabbinic Group Issues Guidelines for Same-Sex Wedding Rituals," Jewish Telegraphic Agency, June 4, 2012, https://www.jta.org/2012/06/04 /life-religion/conservative-rabbinic-group-issues-guidelines-for-same-sex -wedding-rituals; "Gay, Lesbian, Bisexual and Transgender (GLBT) Jews," Women's League for Conservative Judaism, accessed October 1, 2018, http://wlcj.org /resolution/gay-lesbian-bisexual-and-transgender-glbt-jews.

10. CCAR Responsa, American Reform Responsa 146, "Reform Judaism and Mixed Marriage," 1980, https://www.ccarnet.org/ccar-responsa/arr-445-465.

11. Rachel Zoll, "Rabbis for Hire," *Times and Democrat*, September 21, 2007, https://thetandd.com/lifestyles/faith-and-values/rabbis-for-hire/article_d5a1384a-6386-58da-b053-fee4321dfb41.html.

12. InterfaithFamily, *What Attracts Interfaith Families to Jewish Organizations?* InterfaithFamily.com, September 5, 2012, http://www.interfaithfamily.com/about_us_advocacy/What_Attracts_Interfaith_Families_to_Jewish_Organizations.shtml?rd=2.

13. Edmund Case, "Congratulations Washington," *EdmundCase.com* (blog), April 29, 2013, http://www.edmundcase.com/engaging-interfaith-families-jewishly/congratulations-washington, originally published at InterfaithFamily.com.

14. Kerry Olitzky, Paul Golin, and Zohar Rotem, *Listening to the Adult Children of Intermarriage: What Jews with One Parent Need and Want from the Jewish Community* (New York: Jewish Outreach Institute, 2013), 14, https://www.bjpa.org/search-results/publication/18778.

15. Arnold Dashefsky, *Intermarriage and Jewish Journeys* (Boston: National Center for Jewish Policy Studies at Hebrew College, 2008), 30–31, http://www.jewishdatabank.org/Studies/downloadFile.cfm?FileID=2711.

16. Leonard Saxe et al., *Generation Birthright Israel: The Impact of an Israel Experience on Jewish Identity and Choices* (Waltham: Brandeis University, Cohen Center for Modern Jewish Studies, 2009), 29, http://www.brandeis.edu/cmjs/pdfs/Taglit.GBI.10.25.10.final.pdf.

17. Daniel Zemel, "A Letter to My Congregants," InterfaithFamily.com, January 27, 2009, http://www.interfaithfamily.com/news_and_opinion/synagogues_and_the_jewish_community/A_Letter_to_My_Congregants.shtml. Rabbi Richard Block announced a similar change of position. See Marilyn Karfeld, "Two More Reform Rabbis to Marry Interfaith Couples," *Cleveland Jewish News*, February 12, 2010, http://www.clevelandjewishnews.com/archives/two-more-reform-rabbis-to-marry-interfaith-couples/article_c76608eb-80ae-562f-a6c0-2be0ca979e5c.html.

18. James Ponet, "Into the Jewish People," *Tablet*, September 7, 2010, http://www.tabletmag.com/jewish-life-and-religion/44143/into-the-jewish-people.

19. CCAR Task Force on the Challenges of Intermarriage for the Reform Rabbi, *Insights: What We Have Learned and Where Do We Go From Here* (New York: Central Conference of American Rabbis, 2010).

20. CCAR Task Force, *Insights*, 3.

21. Julie Gruenbaum Fax, "Rabbi Reverses Interfaith Marriage Policy," *Los Angeles Jewish Journal*, September 27, 2012, http://jewishjournal.com/news/los_angeles/108425.

22. Fax, "Rabbi Reverses Interfaith Marriage Policy."

23. See Irwin H. Fishbein, "Summary of Rabbinic Center for Research and Counseling 1995 Survey" (Clark, NJ: Rabbinic Center for Research and Counseling, 1995), http://rcronline.org/research.htm. Forty percent of CCAR and RRA members responded to the survey.

24. InterfaithFamily, *Report on InterfaithFamily's 2017 Survey*, 1.

25. InterfaithFamily, 22.

26. InterfaithFamily, 23.

27. InterfaithFamily, 15.

28. Leon Morris, "A Call for a Moratorium on Shabbat Weddings," *New York Jewish Week*, August 24, 2010, http://jewishweek.timesofisrael.com/a-call-for-a-moratorium-on-shabbat-weddings.

29. Evan Moffic, "Jewish Weddings on Shabbat: A Different View," *New York Jewish Week*, August 27, 2010, http://jewishweek.timesofisrael.com/jewish-weddings-on-shabbat-a-different-view.

30. InterfaithFamily, *Report on InterfaithFamily's 2017 Survey*, 1.

31. Angela Buchdahl, "The Power of 'Yes' on Interfaith Officiation," *New York Jewish Week*, March 28, 2017, http://jewishweek.timesofisrael.com/the-power-of-yes-on-interfaith-officiation.

32. See, for example, Zemel, "A Letter to My Congregants"; Fax, "Rabbi Reverses Interfaith Marriage Policy."

33. InterfaithFamily, *Report on InterfaithFamily's 2017 Survey*, 1.

34. Reconstructionist Rabbinical Association, "Resolution on Co-Officiation," 2000, https://therra.org/resolutions/co-officiation.pdf.

35. Julie Wiener, "Sneak Peek: My Page 1 Article/Column on Co-Officiation (and Chelsea, of Course)," *New York Jewish Week*, August 3, 2010, http://jewishweek.timesofisrael.com/sneak-peek-my-page-1-articlecolumn-on-co-officiation-and-chelsea-of-course/.

36. Wiener, "Sneak Peek."

37. Wiener, "Sneak Peek."

38. InterfaithFamily, *Report on InterfaithFamily's 2017 Survey*, 18. Rabbi Buchdahl, in saying that she will not co-officiate, said, "If the wedding is marking the end of a couple's connection to Judaism instead of a new beginning, then I have no proper place there." See Buchdahl, "The Power of 'Yes' on Interfaith Officiation." It's not clear that she meant that co-officiation does mark the end of a couple's connection to Judaism; I don't believe that to be the case.

39. InterfaithFamily, *Report on InterfaithFamily's 2017 Survey*, 17.

40. Wiener, "Sneak Peek."

41. InterfaithFamily, *Report on InterfaithFamily's 2017 Survey*, 1.

42. Edmund Case, "My Interview with Steve and Cokie Roberts," *EdmundCase.com* (blog), April 10, 2011, http://www.edmundcase.com/children-of-intermarriage/my-interview-with-steve-and-cokie-roberts, originally published at InterfaithFamily.com.

43. Adina Lewittes, "Intermarriage: I Do," *Sha'ar Communities*, October 2014, http://shaarcommunities.org/wp-content/uploads/2014/10/YK-2014-Intermarriage-I-Do-1.pdf.

44. Uriel Heilman, "Causing Stir, Prominent Conservative Rabbi Considers Breaking Intermarriage Ban," Jewish Telegraphic Agency, December 18, 2014, http://www.jta.org/2014/12/18/news-opinion/united-states/causing-stir-prominent-conservative-rabbi-considers-breaking-intermarriage-ban.

45. Jeremy Kalmanofsky, "Why I Will Not Simply Accept Intermarriage," *Forward*, March 8, 2015, http://forward.com/opinion/216123/why-i-will-not-simply-accept-intermarriage. For my response to this and other developments at the time, see

Edmund Case, "Three Voices from the Conservative Movement," *Edmund-Case.com* (blog), April 13, 2015, http://www.edmundcase.com/inclusion-and-welcoming/three-voices-from-the-conservative-movement, originally published at InterfaithFamily.com.

46. Seymour Rosenbloom, "It's Time to Allow Conservative Rabbis to Officiate at Interfaith Weddings," Jewish Telegraphic Agency, April 4, 2016, http://www.jta.org/2016/04/04/news-opinion/united-states/op-ed-its-time-to-allow-conservative-rabbis-to-officiate-at-interfaith-weddings; Seymour Rosenbloom, "I Performed an Intermarriage. Then I Got Expelled," *Washington Post*, April 24, 2014, https://www.washingtonpost.com/news/acts-of-faith/wp/2017/04/24/i-performed-an-intermarriage-and-then-i-got-expelled/?utm_term=.1cc19e4363f3.

47. Elliot Cosgrove, "To Officiate or Not at Intermarriages," *New York Jewish Week*, March 15, 2017, http://jewishweek.timesofisrael.com/to-officiate-or-not-at-intermarriages.

48. Cosgrove, "To Officiate or Not at Intermarriages."

49. See Edmund Case, "The Intermarriage Debate Escalates," *EdmundCase.com* (blog), June 20, 2017, http://www.edmundcase.com/inclusion-and-welcoming/intermarriage-debate-escalates; Edmund Case, "More Negative Conservative Officiation News," *EdmundCase.com* (blog), July 10, 2017, http://www.edmundcase.com/wedding-officiation/negative-conservative-officiation-news; Edmund Case, "The Conservative Officiation Debate Continues," *EdmundCase.com* (blog), August 14, 2017, http://www.edmundcase.com/wedding-officiation/conservative-officiation-debate-continues.

50. Ben Sales, "Conservative Movement Reaffirms Intermarriage Ban and Rabbis Ask Why," Jewish Telegraphic Agency, October 20, 2017, https://www.jta.org/2017/10/20/news-opinion/united-states/conservative-movement-doubles-down-on-intermarriage-and-its-rabbis-ask-why.

51. Ben Sales, "Conservative Rabbis Can Now Attend Intermarriages."

16 Status—Recognition and Ritual Participation

1. In 1970, the Conservative movement was the largest Jewish denomination, with 42 percent of American Jews; by the time of the Pew report in 2013, it had been overtaken by the Reform movement, and only 18 percent identified as Conservative (Bernard Lazerwitz et al., "A Study of Jewish Denominational Preferences: Summary Findings," in American Jewish Committee, *American Jewish Yearbook 1997* [New York: American Jewish Committee, 1997], 130, https://www.bjpa.org/search-results/publication/17657; Pew Research Center, *A Portrait of Jewish Americans* [Washington, DC: Pew Research Center's Religions and Public Life Project, 2013], 10, http://www.jewishdatabank.org/studies/downloadFile.cfm?FileID=3088). Most observers agree this is because the Reform movement has been more welcoming to interfaith families. "Realistically, . . . most intermarried couples wanting to seek out Judaism still will gravitate to Reform" (Roberta R. Kwall, "Saving Conservative Judaism," *Commentary*, March 15, 2017, https://www.commentarymagazine.com/articles/saving-conservative-judaism; Jack Wertheimer, *The New American Judaism: How Jews Practice Their Religion Today* [Princeton, NJ: Princeton University Press, 2018], 128).

The policy of the movement's Ramah camps has been not to allow children of mothers from different faith backgrounds to attend (Edmund Case, "Responding to the Intermarriage News," *EdmundCase.com* [blog], March 2002, http://www.edmundcase.com/media/essays/responding-to-the-intermarriage-news, originally published at InterfaithFamily.com).

2. Edmund Case, "What We Can Learn from the InterfaithFamily.com Network Essay Contest," *EdmundCase.com* (blog), September 2003, http://www.edmundcase.com/media/essays/what-we-can-learn-from-the-interfaithfamily-com-network-essay-contest, originally published at InterfaithFamily.com.

3. Kerry Olitzky, Paul Golin, and Zohar Rotem, *Listening to the Adult Children of Intermarriage: What Jews with One Parent Need and Want from the Jewish Community* (New York: Jewish Outreach Institute, 2013), 4, 12, https://www.bjpa.org/search-results/publication/18778. The *Millennial Children* study similarly observes, "In interviews, children of intermarriage described being offended by reference to matrilineal heritage as necessary for Jewish identity. In many cases it was peers with two Jewish parents who challenged them. Even some with a Jewish mother reacted to this as an exclusionary boundary that has little to do with their experience of Jewish identity and living" (Theodore Sasson et al., *Millennial Children of Intermarriage: Touchpoints and Trajectories of Jewish Engagement* [Waltham: Brandeis University, Cohen Center for Modern Jewish Studies, 2016], 30, http://www.brandeis.edu/cmjs/pdfs/intermarriage/MillennialChildrenIntermarriage1.pdf.

4. InterfaithFamily, "What Attracts Interfaith Families to Jewish Organizations?" InterfaithFamily.com, September 5, 2012, http://www.interfaithfamily.com/about_us_advocacy/What_Attracts_Interfaith_Families_to_Jewish_Organizations.shtml?rd=2. In 2007, my teacher Sherry Israel, speaking at a Kansas City Conservative synagogue, said, on the question of day schools admitting the children of mothers from different faith backgrounds, "Here's a family that wants to give a child a Jewish upbringing, and that includes a deep Jewish education. We should say no? Let's find a way to say yes" (Edmund Case, "Two Friends," *EdmundCase.com* [blog], January 22, 2007, http://www.edmundcase.com/conversion/two-friends, originally published at InterfaithFamily.com).

5. Edgar Bronfman, with Beth Zasloff, *Hope Not Fear: A Path to Jewish Renaissance* (New York: St. Martin's Griffin, 2008), 39. Bronfman also said, "Jewish law [should be changed] to recognize paternal, as well as maternal, lineage. . . . Patrilineage was the norm among Jews until the 12th century and the time of Maimonides. We don't have to worry about keeping the bloodlines pure nowadays. We have DNA" (J. Correspondent, "Noted Philanthropist Goes to Bat for Intermarriage," *j. The Jewish News of Northern California*, June 11, 2010, http://www.jweekly.com/2010/06/11/noted-philanthropist-goes-to-bat-for-intermarriage).

6. Andy Bachman, "Patrilineal Promise and Pitfalls," *Forward*, February 16, 2011, http://forward.com/opinion/135475/patrilineal-promise-and-pitfalls.

7. Alana Suskin, "The Non-Jewish Rabbi? The Problem of Patrilineal Descent," MyJewishLearning, August 14, 2013, http://www.myjewishlearning.com/rabbis-without-borders/the-non-jewish-rabbi-the-problem-of-patrilineal-descent.

8. Ben Greenberg, "Patrilineal Jewish Descent: An Open Orthodox Approach," MyJewishLearning, August 13, 2013, http://www.myjewishlearning.com/rabbis-without-borders/patrilineal-jewish-descent-an-open-orthodox-approach.

9. Rachel Gurevitz, "Patrilineal Descent: Why This Rabbi Feels No Angst," MyJewish Learning, August 19, 2013, http://www.myjewishlearning.com/rabbis-without-borders/patrilineal-descent-why-this-rabbi-feels-no-angst.

10. Gurevitz, "Patrilineal Descent."

11. Greenberg, "Patrilineal Jewish Descent."

12. Alana Newhouse, "The Diaspora Need Not Apply," *New York Times*, July 15, 2010, http://www.nytimes.com/2010/07/16/opinion/16newhouse.html.

13. Heidi Hoover, "Israel Doesn't Want a Reform Convert Like Me," *New York Jewish Week*, February 26, 2013, http://jewishweek.timesofisrael.com/israel-doesnt-want-me.

14. Hoover, "Israel Doesn't Want a Reform Convert Like Me."

15. Gurevitz, "Patrilineal Descent."

16. Hoover, "Israel Doesn't Want a Reform Convert Like Me."

17. "Learning Judaism from Giffords," editorial, *Jerusalem Post*, http://www.jpost.com/Opinion/Editorials/Learning-Judaism-from-Giffords.

18. "Who Isn't a Jew?" editorial, *Forward*, January 10, 2011, http://forward.com/opinion/editorial/134958/who-isn-t-a-jew.

19. Some rabbis are now officiating at what they call "affirmation" ceremonies. These ceremonies include the rituals required for conversion, and thereby confer halachic status, on people who already identify as Jewish and do not feel the need for the change of identity that conversion implies. "Some 'patrilineal Jews' choose to immerse in a mikveh to turn aside challenges to their authenticity by satisfying the legal requirement for conversion. However, in such cases, the term 'conversion' can seem inappropriate and even hurtful to someone who has always identified as a Jew and lived a Jewish life. Today, many clergy speak of the ceremony as an affirmation instead, since the individual is affirming their Jewish identity" ("Conversion/Affirmation," Mayyim Hayyim, accessed October 1, 2018, https://www.mayyimhayyim.org/using-the-mikveh/conversion-affirmation).

20. The *Millennial Children* study concluded that "Jewish organizations will continue to adopt different approaches on the question of patrilineal descent according to their religious beliefs. All Jewish organizations, however, can encourage awareness of the strong feelings of Jewish identity and authenticity felt by many individuals who claim Jewish status according to paternity alone" (Sasson et al., *Millennial Children of Intermarriage*, 50).

21. Suggestions have been made over the years to create a status that would entitle people who have not formally converted to Judaism to certain rights and privileges. Rabbi James Ponet, for example, in explaining how he changed his position about wedding officiation, said, "There may be stages of entrance into and levels of engagement with the Jewish people, which might find liturgical expression both in the wedding ceremony and at other lifecycle events going forward. After all, becoming a Jew, like becoming a person, takes a lifetime" (James Ponet, "Into the Jewish People," *Tablet*, September 7, 2010, http://www.tabletmag.com/jewish-life-and-religion/44143

/into-the-jewish-people). The most often advanced status is that of *ger toshav*, as ably spelled out in Amichai Lau-Lavie, *Joy: A Proposal*, Lab/Shul, June 2017, http://amichai.me/wp-content/uploads/2017/06/Welcome_Book_2017.pdf. Creating a new status with required characteristics will serve to exclude those who don't make the defined grade, which runs counter to a radically inclusive approach.

22. Nancy tells her story in her remarkable book, *Both Sides Now: A True Story of Love, Loss and Bold Living* (Miami: Books & Books Press, 2014).

23. Related issues of whether partners from different faith traditions could be voting members of synagogues and take leadership positions have been frequently debated in Reform synagogues since the 1990s. Negative decisions on those issues have been off-putting to interfaith couples. The Reform movement published a set of materials to help synagogues develop their positions. Commission on Outreach and Synagogue Community, *Defining the Role of the Non-Jew in the Synagogue* (New York: Union of American Hebrew Congregations, 2003). In March 2017 the United Synagogue of Conservative Judaism passed a resolution to "allow individual congregations to decide whether to grant membership to non-Jews." A United Synagogue leader said they wanted to "deepen the sense of welcome for those married to people of another faith," and a Rabbinical Assembly leader said they believed "in the idea that synagogue life should be open to those who wish to be part of the Jewish community and [that] we are enriched by their presence" (Lauren Markoe, "Conservative Synagogues Can Now Accept Non-Jews As Members," ReligionNews.com, March 7, 2017, http://religionnews.com/2017/03/07/conservative-synagogues-can-now-officially-accept-non-jews-as-members). Daniel Solomon, a *Forward* writer, questioned whether the partners from different faith traditions would be "second-class citizens" (Daniel Solomon, "Conservatives Welcome Non-Jews—But Will They Be Second-Class Citizens in the Synagogue?" *Forward*, March 30, 2017, http://forward.com/news/366767/conservatives-welcome-non-jews-but-will-they-be-second-class-citizens-in-sy). He shared with me that the United Synagogue was going to issue guidelines reiterating that people who are not Jewish cannot serve on a synagogue board and that people who are not Jewish cannot handle the Torah during services.

24. Eric H. Yoffie, "A Call to Outreach," *Reform Judaism*, Fall 1999, quoted in Edmund Case, "We Need a Religious Movement That Is Totally Inclusive of Interfaith Families," *EdmundCase.com* (blog), March 2000, http://www.edmundcase.com/media/essays/we-need-a-religious-movement-that-is-totally-inclusive-of-intermarried-jewish-families, originally published at InterfaithFamily.com.

25. There is a concept in Jewish law of the *shaliach tzibur* (leader of the service) (Congregation Sinai, "Standards for Shichei Tzibbur, Torah & Haftarah Changers, and Gabbaim," *Sinai-SJ.org*, accessed October 1, 2018, https://sinai-sj.org/be-a-service-leader-reader/service-leader-standards). I have heard people argue that only a Jew should say a prayer as a representative of the Jewish people while publicly leading a prayer service; partners from different faith traditions could privately say the same prayer while sitting in the pews, but not publicly from the bimah. But the people sitting in the pews are not aware of this distinction. It leaves partners from different faith traditions excluded from fully participating in their child's bar or bat mitzvah

and wondering, if they shouldn't say the prayers publicly, whether it's appropriate to say them privately. The net effect is to distance people instead of drawing them in.

26. Quoted in Case, "We Need a Religious Movement."

27. Case, "We Need a Religious Movement." Jack Wertheimer made the same point in a debate with me in the Back Page feature of the *Jerusalem Report* in 2002, when he said that interfaith couples' decisions about engagement have "little to do with the posture of the Jewish community and everything to do with a family's negotiation of the fault line created by intermarriage" ("Should Efforts Be Made to Draw Interfaith Couples into the Jewish Community?" *Jerusalem Report*, December 16, 2002, 56, https://www.highbeam.com/doc/1P2-10029353.html). See also Jack Wertheimer, "New Outreach to Intermarrieds Makes Wrong Assumptions," *New York Jewish Week*, December 13, 2011, http://jewishweek.timesofisrael.com/new-outreach-to-intermarrieds-makes-wrong-assumptions.

28. Some converts say that giving non-converts the same rights and benefits devalues their conversion. Harold Berman, with his wife, Gayle, a convert, founded an organization to help intermarried families who wish to explore becoming traditionally observant Jewish families, as they did. See Harold Berman, *Doublelife: One Family, Two Faiths and a Journey of Hope* (New York: Longhill Press, 2013). It's wonderful if partners who aren't Jewish decide to convert and become traditionally observant, but this is not likely to happen very often. Berman says it is insulting to converts to treat people who had not converted as equals. I would hope that what motivates converts is a desire to integrate how they identify with how they live, not enjoying ritual participation that is barred to people who have not converted.

29. InterfaithFamily, "What Attracts Interfaith Families to Jewish Organizations?"

30. When the Chasidic rabbi who is also the publisher of the Boston *Jewish Advocate* took the position that people who are not Jewish should not attend Passover Seders, I wrote a letter to the editor, rhetorically asking if the rabbi really wanted the thousands of partners from different faith traditions in interfaith relationships to absent themselves from their families' Seders. See Edmund Case, "Striving for a More Inclusive Approach to Safeguard Our Future," *Jewish Advocate*, May 13–19, 2005, 23.

31. On the issue of permitting non-Jewish family members to participate in life-cycle events, including taking part in the symbolic passing of the Torah during a bar or bat mitzvah, Sherry Israel said, "People who study these matters say the *bimah* isn't sacred space. . . . There is no prohibition against non-Jews touching a Torah. Take the situation of the non-Jewish mother who has done all this work raising the child. Hasn't that mother been helping pass the tradition?" (Case, "Two Friends").

32. Edmund Case and Jodi Bromberg, "Promote Jewish Engagement, Not Inmarriage," *eJewishPhilanthropy*, January 29, 2014, http://ejewishphilanthropy.com/promote-jewish-engagement-not-in-marriage.

33. Rabbi Adam Morris also "fervently believes" that sanctifying an interfaith couples' covenant with a Jewish ceremony should be an option (Adam Morris, "The Importance of Whom We Marry," Micahdenver.org, November 14, 2003, http://micahdenver.org/2003/11/the-importance-of-whom-we-marry). For many years, Rabbi Morris was the only congregational rabbi in Denver who would officiate for interfaith couples,

to the best of my knowledge. In 2018, Rabbi Joe Black, of Temple Emanuel in Denver, announced that he had changed his position and would officiate under certain conditions (Ari Feldman, "Rabbi Will Do Interfaith Weddings—If the Kids Are Jewish," *Forward*, July 29, 2018, https://forward.com/news/national/406825/rabbi-will-do-interfaith-weddings-if-the-kids-are-jewish).

34. In July 2013, I got a distressed call from a friend. The teenage daughter of close family friends had been killed while on a bicycle trip. Her father was Jewish, her mother was Christian; they had belonged in the past to a Reform synagogue but at the time were members of an Episcopal church. They had not been able to find a rabbi who was willing to participate in their daughter's funeral at the church. I quickly called a rabbi InterfaithFamily often recommended to interfaith couples. After hearing the circumstances, he said, "Of course I will help them." The grieving parents shouldn't have been rejected in the first place. While I disagree with rabbis who won't officiate at weddings of interfaith couples, I understand the logic that they are not certain about what the Jewish engagement of the couple and any children will be. I don't understand why a rabbi would not participate in a funeral, even in a church, by offering Jewish words and rituals to comfort bereaved Jewish relatives.

35. Karen Wall, "Jewish Cemetery Welcomes Interfaith Family Members in Toms River," *Toms River Patch*, December 4, 2017, https://patch.com/new-jersey/tomsriver/jewish-cemetery-welcomes-interfaith-family-members-toms-river; Frances Kraft, "New Cemetery for Interfaith Couples Opens in the GTA," May 3, 2018, http://www.cjnews.com/news/canada/new-cemetery-for-interfaith-couples-opens-in-the-gta.

17 Intermarried Rabbis

1. CCAR Responsa 5761.6, "May a Jew Married to a Non-Jew Become a Rabbi?" March 2002, https://www.ccarnet.org/ccar-responsa/nyp-no-5761-6.

2. Edie Mueller, "Why I'm Not a Rabbi," InterfaithFamily.com, accessed October 1, 2018, http://www.interfaithfamily.com/spirituality/spirituality/Why_Im_Not_a_Rabbi.shtml.

3. Jeremy Gillick, "The Coming of the Intermarried Rabbi," *New Voices*, April 23, 2009, http://newvoices.org/2009/04/23/0007-3.

4. Edmund Case, "Where Might Interfaith Families Find Welcoming Jewish Communities?" *EdmundCase.com* (blog), February 15, 2017, http://www.edmundcase.com/inclusion-and-welcoming/where-might-interfaith-families-find-welcoming-jewish-communities.

5. Edmund Case, "Rabbinical School and the Interfaith Marriage, Part 2," *EdmundCase.com* (blog), May 5, 2009, http://www.edmundcase.com/intermarried-rabbis/rabbinical-school-and-the-interfaith-marriage-part-2, originally published at InterfaithFamily.com.

6. Marissa Brostoff, "Big Tent Country," *Tablet*, August 10, 2009, http://www.tabletmag.com/jewish-life-and-religion/13034/big-tent-country.

7. Daniel Kirzane, "Debatable: Should Our Seminary Admit Students with Non-Jewish Partners?" *Reform Judaism*, Spring 2013, https://reformjudaismmag.org/past-issues

/spring2013/seminary-admit-students-non-jewish-partners. For further discussion of the debate, see Edmund Case, "Intermarried Rabbis and Intermarriage Attitudes," *EdmundCase.com* (blog), April 4, 2013, http://www.edmundcase.com/intermarried-rabbis/intermarried-rabbis-and-intermarriage-attitudes, originally published at InterfaithFamily.com.

8. Mark Miller, "Rabbis Married to Gentiles?" *Times of Israel*, March 25, 2013, http://blogs.timesofisrael.com/rabbis-married-to-gentiles.

9. Aliza Worthington, "Rigidity Is the Real Threat to Jewish Continuity," *Times of Israel*, March 27, 2013, http://blogs.timesofisrael.com/rigidity-is-the-real-threat-to-jewish-continuity.

10. Adin Feder, "The Threat of Warrantless Hatred," *Times of Israel*, April 1, 2013, http://blogs.timesofisrael.com/113854.

11. Ellen Lippman, "Reform Rabbi Urges Hebrew Union College to Reconsider Decision on Intermarriage," *Forward*, May 17, 2013, http://forward.com/opinion/176823/reform-rabbi-urges-hebrew-union-college-to-reconsi. Paul Golin added his perspective: "Rabbis with nontraditional families like my own make me feel more included. Conveying why Judaism is still relevant to them provides me with access I wouldn't feel elsewhere" (Paul Golin, "What Intermarried Rabbis Can Teach Us," *New Jersey Jewish News*, July 24, 2013, https://njjewishnews.timesofisrael.com/what-intermarried-rabbis-can-teach-us).

12. Lippman, "Reform Rabbi Urges Hebrew Union College."

13. Reconstructionist Rabbinical College, "RRC Removes Ban on Admitting/Graduating Intermarried Rabbinical Students," September 30, 2015. The policy change is referred to at https://archive.rrc.edu/news-media/news/rrcs-non-jewish-partner-policy-announced.

14. Jane Eisner, "Why We Shouldn't Accept Rabbis Who Marry Non-Jews," *Forward*, October 8, 2015, http://forward.com/opinion/editorial/322258/why-rabbis-shouldnt-marry-non-jews.

15. Eisner, "Why We Shouldn't Accept Rabbis."

18 Working with Families *Doing Both*

1. Edmund Case, "How Should American Jewry Respond to the National Jewish Population Survey?" *EdmundCase.com* (blog), accessed October 1, 2018, http://www.edmundcase.com/media/essays/how-should-american-jewry-respond-to-the-national-jewish-population-survey-reach-out-to-intermarrieds, originally published in the *Forward* and reprinted at InterfaithFamily.com; Edmund Case, "Interfaith Families Raising Jewish Children" (speech, General Assembly of the United Jewish Communities, Philadelphia, PA, November 20, 2002), http://www.edmundcase.com/media/in-the-news/interfaith-families-raising-jewish-children, originally published at InterfaithFamily.com.

2. Susan Katz Miller, *Being Both: Embracing Two Religions in One Interfaith Family* (Boston: Beacon Press, 2013), xvii.

3. Deborah Goldman, "Jesus, the Most Influential Rabbi in History," ReformJudaism.org, August 9, 2016, http://reformjudaism.org/blog/2016/08/09/jesus-most-influential -rabbi-history.

4. "A New Era for Reform Jews," Jewish Telegraphic Agency, December 4, 1995, http:// www.jta.org/1995/12/04/archive/a-new-era-for-reform-jews-part-1-children -educated-in-2-faiths-barred-from-reform-schools.

5. Sarah Podenski Sinderbrand, "I'm the Christian spouse of a Jewish man," Facebook, November 12, 2013, https://www.facebook.com/interfaithfamily/posts /10151769377901918.

6. Susan Katz Miller, "Being 'Partly Jewish,'" *New York Times*, October 31, 2013, http:// www.nytimes.com/2013/11/01/opinion/being-partly-jewish.html.

7. Miller, *Being Both*, 76.

8. Miller, 74–75.

9. Miller, "Being 'Partly Jewish.'"

10. Miller, *Being Both*, 16.

11. Miller, "Being 'Partly Jewish.'"

12. Miller, *Being Both*, 42.

Road Map Three   A Serious Campaign to Engage Interfaith Families

1. There has also been a great deal of attention given to engagement of LGBTQ Jews, another worthy cause. The rate of interfaith relationships is much higher among LGBTQ Jews than among straight Jews; for example, while 22 percent of married Jews in New York were intermarried as of 2011, 44 percent of LGBTQ married Jews were intermarried (Steven M. Cohen, Jacob B. Ukeles, and Ron Miller, *Jewish Community Study of New York: 2011* [New York: UJA-Federation of New York, 2012], 249, http://www.jewishdatabank.org/studies/downloadFile.cfm?FileID=2852.

2. Theodore Sasson et al., *Millennial Children of Intermarriage: Touchpoints and Trajectories of Jewish Engagement* (Waltham: Brandeis University, Cohen Center for Modern Jewish Studies, 2016), 50, http://www.brandeis.edu/cmjs/pdfs/intermarriage /MillennialChildrenIntermarriage1.pdf.

19 Building a Future of Programmatic Efforts

1. Speaking at a Jewish Outreach Institute conference, Rukin, a past leader of the Boston federation, Hillel, and the Hebrew Immigration Aid Society, asserted that allocations of funding for outreach to intermarried families had been lost in favor of programs that followed a strategy to "infuse the core Jews with greater knowledge, affiliation and commitment." Rukin said that "fifteen years later . . . the demographics of affiliation and intermarriage have not changed" (Michael Rukin, *"Teruah*: The Train Is Leaving the Station!" [speech, Jewish Outreach Institute Conference, Atlanta, GA, December 4, 2005]). Other voices have recognized the need for significant efforts to engage interfaith families in Jewish life and community. A 1994 federations' task force said, "The Jewish community has the choice to respond with a broadened array of opportunities to engage the intermarried in communal life and community

services." It added, "With Federation leadership, services to the intermarried can be part of a total communal effort" (Council of Jewish Federations, *Jewish Community Services to the Intermarried: Report of the Task Force on the Intermarried and Jewish Affiliation* [New York: Council of Jewish Federations, 1994], 2, 4). InterfaithFamily advocated for "programs specifically aimed at welcoming interfaith families" from the outset (Edmund Case, "Discouraging Intermarriage Is Not the Way to Preserve Jewish Identity," *EdmundCase.com* [blog], May 2001, http://www.edmundcase.com /media/essays/discouraging-intermarriage-is-not-the-way-to-preserve-jewish -identity, originally published at InterfaithFamily.com; Edmund Case, "Interfaith Families Raising Jewish Children" [speech, General Assembly of the United Jewish Communities, Philadelphia, PA, November 20, 2002], http://www.edmundcase.com /media/in-the-news/interfaith-families-raising-jewish-children, originally published at InterfaithFamily.com; Edmund Case, "How Should American Jewry Respond to the National Jewish Population Survey?" *EdmundCase.com* [blog], accessed October 1, 2018, http://www.edmundcase.com/media/essays/how-should-american-jewry -respond-to-the-national-jewish-population-survey-reach-out-to-intermarrieds, orig- inally published in the *Forward* and reprinted at InterfaithFamily.com).

2. Edmund Case and Kathy Kahn, "Engaging the Intermarried," *Forward*, November 17, 2006, http://forward.com/opinion/8451/engaging-the-intermarried. Critics of intermarriage responded that outreach was ineffective, and they said the 60 percent rate was not influenced by Boston's outreach efforts. Steven M. Cohen questioned how "Jewish child" was defined, and Steven Bayme questioned the seriousness and sustainability of the children's Jewish connection (Nathaniel Popper, "Boston Study Shows 60% of Interfaith Kids Raised Jewish, *Forward*, November 17, 2006, http://forward.com/news/8446/boston-study-shows-60-of-interfaith-kids-raised; Micah Sachs, "Our Op-ed in the Forward," InterfaithFamily.com, November 16, 2006, http://www.interfaithfamily.com/blog/iff/other-religions-2/our-op-ed-in-the-forward).

3. "Funding Proposal for the Interfaith Initiative," September 23, 2008.

4. UJA-Federation of New York, *Report of the Task Force on Welcoming Interfaith Families* (New York: UJA-Federation of New York, 2011), 5.

5. Alyssa Schmidt, "jHUB Sees Success 'Welcoming' Interfaith Families to Jewish Cleveland," *Cleveland Jewish News*, June 22, 2018, https://www.clevelandjewishnews .com/news/local_news/jhub-sees-success-welcoming-interfaith-families-to-jewish -cleveland/article_f90a1fc6-74b2-11e8-bbff-87717ea65564.html.

6. The program's website is https://www.honeymoonisrael.org.

7. InterfaithFamily, "What Attracts Interfaith Families to Jewish Organizations?" Inter- faithFamily.com, September 5, 2012, http://www.interfaithfamily.com/about_us _advocacy/What_Attracts_Interfaith_Families_to_Jewish_Organizations.shtml?rd =2. In another survey, 61 percent said that the program title "Raising a Jewish Child in Your Interfaith Family" would be more likely to interest them than the title "Rais- ing a Jewish Child" (InterfaithFamily, "Do Interfaith Families Prefer Programs Marketed as "For Interfaith Families? A Report on InterfaithFamily.com's Annual Holiday Surveys," InterfaithFamily.com, October 2011, https://www.interfaithfamily .com/about_us_advocacy/Interfaith_Families_Program_Preferences). Arnold Eisen

supported "special programming" for the intermarried back in 2000: "More import-ant, one wants to . . . work . . . to increase the percentage of intermarried families who do live substantially Jewish lives and raise Jewish children. We can accomplish this in part . . . by welcoming intermarried families, providing special program-ming as needed" (Arnold Eisen, "A Reply to Ed Case's Review of *The Jew Within*," *EdmundCase.com* [blog], January 2001, http://www.edmundcase.com/media/essays /an-intermarried-perspective-on-the-jew-within-by-steven-m-cohen-and-arnold -m-eisen; originally published at InterfaithFamily.com).

8. InterfaithFamily, "Do Interfaith Families Prefer Programs."

9. Edmund Case, "Programs Targeted to Interfaith Couples," *EdmundCase.com* (blog), March 16 2009, http://www.edmundcase.com/engaging-interfaith-families-jewishly /programs-targeted-to-interfaith-couples, originally published at InterfaithFamily.com.

10. Case, "Programs Targeted to Interfaith Couples.

11. Edmund Case and Jodi Bromberg, "Birthright Israel and Intermarriage," *eJewish-Philanthropy*, September 11, 2014, http://www.ejewishphilanthropy.com/birthright -israel-and-intermarriage.

12. Leonard Saxe et al., *Beyond 10 Days: Parents, Gender, Marriage, and the Long-Term Impact of Birthright Israel* (Waltham: Brandeis University, Cohen Center for Mod-ern Jewish Studies, 2017), 12, https://www.brandeis.edu/cmjs/pdfs/jewish%20futures /Beyond10Days.pdf.

13. In 2006, a major city federation executive, when I urged him to try to reach a 60 per-cent level of interfaith families raising their children as Jews in his community, said, "If only we knew what to do." The executive director of a major foundation once told me, "We like to fund programs that work," implying that outreach programs didn't.

20 Model Pathways to Engagement

1. The theory of change described in this chapter is based on one developed by Inter-faithFamily with significant assistance from Rosov Consulting.

2. Edmund Case, "What We Can Learn from the InterfaithFamily.com Network Essay Contest," *EdmundCase.com* (blog), September 2003, http://www.edmundcase.com /media/essays/what-we-can-learn-from-the-interfaithfamily-com-network-essay -contest, originally published at InterfaithFamily.com.

3. Edmund Case, "Let's Encourage the Jewish Journeys of Interfaith Families," *EdmundCase.com* (blog), July 13, 2006, http://www.edmundcase.com/media/essays /lets-encourage-the-jewish-journeys-of-interfaith-families, originally published at InterfaithFamily.com.

4. Case, "Let's Encourage the Jewish Journeys."

5. Scot Landry, "1060 AM WQOM Responds to Defacing of its 'Try God' Billboard," *Good Catholic Life*, August 23, 2013, http://www.thegoodcatholiclife.com/2013 /08/23/1060-wqom-responds-defacing-try-god-billboard.

6. The Foundation for Jewish Camp recognizes that "the opportunity to engage the children of mixed married families" is "particularly important. . . . Camps need to rec-ognize that messages which testify to their Jewish cultural depth and sophistication

. . . probably alienate parents (and children) who feel ill-at-ease or unfamiliar with more intense Jewish cultural environments, such as may be symbolized by use of Hebrew letters and phrases" (Steven M. Cohen and Judith Veinstein, *Recruiting Jewish Campers: A Study of the Midwestern Market* [New York: Foundation for Jewish Camp, 2013], http://bjpa.org/Publications/details.cfm?PublicationID=4957); see also Edmund Case, "What the Camp Study Was Really About," *EdmundCase.com* [blog], July 27, 2010, http://www.edmundcase.com/uncategorized/what-the-camp-study-was-really-about, originally published at InterfaithFamily.com). Similarly, community day schools can ensure that advertising and marketing materials emphasize acceptance of the children of interfaith families, the diversity of the community, the diversity of Jewish religious observance of students, and the atmosphere of tolerance at the school, as well as clearly articulate policies regarding patrilineal children, interfaith dating, and allowing students to bring dates from different faith traditions to events like the prom (Micah Sachs and Edmund Case, "Marketing Day Schools to Interfaith Families," InterfaithFamily.com, October 25, 2006, http://www.interfaithfamily.com /blog/iff/passover-and-easter/marketing-day-schools-to-interfaith-families).

7. Quoted in Case, "What We Can Learn."

8. The results of the One8 Foundation research, which was conducted by the firm Continuum, are contained in an unpublished presentation, *Interfaith Insights & Workbook*.

9. InterfaithFamily, "What Attracts Interfaith Families to Jewish Organizations?" InterfaithFamily.com, September 5, 2012, http://www.interfaithfamily.com/about_us _advocacy/What_Attracts_Interfaith_Families_to_Jewish_Organizations .shtml?rd=2.

10. Case, "What We Can Learn."

11. One8 Foundation, *Interfaith Insights & Workbook*.

12. Ruth Nemzoff's book on parenting adult children is *Don't Bite Your Tongue: How to Foster Rewarding Relationships with Your Adult Children* (New York: Palgrave MacMillan, 2008).

13. Theodore Sasson et al., *Millennial Children of Intermarriage: Touchpoints and Trajectories of Jewish Engagement* (Waltham: Brandeis University, Cohen Center for Modern Jewish Studies, 2016), 36, http://www.brandeis.edu/cmjs/pdfs/intermarriage /MillennialChildrenIntermarriage1.pdf.

14. Jim Keen, *Inside Intermarriage: A Christian Partner's Journey Raising a Jewish Family* (Springfield, NJ: Behrman House, 2017), 47.

15. Union for Reform Judaism, "Yours, Mine and Ours for Interfaith Couples," ReformJudaism.org, accessed October 1, 2018, https://reformjudaism.org/reform -jewish-outreach-boston/yours-mine-ours.

16. See Marion Usher's book describing her experience, *One Couple Two Faiths: Stories of Love and Religion* (Washington, DC: Marion Usher, 2018).

17. Esther Perel, "Ethnocultural Factors in Marital Communications Among Intermarried Couples," *Journal of Jewish Communal Service* 66, no. 3 (January 1990): 246, https://www.bjpa.org/search-results/publication/4.

18. Perel, "Ethnocultural Factors in Marital Communications," 248, 251.

19. Perel, "Ethnocultural Factors in Marital Communications." 251–252.
20. Available at https://www.ccarpress.org/shopping_product_detail.asp?pid=50251.
21. Usher clearly states at the beginning of the workshop that one of her goals is to encourage the couples to make Jewish choices. She talks about having a "lead religion" in the home, while acknowledging that an interfaith couple will always have the presence of another religious tradition. Some couples end their relationships when they realize the importance to each of them of raising a child in their own faith; Usher describes that as a positive outcome of her workshop as well. Marion Usher, *Love and Religion: An Interfaith Workshop for Jews and Their Partners*, August 12, 2014, http://www.jewishinterfaithcouples.com/category/videos/, quoted in Edmund Case, "Love and Religion—A Must See!" *EdmundCase.com* (blog), December 8, 2009, http://www.edmundcase.com/discussion-groups-for-couples/love-and-religion-a -must-see, originally published at InterfaithFamily.com.
22. One8 Foundation, *Interfaith Insights & Workbook*. See n. 8 above.
23. One8 Foundation, *Interfaith Insights & Workbook*.

21 The Positive Impacts That Can Be Achieved

1. Steve Lipman, "Intermarriage Now Seen As 'In the Mainstream,'" *New York Jewish Week*, November 1, 2016, http://jewishweek.timesofisrael.com/intermarriage -now-seen-as-in-the-mainstream.
2. Jodi Bromberg and Edmund Case, "What We Learned at the Interfaith Opportunity Summit," *eJewishPhilanthropy*, November 6, 2016, http://ejewishphilanthropy.com /what-we-learned-at-the-interfaith-opportunity-summit/#more-98333.
3. Bromberg and Case, "What We Learned." One newer programmatic effort at the Los Angeles Jewish Federation, NuRoots, www.nuroots.org, is built on a community organizing model and involves meeting people where they are, building relationships one-on-one, connecting them with others with similar interests, and providing content from Jewish wisdom and tradition that addresses their interests and helps them do Jewish things.
4. All references in the remainder of this chapter, unless otherwise noted, are drawn from the following unpublished evaluations by Rosov Consulting:
   • *InterfaithFamily/Philadelphia Pilot Evaluation, Executive Summary*, July 30, 2015
   • *An Impact Study of InterfaithFamily's Your Community Initiative*, August 2016
   • *Early Outcomes of the Honeymoon Israel Experience: Contributing to Couples' Jewish Journeys*, September 2016
   • *Opening Doors to Cleveland Jewish Life, Findings from a jHUB User Study*, April 2018
5. Efforts can be designed and implemented to achieve particular desired outcomes. The authors of the 2011 New York study, noting that 90 percent of intermarried households that join synagogues give Jewish education to their children, write, "Perhaps expanding congregation-based efforts to engage intermarried households is worth pursuing" (Steven M. Cohen, Jacob B. Ukeles, and Ron Miller, *Jewish Community Study of New York: 2011* [New York: UJA-Federation of New York, 2012],

28, http://www.jewishdatabank.org/studies/downloadFile.cfm?FileID=2852). If one thinks interfaith families would be more engaged if they had more Jewish social connections, one could try to "connect the intermarried socially to other Jews," as the New York Study also recommends (162).

Conclusion

1. Edmund Case, "Breaking New Ground with Jewish Leaders," *EdmundCase.com* (blog), November 23, 2008, http://www.edmundcase.com/inclusion-and-welcoming /breaking-new-ground-with-jewish-leaders, originally published at InterfaithFamily .com.

2. Rick Jacobs, "The Genesis of Our Future" (keynote address, Union for Reform Judaism Biennial, San Diego, CA, December 11–15, 2013), https://urj.org/blog /2013/12/12/genesis-our-future.

3. Gary Rosenblatt, "A Call for Audacious Hospitality," *New York Jewish Week*, January 24, 2014, http://www.heritagefl.com/story/2014/01/24/opinions/a-call-for-audacious -hospitality/2101.html.

4. "Intermarriage Rorschach Test," editorial, *Forward*, January 16, 2014, http://forward .com/opinion/editorial/191024/intermarriage-rorschach-test.

5. Jodi Bromberg and Edmund Case, "What We Learned at the Interfaith Opportunity Summit," *eJewishPhilanthropy*, November 6, 2016, http://ejewishphilanthropy.com /what-we-learned-at-the-interfaith-opportunity-summit/#more-98333.

6. Council of Jewish Federations, *Jewish Community Services to the Intermarried: Report of the Task Force on the Intermarried and Jewish Affiliation* (New York: Council of Jewish Federations, 1994), 8.

7. Theodore Sasson et al., *Millennial Children of Intermarriage: Touchpoints and Trajectories of Jewish Engagement* (Waltham: Brandeis University, Cohen Center for Modern Jewish Studies, 2016), 30, http://www.brandeis.edu/cmjs/pdfs/intermarriage /MillennialChildrenIntermarriage1.pdf.

8. Ron Heifitz, *Leadership Without Easy Answers* (Cambridge, MA: Harvard University Press, 1994), 130–49.

9. Jack Wertheimer and Steven M. Cohen, "The Pew Survey Reanalyzed: More Bad News, but a Glimmer of Hope," *Mosaic*, November 2, 2014, https://mosaicmagazine.com /essay/2014/11/the-pew-survey-reanalyzed. A similar pessimistic view was expressed in the most recent demographic study of Jews in the United Kingdom, but progressive voices in Britain are taking a more enlightened view. See Edmund Case, "Intermarriage in Britain: Tragedy or Opportunity?" *eJewishPhilanthropy*, October 10, 2016, http://ejewishphilanthropy.com/intermarriage-in-britain-tragedy-or-opportunity/?.

10. Chip Edelsberg and Jason Edelstein, "The Ever-Renewing People," *Mosaic*, November 19, 2014, https://mosaicmagazine.com/response/2014/11/the-ever-renewing-people.

11. Edelsberg and Edelstein, "The Ever-Renewing People."

12. Edelsberg and Edelstein, "The Ever-Renewing People."

13. Gary Rosenblatt, "Douglas Taking Jewish Pride on the Road," *New York Jewish Week*, January 20, 2016, http://jewishweek.timesofisrael.com/douglas-taking-jewish

-pride-on-the-road. The Genesis Prize is a one-million-dollar annual award made to renowned individuals who inspire others through their engagement and dedication to the Jewish community (www.genesisprize.org).

14. Gary Rosenblatt, "Genesis Prize Taps Michael Douglas," *New York Jewish Week*, January 14, 2015, http://jewishweek.timesofisrael.com/genesis-prize-taps-michael-douglas.

15. Mikhail Fridman, "The Genesis Prize: Reflecting on Jewishness," *Jerusalem Post*, June 18, 2015, http://www.jpost.com/Opinion/The-Genesis-Prize-Reflecting-on-Jewishness-406530.

16. Marcy Oster, "Michael Douglas Salutes Son, Famous Dad in Accepting Genesis Prize for Jewish Commitment," Jewish Telegraphic Agency, June 18, 2015, http://www.jta.org/2015/06/18/news-opinion/israel-middle-east/michael-douglas-salutes-son-famous-dad-in-accepting-genesis-prize-for-jewish-commitment.

17. Edmund Case, "Mazel Tov, Michael Douglas—and Our Cause," *EdmundCase.com* (blog), June 18, 2015, http://www.edmundcase.com/inclusion-and-welcoming/mazel-tov-michael-douglas-and-our-cause, originally published at InterfaithFamily.com.

About the Author

Edmund Case is the founder of the Center for Radically Inclusive Judaism. He founded and served from 2001 to 2016 as CEO of Interfaith-Family, which grew to become the leading nonprofit working to engage interfaith families in Jewish life and community. Past president of Temple Shalom of Newton, Massachusetts, he served on a Reform movement regional outreach committee and a Combined Jewish Philanthropies of Boston task force on services to the intermarried. In 1999 he earned a master's degree in Jewish communal service from the Hornstein Program at Brandeis University, after graduating earlier from Yale and Harvard Law School and practicing law for twenty-two years. He is coeditor of *The Guide to Jewish Interfaith Family Life: An InterfaithFamily.com Handbook* (Jewish Lights Publishing) and has written extensively on intermarriage issues. His wife, Wendy, converted to Judaism after they had been married for thirty years. Their two children, both intermarried, are raising their four grandchildren with Judaism.

If you would like to contact Ed to speak to your group or at your event, please visit the website of the Center for Radically Inclusive Judaism, www.CFRIJ.com, or email info@CFRIJ.com.

Made in the USA
Middletown, DE
15 March 2019